MORE QUESTIONS THAN ANSWERS

Reflections on a Life in the RUC

MORE QUESTIONS THAN ANSWERS

Reflections on a Life in the RUC

KEVIN SHEEHY

Gill & Macmillan

Gill & Macmillan Ltd
Hume Avenue, Park West, Dublin 12
with associated companies throughout the world
www.gillmacmillan.ie

© Kevin Sheehy 2008
978 07171 4396 2

Index compiled by Cover to Cover
Typography design by Make Communication
Print origination by O'K Graphic Design, Dublin
Printed and bound in Great Britain by MPG Books Ltd,
Bodmin, Cornwall

This book is typeset in 12/14.5 pt Minion

The paper used in this book comes from the wood pulp
of managed forests. For every tree felled, at least one
tree is planted, thereby renewing natural resources.

A CIP catalogue record for this book is available from
the British Library.

5 4 3 2 1

Dedicated to the memory of

Paul Sheehy, Philip Boyd,
Mervyn Mitchell, Frank Murray,
Austin Wilson, John Bennison,
Ray Christie, Robert 'Roy' Leslie,
John Hallawell, Russell Turkington,
Colleen McMurray, Jackie Montgomery,
Jerry McCabe, Bernard Moane
and Veronica Guerin
—all of whom opposed violence
and sought justice.

CONTENTS

PREFACE

This is the story of my life in the Royal Ulster Constabulary between 1970 and 2001, and the influences that helped prepare me for it. Had these been different, no doubt I would have another story to tell. But this is the way it was.

In any organisation, be it priesthood, the medical or teaching profession, membership of a political group of whatever hue, or the police, you will always find a range of humanity—from the morally idealistic and generous to the outright scoundrel. The RUC was no different from any other in this respect.

It was my privilege to work with people of the highest integrity, individuals committed to making a difference on behalf of the community—and my burden to have to endure the proximity and hostility of those who, in popular parlance, can only be described as 'scumbags'.

I was also obliged to work within certain constraints which I found difficult—at times exceedingly so—whether imposed by central government or Special Branch. Throughout, I tried to remain faithful to the example set by my father—of integrity, courage, hard work and loyalty to colleagues. In the end, it seems that this was not enough—like many others who have given their best years to their profession, I left with more questions than answers ...

Chapter 1 ∾

| MY EARLY LIFE

I was born on 22 April 1948, in 42 North Queen Street, Belfast, the third child of my parents, Joseph and Philomena. The house, owned by my maternal grandfather, Charles Loughran, was a two-storey terraced property built of fine brick with a solid tile roof. The downstairs had been converted into a barber's shop with a counter for the sale of confectionery, basic groceries, stationery, comics and newspapers.

It was functional rather than comfortable—particularly on a cold, wet, blustery night. The toilet was in the backyard. For a little boy it presented the most precarious of perches: legs dangling over a bottomless pit, terror-stricken at the thought of a passing rodent nibbling my frozen toes.

My mother's father had served in the Great War in France as a barber to the generals. He returned with a 'Blighty' wound—and several commendations for his barbering services. The shop became a drop-in centre for local personalities such as Rinty Monaghan, World Flyweight champion. They came for the warm and friendly atmosphere and the rich exchange of stories—whether they also wanted a haircut or shave was quite incidental. The story-telling was fuelled by frequent (hairy) cups of tea made in the tiny scullery. As lunchtime approached, Grandad would report to his diminutive wife, Annie, that he had done x number of heads of hair and chins, receive his pay and breeze across the road, his cronies in tow, to the local watering-hole, Hannigan's Bar, leaving behind his son, Jimmy (my mother's older brother), and a hired hand to carry on in his absence.

On occasions the drinking was excessive and led to rows. Grandmother was a religious woman and strongly disapproved of intemperate behaviour. On one occasion, a neighbour advised her to bar the door—but he kicked it in.

There was, however, another side to Grandfather: he was a keen observer of political and social events and devoured the newspapers of the day. Behind this habit was a highly principled social conscience. In 1903 he had helped launch the Belfast Labour Representation Committee, affiliated to the Irish trade union movement, and two years later campaigned for its first candidate, William Walker, in a by-election in north Belfast. Ramsay MacDonald, the future Labour Prime Minister, was Walker's election agent[1], and visited Grandfather during the campaign.

The Belfast I was born into was poor but full of indelible memories: horse-drawn vehicles carrying all sorts of goods; the bleach man selling his wares in milk and lemonade bottles, the coal-brick man and the pigs' swill man; old widowed women attired in heavy black shawls draped around their heads and shoulders—a practice I still see in the Greek islands.

There was a wonderful community spirit. Uncle Jimmy had by now taken over the shop, and had converted the long, narrow hallway under the stairway into a veritable Aladdin's cave of comic strips and adventure/true romance/detective novels. I spent many happy hours browsing through its contents, rubbing shoulders with the locals, for whom it was a precious lending library. Jimmy was generous to a fault and often gave bread and other groceries to women who had no money. At the end of the day's business, he would visit old fellas who were housebound and give them a shave/haircut, before heading home to his wife, Maggie.

Maggie Corrigan was another remarkable person. Though unable to read or write, she had an incredible business brain and was a legend in the Markets area where she ran a stall. Maggie and Jimmy held a unique record: Ireland's longest engagement (it lasted thirty-six years before they took the plunge). They were such generous souls; I was pleased to have them as my godparents.

Grandfather never had any respect for Jimmy. He often told his cronies that Jimmy could not organise a piss-up in a brewery. But Uncle Jimmy ran the best poker school in town during World War Two. Sessions sometimes lasted a whole week and were much frequented by American GIS, bringing with them a multitude of contraband goods, including silk nylons, chocolates, cigarettes and perfume. One night, the military police raided the game. Jimmy was caught red-handed, sitting on one of the contraband containers, and ended up spending a week in Crumlin Road jail at His Majesty's pleasure.

When my parents got married in St Patrick's Church, Donegall Street, in April 1944, the reception was held in the shop. An American sergeant arrived with a jeep full of tinned foodstuffs, chocolates, etc.— the sort of fare unknown in Belfast during the war years.

My mother, Mena, was born in July 1922, the youngest of the Loughran family. She was mad keen on Irish dancing and frequented the Ard Scoil in Divis Street, Lower Falls. She and Dad had been going together from the ages of fourteen and fifteen respectively. Dad was so rarely out of NO. 42 that Uncle Jimmy called him the 'Breakfast, Dinner and Tea Kid'.

When Mum left school (Star of the Sea at the top of New Lodge Road), she was employed by the Albion Clothing Company in Sandy Row. It was a Protestant firm, but one of the supervisors, by the name of May Maltman, got her a job as a stitcher. The wages were pretty good. Mother worked there until she married. She was regarded by many as a local beauty and Uncle Jimmy frequently remarked how lucky Dad was to win her affection.

My father Joseph was born in April 1921 and lived for many years in 29 Ship Street, in the docks area of Belfast. He was the eldest of six boys and three sisters. His parents were Felix and Clara; both died before their time, Clara at forty-six, Felix around fifty.

'Sailor town', as the area was known, was predominantly a working-class, Catholic district, bordered on the north side by Tiger's Bay, a Protestant area. Religious tensions were never far from the surface and inter-communal riots were frequent. Unemployment in the area was high, with most families dependent on casual labour at the docks. Grandfather Sheehy was fortunate: he worked as a 'checker', which meant he had a steady job. He was required to check the cargo manifest and ensure that freight was unloaded into the designated warehouse.

After his schooling with the Christian Brothers in Harding Street, Dad worked for a while as an assistant chef at the Grand Central Hotel, Royal Avenue, but the wages were not good and inevitably he ended up seeking employment in the docks.

Religious divisions were much in evidence on the quayside. Most

Catholics worked at the shallow dock, which handled ships of only moderate size; Protestants worked the deep water docks, which serviced bigger boats with larger cargoes and, as a result, were guaranteed higher wages. Father chose this end because of the prospect of better money. He laboured in the holds of ships, loading cargo onto a sling so that it could be lifted by crane onto the quayside. It was difficult and dangerous work, excessively hot in summer, exposed to the elements in winter. He suffered frequent rib and wrist injuries and on one occasion was hospitalised for eight weeks with a compound leg fracture, from which he never quite recovered. He had a reputation, fully deserved, for being a reliable, hard-working colleague; and although he did not drink, smoke or curse, he knew how to buy his round in the local pubs frequented by his workmates.

Father made several life-long friendships with his Protestant colleagues. Sadly this was not sufficient to gain him union membership, which meant that for years he was classified as a casual labourer. John Campbell, the distinguished Belfast poet and novelist, writes sympathetically about the lives of dockers.[2] He describes with pathos the ritual of hundreds of men standing about in the early morning rain hoping to be selected by gangers for a day's work. Blue badge holders, as full members of the Belfast Dockers Union, were chosen first and got the less dirty and best-paid jobs; red badge holders, also union members but not of the dockers' branch, were chosen next; then non-union casuals (my father's category). Inevitably, too many men for too few jobs meant that religion was often a factor in the selection process.

My father left for work each morning at 6.10 a.m. and was frequently home before we left for school. My mother understood his dispirited and embarrassed look and was quick to console him. I often left for school with a heavy heart. Dad retained his socialist principles all his life and never once in my presence expressed bitterness about his experiences in the docks.

He was a talented ballroom dancer with a reputation among enthusiasts in Belfast. Other interests included cycling (he thought nothing of cycling a hundred miles in a day) and Gaelic games, which he played to county level. He was an enthusiastic supporter of Belfast Celtic soccer club with whom he had a trial in goals, but any hopes of further involvement were terminated by the directors' decision to close the club following an outbreak of sectarian violence at Windsor Park, the home of Linfield, in December 1948.

Dad had no tolerance for sectarian demonstrations of any kind and strongly disapproved, for example, when some Celtic supporters directed Nazi salutes at rival supporters each time their team scored a goal.

In 1955, my parents, anxious that their expanding family should grow up in a more fulfilling environment, bought a house in Glengormley, a small suburb on the northern fringes of Belfast. The fine, semi-detached, four-bedroom house cost £1,650 (a considerable sum of money in those days); it was made possible by Dad's successful claim following his horrific leg injury in the docks. Nevertheless, it was a brave financial gamble, for the success of the venture depended on him continuing to earn a wage. There would be desperate times ahead, testing my parents' resolve to the limit, but that resolve was vindicated.

The location afforded uninterrupted views of the beautiful, ancient hills of Ben Madigan—known as Cave Hill because of the five caves on its highest precipice. There was a working farm to the rear of the house, which gave me my first contact with cattle, sheep and rabbits. I developed a fondness for these gentle creatures; later in life it encouraged me to challenge conventional morality with regard to man's exploitation of animals and the environment. The farmer sold an array of fresh vegetables and eggs, which supplemented produce from Dad's wonderful, weed-free vegetable garden.

Events elsewhere in Northern Ireland caused him great concern. In December 1956 the IRA attacked several locations. The place names were unknown to me and seemed far away. For the first time I was aware that my parents were concerned about issues other than the family. Dad was worried that the paramilitary campaign would worsen the position of Catholics and lead to a rise in unemployment. My parents were devout Roman Catholics, conventional believers in the righteousness of the Church and the authority of the Pope. Each night the family knelt and said the Rosary. On more than one occasion, when a serious incident had occurred, prayers were offered for peace. They were distressed when one young policeman was shot dead. Their anxiety was undoubtedly heightened by the fact that several members of our extended family were serving members of the RUC. Two would later rise to the rank of Head Constable.

Father O'Rawe, our local priest and close family friend, frequently condemned the violence. I am grateful that the views of my parents and other people close to me encouraged me to reject republican violence from this point in my life. Other pupils I encountered during my time at St Malachy's College were moulded by different circumstances and became influential figures in the republican movement during the decades of the Troubles.

As regards my education at this time, it is still a bit of a mystery to me why I was sent to three primary schools before the age of eleven. Perhaps my father was determined that I should receive the quality of education he had been denied. In 1957, I was sent to the Star of the Sea School in north Belfast. By the end of the academic year, I was declared top pupil and awarded a prize of one shilling. He still was not convinced; the following year I was sent to the newly opened Christian Brothers school at Park Lodge on the Antrim Road. My teacher, Brother Holian, decided that I and several other pupils were educationally deficient and provided extra tuition every Saturday morning. He was an imaginative and inspirational teacher. As a result of his selfless dedication I managed to pass the Eleven Plus, which gave me the required entrance qualifications for St Malachy's College. Brother Holian loved Gaelic games and entered a school team in a prestigious under-12 Belfast football league. I rewarded his kindness by being one of his star performers in the school's victorious path to the championship.

My early teenage years were fairly routine but pleasant: school during the week, sport and more sport at weekends. Every so often, a traumatic event would disrupt this tranquil routine: a friend's death in a car accident; another after a fall at school; a neighbour lost in a collision between oil-tankers in the Pacific; the sudden death of a friend's father. I found comfort in praying for them in the family's nightly Rosary.

Money was an issue for me from the age of fourteen—like other young people, I wanted to buy records and new clothes. At every opportunity, I took temporary jobs: as a gardener, or helping my Uncle Vincent, who was a builder. At sixteen, I travelled with a number of friends from St Malachy's to work in a fruit-canning factory in King's Lynn, Norfolk. The hours were long (4 a.m. until 10 or 11 p.m.), but the wages were good. We stayed in the Bowling Green Inn, an Irish-owned pub in town. Fifteen people shared five beds and at weekends lots were drawn to determine the order of the bath. A draw higher than six meant that a wash at the sink was more beneficial.

During this time I met labourers from the west of Ireland who, because of lack of work at home, travelled to England every January and stayed until December. They lived frugally and sent as much money as they could afford to their families back home. They were pleasant men, but always seemed forlorn and lonely. Each night they played Johnny McEvoy's 'Pretty Brown Eyes' fifty or sixty times on the juke-box and made us feel as homesick as they were.

I attended St Malachy's College from 1959 to 1966. The staff comprised lay and clerical teachers. Few of them considered me scholarly, but they succeeded in getting sufficient effort out of me to pass examinations. My religious knowledge teacher, Father Des Wilson, impressed me as a liberal, progressive theologian. It was his hope that we would be as thoughtful in religious matters as in history, geography, science, etc. He stressed the importance of having a social conscience and of working with others for the benefit of all. He himself was deeply involved in the ecumenical movement and believed that Northern people had the capacity to work together and make a good future for everyone. I have fond memories of St Malachy's and am grateful to many of the fine teachers who worked hard to prepare me for adult life.

A great deal of my time was spent on the sports field representing the school in Gaelic football, hurling, athletics, soccer and basketball. Father John O'Sullivan, my maths teacher, was soccer-mad and during my last year he sought permission from the Principal, Father Larkin— an austere Catholic conservative and a devotee of Gaelic culture—to enter a soccer team in the Ulster Grammar Schools' League. The request was granted—on condition that the team did not use the school name or play in the school colours. Father O'Sullivan purchased a set of jerseys and several footballs and entered the team under the disappointingly ordinary name of Carlisle United (after nearby Carlisle Circus). It was a wonderfully exciting competition and under the inspirational guidance of our fine captain, Jackie McManus, we remained unbeaten all season and finished top.

During the competition, I was watched several times by the legendary football scout Bobby McAuley. He invited me to a number of trial matches at the Oval, the home of Glentoran Football Club, situated in the heart of Protestant east Belfast. Gibbie McKenzie, the manager there, liked what he saw and signed me under contract. On the first training night of the new season, I identified myself to a gateman at the ground. He told me the team was training at Celtic Park, which was situated in Catholic west Belfast. I made my way to Celtic Park and found that a greyhound meeting was in progress. The gateman there chased me when I told him I had come to train with Glentoran. My father was very angry and despite approaches from the Glentoran management, I was not allowed to return.

In my final year at St Malachy's, Professor Kennedy, my slightly eccentric but scholarly history teacher, organised a trip around sites of historical importance in Dublin. Our guide for the day was R.B. McDowell, the distinguished and charismatic Trinity historian. He was dressed in a small flattened hat, a Dr Who length scarf (despite it being a hot summer's day) and a suit which Professor Kennedy later suggested he had worn for the last thirty years. He walked at breakneck speed and imparted information, often inaudibly, as we struggled to keep up. Eventually he took us through an archway at the Dame Street entrance to Trinity College into a spacious cobbled square of magnificent Georgian buildings and manicured lawns. It was the most awe-inspiring and blissful moment of my life. Only the experience of entering the Vatican matched the pleasure of that moment. I resolved to enter Trinity as a student—which I did, after securing the required entrance qualifications.

As a prelude to entering the college, I was required, as a Catholic, to seek the written permission of John Charles McQuaid, the Archbishop of Dublin. In the 1950s, he had publicly declared that it was a 'mortal sin' for Catholics to attend Trinity. I contacted the Archbishop out of deference to my parents—but I had resolved to enrol whether he granted or withheld permission.

The four years I spent at Trinity were the most fulfilling and stimulating of my life. The grandeur of the buildings, the history of the college, the distinguished academics on the staff, the Philosophical and Historical Debating Societies, the Boat Club and the Trinity Ball left me with such pleasurable memories.

It was during this time that I took an interest in the civil rights movement in the North. Its declared aim was to seek redress for anyone who had suffered discrimination, particularly as a result of housing allocation, employment practices and manipulation of voting procedures in local government elections. I was hopeful of a positive response from the Stormont government. Catholics for many decades had protested their grievances, but they were not the only victims. Catholic-dominated businesses and councils had also disadvantaged Protestants when they got the opportunity.

Perhaps I was being naively optimistic to hope that ending such practices would encourage dialogue and respect between the two communities—which, in turn, could possibly secure a peaceful and prosperous future for all the people of Northern Ireland.

In 1968, Ivan Cooper, a civil rights activist in Londonderry, declared: 'I love the constitution of this country. I love its flag and all it stands for. I am a loyal Protestant who is seeking civil rights for all the people of the country, Catholic as well as Protestant.'[3] I was a loyal Catholic and my sentiments were the same.

Tensions increased in June 1968 when a council house was allocated to a nineteen-year-old Protestant, leading to allegations of discrimination. A number of people squatted in the house in protest, including the Nationalist MP at Stormont, Austin Currie; but they were evicted. The incident led to a further protest march involving two thousand people.

Loyalists planned counter-demonstrations any time the civil rights movement took to the streets. Like most other people in the country, I watched with a sense of foreboding as a major march was planned for Londonderry on 5 October. The Protestant Apprentice Boys planned to walk the same route. The decision of the Home Affairs Minister, Bill Craig, to ban the civil rights march seemed reasonable in the circumstances. I was really surprised when the organising committee, after their commitment to peaceful protest, announced their intention to defy the ban and risk confrontation with the Apprentice Boys.

The television pictures from Londonderry on the day of the march were shocking. Much of the footage concentrated on policemen attacking civil rights marchers with batons. Many people were hurt, including Gerry Fitt, the Westminster MP, who received a head wound. Later in the day, the situation deteriorated as hundreds of rioters threw petrol bombs and stones at the police. Over the following weeks, allegations from marchers and nationalists of police brutality were countered by many unionists (including Craig), who claimed that the civil rights movement had been infiltrated by the IRA and communists.

The controversy did not stop me from joining a students' march from Queen's University to Belfast City Hall. I expected the protest to be peaceful, and that speakers representing the group would present intelligent and measured arguments defending civil rights for all. A loyalist counter-group reached the front of City Hall ahead of us, so the organisers of our march told us to sit down in Linen Hall Street, where we sang protest songs, including the Joan Baez anthem, 'We Shall Overcome'. About half an hour into the sit-down, some of the protestors started to chant 'ss RUC'. Disturbed and bitterly disappointed when more and more joined in, I left in disgust.

My spirits rose again when, a month later, the Northern Ireland Premier, Terence O'Neill, announced that he would introduce reforms to remove many of the grievances. Street protests were called off to give him time to implement his reforms. But he had under-estimated the strength of opposition within his own party. As a result, public order deteriorated and there were violent clashes between protesters and loyalists.

In late December, members of the People's Democracy announced their intention to march from Belfast to Londonderry early in the new year. Many members of protest groups in the two cities anticipated a violent reaction because the route chosen passed through loyalist areas. I decided I would join the march at Glengormley—as a Catholic unionist holding a Union flag. This would clearly demonstrate that civil rights were about equality and respect and nothing else. My parents were horrified and got up at first light to dissuade me. When quiet persuasion failed, Dad announced that he would forcibly prevent me from leaving the house. I knew he meant it. The combination of his determination and my mother's tears kept me at home.

I have mixed feelings about that day. When I think of the merciless violence meted out to the marchers at Burntollet Bridge, I feel relief that I did not go; when I consider the political significance of the occasion, I regret not being there.

During my time at Trinity, I met a wonderful girl, Rosalind, from Northern Ireland. She became my partner for almost thirty years and remains a dear and special friend. She was a passionate and devout ethical vegetarian and helped advance my feelings and beliefs on animal welfare issues and the environment.

As much as I loved Dublin and enjoyed the pubs and the wonderful traditional music of the Dubliners, the Press Gang, the Chieftains, Planxty and Christy Moore, my happiest moments were within the confines of the college grounds. I took rooms in the Front Square for my last year and sometimes did not leave the complex for weeks on end.

I was a hard-working and enthusiastic student and spent endless hours in the magnificent library complexes reading and researching subject matter. But I lacked the imaginative intelligence of a scholar. How I regretted not working at school! In 1970, much to my delight, I graduated with a BA degree in History and English.

The following week, Rosalind and I left for a three-month trip to the USA. We stayed with my relatives for a short time in New York before travelling by Greyhound bus to Montreal and Lake Ontario, where we enjoyed the majestic beauty of Niagara Falls. Then on to Detroit and Chicago, the Midwest (Yellowstone Park), the Rockies, Yosemite Natural Park and the Grand Canyon before eventually attending a family wedding in California. On our return journey, we visited Las Vegas, where we saw Elvis Presley perform; then Disney World and north to Washington, then Boston to meet my old friend, Pat Finucane, who later became a well-known solicitor in Belfast before his callous murder at the hands of loyalist paramilitaries.

I had first met Pat in 1968 in King's Lynn. He worked at the same factory as me (Lin Can) and stayed at the Bowling Green Inn. We met up afterwards on several occasions through football. During the 1969 season in King's Lynn, we were getting reports about the deteriorating political situation back home. Just how serious it was became clear to us all when Pat had to return abruptly in August when his family was burnt out of their home during an inter-communal riot. He arrived in Trinity later that year. One night he invited himself to dinner at our student digs—and ended up staying for a year. We both played soccer for Trinity and became good friends. I introduced him to his future wife, Geraldine—an old friend and former schoolmate of Rosalind's.

During the Boston reunion with Pat and Geraldine, we became aware of our differing political views on what was happening back home. I told Pat at that stage that I was going to join the RUC and he made it clear that his sympathies lay with the republican movement. We agreed to differ; I respected his views and we remained close friends until his death.

Within twenty-four hours of my return to Northern Ireland, my father ordered me to discard the long hair and the beads and enter the real world.

Chapter 2 ∾

I JOIN THE RUC

In September 1970 I responded to an RUC recruitment advert in the *Belfast Telegraph*. A serving chief inspector visited me at home, explaining that as I was the first Catholic college graduate to apply to the RUC, the police would like to arrange a photo-shoot and interview with the *Belfast Newsletter*, which duly took place.[4]

I was photographed with Jennifer Higginson, the first ever college graduate to join the RUC ranks; she had recently completed her training course in Enniskillen. I told the newspaper that I had decided to join the police force because of the situation in Northern Ireland. 'I feel that the RUC is the one body that can bring peace to Northern Ireland and restore stability.'

On 6 December, I arrived at the training centre in Enniskillen. Opened in 1936, the 'Depot' (as it was known) was a fine, spacious complex with a large square at the front used for parades and marching. We were 'greeted' by a senior sergeant; it became obvious very quickly that the regime was not conducive to one who had just returned from California wearing Indian moccasins and beads.

We lived and breathed and had our being in strict accordance with the tick of the clock: breakfast at 8 a.m., inspection immediately afterwards, when boots, uniform and hair were expected to conform to strict regulation. This was followed by a period of double-time drill around the complex to get the blood flowing; then into the classroom for intensive instruction, morning and afternoon. Topics covered were law and police procedures.

After years of being cooped up in classrooms/lecture halls, this did not pose a problem for me personally, but others had left school some time before and were coming from a working background; they found a return to the classroom a real ordeal.

Another inspection followed after lessons; then tea and recreation. I played football in the gym most evenings for a couple of hours, followed by a similar time studying, then bed by 10.30 p.m. on the dot, no matter what was on TV (even Man. Utd and Liverpool).

For the first five weeks, I shared a small dormitory with seven others. Two of them were much older than the rest of us. They were early risers, having worked for several years in the shipyard; they had the dormitory cleaned, polished and ready for inspection before I was awake. They even provided us with tea in bed—not strictly true in my case. Such was my fear of failing the bed inspection that I made a substitute one of sheets and blankets on top of the official bed, leaving it undisturbed and in pristine condition for the sergeant when he made his rounds.

During the first weeks, I was ordered three times to get my hair cut. On the third occasion, even the barber decided that it was not necessary. We had a cup of tea instead and agreed that the order was probably the regime's way of showing who was boss.

Because we were a uniformed organisation, footwear was important. At our own expense, we had to provide two pairs of black, laced boots—one for everyday use, the other for inspection. They had to be polished until they were gleaming. The process involved heating a spoon over a candle and applying it gently to toe and heel, followed by layers of polish, using a 'spit-and-polish' technique. A damp cloth was applied in a gentle, clockwise movement until the desired sparkle was achieved. On my first night, I spent hours trying to master the technique, failing miserably. Some of the other recruits noticed and for the rest of our training, they loaned me their everyday boots, which they had managed to maintain to the standard of their reserved ones.

Infringements of the rules resulted in punishment—a real nuisance and designed to prevent any reoccurrence. One day, I was seconds late for both the morning and afternoon inspection. The sergeant ordered me to do security duty around the inside of the perimeter wall every evening for two weeks, from 6 to 8 p.m. The fact that he was also in charge of the soccer team and appreciated that I was one of his 'stars' didn't help; he was determined to show no favouritism. Bearing in mind that my equipment consisted of a torch and a whistle and that this was the middle of winter, I found it hard to convince myself that it had any value whatsoever.

On another occasion, I was determined to visit Rosalind, who was still in Dublin. It meant getting to Enniskillen Bus Station by mid-afternoon on the Friday. I knew it was a waste of time trying to get permission. At substantial personal risk, a fellow recruit and good friend smuggled me out in the boot of his car. I then had until Sunday evening at 10 p.m. to get back (we were allowed home at weekends). An engine failure at Connolly Street Station, however, derailed my plans. I did not get back until Monday afternoon and missed an examination. I can't remember how many mornings I had to spend on show parade at 7.30 a.m. as punishment.

The other seventy-four recruits in my squad were from every county in Northern Ireland and represented a cross-section of society. The majority were aged between eighteen and twenty; but others, as I have indicated, were older. Most were from a working-class Protestant background—probably the mainstay of RUC recruitment at that time. Over the coming weeks, it became obvious that they did not know much about Catholics or Catholicism and took for granted that Catholics automatically supported a United Ireland and republicanism. These were sincerely held beliefs but were never expressed with bitterness or hostility. At no time were they threatening or offensive to me. I explained my political point of view—they found it hard to believe that I was a unionist like themselves. Over the next ten weeks, it prompted many late evening discussions which were sometimes heated but never acrimonious.

Early in the training programme, each recruit was asked to give some background information about himself to the class. I referred to my slight involvement in the civil rights campaign and told them of my participation in the sit-down protest at Linen Hall Street. This caused a cooling in some relationships.

Overall, I really enjoyed my time in Enniskillen. I forged many friendships and was always pleased to meet former recruits during the next thirty years of service.

From Enniskillen, we took up residence in Castlereagh police station, where we undertook an intensive four-week course in driving and swimming. Specialist police driving instructors took us out three at a time for day-long courses of instruction. On two days a week, we had swimming and life-saving training at Newtownards swimming pool.

It was during this month that the reference to civil rights returned to haunt me. Each evening we went to Donegall Pass for tea. On one of these occasions, I was summoned from the table by a member of Special Branch. He asked me why I had not declared my involvement in the civil rights movement during my interview. He produced a photograph allegedly of me pushing a police vehicle into Newry Canal during a riot which followed a civil rights march in the town in January 1970. I told him it was ludicrous: I had not been on the march; the photograph could not be of me; my involvement in the organisation had been short-lived because I believed that trouble-makers had infiltrated the organisation; in all, I had participated in one march in Belfast. He was not satisfied, but before he could continue, I walked away. I was disturbed by this incident for some time but did not think I could approach anyone in authority about it.

The security situation continued to deteriorate and rioting in Belfast was a daily occurrence. We were frequently sent to support other police on the front line in various parts of the city, although we were not trained or properly equipped for this task. I was shocked at the amount of hatred shown by the rioters, both loyalist and republican. It brought home to all of us the dangers facing police officers in Northern Ireland.

Chapter 3 ∾

EARLY CAREER IN THE RUC

In April 1971 I finished my training at Enniskillen and was posted to Downpatrick, a historic county town with many fine Georgian houses. As we drove along a straight stretch of road, I spotted the splendid spire of Down Cathedral—confirmation that I had arrived to start my police career. After a warm welcome at Downpatrick police station, I was shown to a small room at the top of the building with an iron bed, a wash-hand basin and a wardrobe. The sergeant handed me a duty-rota: I was to report that evening for night duty at 11.45 p.m. It was a three-man shift: the sergeant and I in a police car and a constable on guard in the station—he was also responsible for answering the telephone and passing radio messages to the vehicle.

I drove around the town for a short time until the sergeant told me to park in Market Street so that he could check that the nearby business premises were secure. During training, new recruits had been advised to do this at every possible opportunity while on night duty. At 3.45 a.m., the sergeant returned to the vehicle substantially inebriated. He told me to drive to the police station for refreshments. Attempts to contact the guard by banging on the door, sending radio transmissions and using a nearby public telephone were unsuccessful. We left the station and the sergeant directed me to a laneway off the Strangford Road, adjusted his seat and told me to waken him at 7.40 a.m. We finally entered the station cold and hungry in time to see the guard carrying two pillows and a blanket upstairs.

During the next number of months, I was involved in other bizarre episodes, such as the time a uniformed constable lay on the ground beneath a parked car in St Patrick's Avenue so that he could arrest a drunken cyclist. This unfortunate cyclist left the same licensed premises every evening at the same time. The method of his capture caused great mirth among a group of townspeople, who gathered to watch; it embarrassed me a great deal.

A couple of months into my posting at Downpatrick, I organised a football match between locally based police officers and young men from the town, in an attempt to further community relations. A sizable crowd watched in amazement as I flattened one of the opposition after he had spat in my face. He obviously resented being tackled in the nether regions.

My greatest humiliation happened after I arrested a car driver on suspicion of being drunk. He cried copiously and became distressed. After a bit of persuasion I agreed to let him call at his home nearby to explain his predicament to his wife. Once in the house, he refused to come out. I eventually gained access and was attacked by other members of the family. During the fracas, a settee was inadvertently pushed against a lighted gas-fire and burst into flames. Some time late the inspector and the fire brigade arrived to restore order. I started to believe I was accident-prone.

On one occasion during night duty, I was preparing a report for court when a colleague accidentally discharged a shotgun he had been cleaning. It blew a hole in the wall just in front of me. The following week, I was going upstairs with another officer when he dropped his Webley revolver. I felt the heat of the bullet as it creased my trouser leg and hit the wall. We laughed off both incidents, probably out of relief that no one had been injured.

It was not possible to keep the pain and anguish of life at bay. During the next number of months I investigated car accidents involving serious injury and death, sudden deaths as a result of illness, serious public order assaults and instances of domestic violence. I quickly realised that my training as a recruit had merely provided a basic framework; the ability to deal with incidents as they happened required initiative, courage and great mental strength.

The businesslike nature and chilling finality of post-mortem examinations was difficult to handle. Occasionally the pathologist asked me to take notes while he dictated his findings; on more than one occasion because of a heavy work schedule he broke off from an examination of the body for lunch.

The process of telling people that their loved ones had died caused me the most anguish. I felt frightened at such moments—frightened of how the person would react, frightened that I would not know what to do next. A slight pause in conversation or a moment of quietness caused me great embarrassment. In training, we were told not to leave the person alone after delivering sad news, unless they specifically requested it. It was always a relief when a family member or friend arrived to give comfort.

On 18 September 1971 one of my closest friends from training days in Enniskillen, Roy Leslie, was shot dead in Strabane town centre. I heard the news just before leaving for work the following morning. For the first time since childhood I cried. A couple of days later I attended Roy's funeral in Moy. He had lived with his mother in a small cottage just outside the village. She embraced me when I told her who I was and took me into her bedroom, where she produced a diary entry which Roy had made while in Enniskillen. It referred to the weekly five-mile road races that were part of our training. In this particular entry Roy expressed his determination 'to beat the Sheik'. (I was given the nickname because I had black hair and a moustache and it was an abbreviation of my surname.) I won every race during the ten-week course; Roy invariably came second.

In November of that year, I was transferred to Bangor. The religious tensions, so evident throughout Northern Ireland, were patent in the town. Many young men from east Belfast and the Shankill Road area frequented the pubs and clubs in Queen's Parade and the lower end of High Street. Violent incidents were common occurrences at weekends and involved many of the Belfast boys. Most had loyalist paramilitary connections and some would develop infamous reputations in the years ahead; others would meet violent deaths, while many served long terms of imprisonment. Strange to say, I got on well with them and never encountered serious problems, even though I had to arrest quite a few of them.

Many local youths were also involved in the violence, and housing estates like Kilcooley and Whitehill were fertile recruiting grounds for militant groups. I had many run-ins with them.

Fatal and serious car accidents were a common occurrence. One lovely summer's day six elderly people were killed in a head-on collision on the dual carriageway between Holywood and Bangor. I was sent to the scene shortly after the accident to assist with traffic control. I saw sights that day that still cause me great anguish. On the same stretch of carriageway a sixteen-year-old girl was knocked down and killed. This was particularly distressing as I had to tell her parents that she was dead, arrange for her father to formally identify the body, attend the post-mortem and return the girl's ring and other personal items to the family.

Other instances that caused me great upset involved telling an 83-year-old widowed woman that her son had been knocked down and killed in a hit-and-run accident. After completing the examination of the accident site, I called to her house at 1.30 a.m. She took me into the kitchen and pointed to a small glass of milk and a biscuit sitting on the table which she had left out for him. It was a heart-breaking moment.

I recall with sadness a long walk up a driveway to tell a woman watching at the window that her husband had died of a heart attack while travelling home by train from work.

Life in the police was unpredictable; no two days were ever the same. At the start of each shift, the senior sergeant assigned us various tasks. Much of the work was routine: visiting shops and homes that had been burgled; dealing with shoplifters; stolen cars; and assault cases. Situations that appeared ordinary could suddenly develop into something more serious. One night I went to a domestic dispute involving a drunken husband. After some effort, things seemed to quieten down and I was about to leave. Without warning, he smashed the television and front window. I tried to restrain him and he stabbed me in the leg with a piece of glass.

In August, I was sent to Grey's Point outside Helen's Bay, where workmen had spotted a body in the water. I was distraught when I realised it was the body of a seven-year-old girl who had gone missing with her father days earlier after their dingy capsized in Belfast Lough. A number of weeks later, the father's body was found floating in shallow water off Crawfordsburn beach. As we removed it from the sea, the skin peeled from the legs and arms. It distressed me and the crowd of onlookers who had gathered to watch.

On the night of 23 March 1972, I was patrolling around Bangor in a police car with another officer. We were told that two vehicles, a Ford Zodiac and an Austin Maxi, had been abandoned in Main Street. I asked the control room staff in the station to check the ownership details with the Taxation Office. Almost immediately, we were informed that the IRA had telephoned a bomb warning and that the two cars had been hijacked.

We cordoned off the street and evacuated people as quickly as possible. Sirens wailed as firemen, police and army bomb experts raced to the scene. Half an hour later, a man rushed up to me and told me that his elderly mother lived in a flat close to one of the abandoned cars. He gave me a key and I dashed up to the flat. She was fast asleep, blissfully unaware of the commotion and danger outside. I helped her put on a dressing-gown and carried her down the stairs onto the street and past the bomb. A few minutes later, it exploded, devastating the flat and adjoining shops. The second bomb went off a short time later.

At 6 a.m. one morning a postman ran into Bangor station in an agitated state and told us that he had found the body of a man in a garden at Southwell Road. An experienced sergeant and I went to the scene; we discovered the remains of an elderly man dressed in pyjamas. He had a bread-knife sticking out of his chest. Neighbours told us that the man's son was a psychiatric patient in a secure wing of Downshire Hospital, Downpatrick. We soon learned that he had gone missing from the hospital a few days previously. In a short time we traced him to a flat in a nearby street; he was covered in blood. On the way back to the station he said that he had stabbed his father believing him to be the Devil. The man was charged with murder and remanded back to the Downshire Hospital. Each morning of his trial I had to collect him from the secure wing of the hospital. I sometimes had to sit in the ward for fifteen or twenty minutes before he was produced. It gave me a shocking and unnerving insight into the effects of mental illness.

In November 1972 I was seconded to the Criminal Investigation Branch in Bangor. Because I lived in the station and was readily available, I dealt with many of the burglaries, car thefts, robberies and assaults that occurred after midnight. On my third night as a CID officer, I investigated the death of a woman in Donaghadee who died when her electric blanket caught fire. In December, a Catholic man was shot in the chest on the Clandyboye Road by the Red Hand Commando. I accompanied the injured man in an ambulance to Ards Hospital. There was no medic in attendance and I quickly realised that my first aid training was of no value: sadly he died a short time later in hospital.

I was kept busy as bombings, shootings, robberies and burnings connected to the deteriorating public order situation took hold in Bangor. On one occasion, a man went into a wooded area to relieve himself and found a gun hidden in undergrowth. It so happened that I was the only detective available to respond to his call. During a lengthy search, I recovered a rifle, a sub-machine-gun, a pistol and twelve sticks of gelignite. I returned to the station thinking I was a bit of a hero; but smiles turned to profound embarrassment when the station had to be evacuated while the gelignite was removed by an Ammunition Technical Officer.

In December 1973 I was a member of a team set up to investigate a spate of IRA bombings and shooting incidents in the area, which had left one police officer dead, another blown up and seriously injured and a CID officer shot and critically wounded. Premises in Downpatrick, Ardglass and Ballynahinch had been damaged or destroyed. A major breakthrough occurred when uniformed officers stopped to speak to two men on a road outside Ardglass. They told the officers that their vehicle had broken down. The officers offered to push the vehicle to get it going and became suspicious when the engine started easily. They checked a nearby laneway and discovered a bomb. On 13 December, five men from Downpatrick were arrested. Over the next two days I and other detectives interviewed them about the incidents. The following day I helped interview two further suspects. By the end of the week admissions had been obtained in relation to most of the thirty-nine bombings and the wounding of two police officers. Later that year the seven men were convicted and received prison sentences ranging from twelve to thirty-five years.

I was on this inquiry for the next eight months, but still had to assist in major investigations in Bangor, such as the fire-bombing of shops on 30 July 1974 which caused massive damage; the death of a man in a domestic dispute in Donaghadee; the fatal shooting of a young woman by her boyfriend; and the murder of a sixteen-year-old Catholic youth at an 11 July bonfire in Valentine playing fields in Bangor. Two suspects were arrested the following morning. The suspect I was detailed to interview answered questions put to him by my colleague but refused to speak to me because I was a 'Taig'. By lunchtime, no admissions had been made and the interviewers left for lunch. I was told to stay with the suspect while he ate his food.

Eventually he spoke and told me how much he hated the IRA and Catholics. He conceded that I was probably all right because I was in the police. He went silent for a few moments, then asked for a Bible. I went to my room and recovered an inscribed copy of the New Testament which had been presented to me by the Christian Police Association when I joined the police—every new recruit got one. (It remains one of my most treasured possessions.) When he opened the book and saw the personal inscription to me, he looked at me for some minutes and said, 'You're okay.' He read for a short time and then told me that he had murdered Michael Browne. He and his companion, who also made admissions, were sentenced to life imprisonment.

The bomb unit was also busy investigating the activities of the UVF, who were responsible for a number of bombing incidents. A major break-through in the investigation came when a purple Ford Capri was seen leaving the scene of an explosion in Kircubbin. Inquiries with the Tax Office, which has details of all licensed vehicles in Northern Ireland, highlighted a small number of owners of purple Ford Capris in north Down. One was traced to Donaghadee. I was sent to interview the owner, but he was not at home. Details given by his unsuspecting mother about his movements the previous Saturday night contradicted the story he gave when he returned home. He was arrested with a number of other suspects. Several weapons and a substantial amount of explosives were recovered. They all made admissions about a series of bombings and eventually received long prison sentences.

It was during this period that I met Detective Constable David Morwood, who in my view was the best detective in the force. He was an intelligent and very shrewd man. He knew how to obtain intelligence, how to analyse and put it to good use; he was a fantastic interviewer and a popular and influential colleague. He taught me everything he could about investigative policing. He was a dear and valued friend until his death in 2005.

The Ulster Workers' Council Strike of May 1974 was a worrying and confusing time. On the first afternoon of the strike a colleague and I were patrolling in a police car when we were sent to a reported burglary in the Kilcooley Estate. As we drove up the hill from the Clandeboye Road end I saw thirty or forty youths standing across the road. Some of them were masked and some were carrying wooden clubs. I did not slow down and drove through them. I immediately reported their presence to the control room at Bangor station. Within minutes, a senior officer ordered us not to have any contact with the youths and directed us to move out of the area. They blocked the road menacingly when we attempted to leave the estate. We drew our guns in a way that was clearly visible to them and drove through without any trouble. Later in the evening we saw masked men parading through various areas of Bangor. On the Skipperstone Road they sarcastically saluted and gave us an 'eyes right' as they passed in military formation.

On the following three mornings, I had examinations at Jordanstown College—as part of a Higher National Certificate in Police Studies. Because I lived in Hawthornden Road in east Belfast, I had to pass through a massive roadblock of armed and masked men at the junction of Newtownards Road and Beersbridge Road. I had to produce my police warrant card, which they took away and showed to their 'commanders'. After a short time, they returned the card and told me I was free to pass. It was a frightening experience. I eventually arrived at the examination hall forty-five minutes late but managed to pass all the examinations. Later the same year I sat the Sergeants' Promotion Examination and was awarded the second highest marks in the force.

———

To this day, it is difficult to understand the thinking of government in its handling of the strike, but I feel that the integrity of policing was damaged by our seeming inability and lack of resolve to influence events. Most moderate people, particularly the business community and hard-working people trying to get to their place of employment, felt intimidated and betrayed. I think, for their sakes, we should have taken on the strikers and kept the roads open. Even if this had not succeeded, there would have been more honour in failure than in doing nothing.

As a prelude to being promoted to the rank of Sergeant, I had to attend a pre-promotion course at Connswater, a police training establishment in the east of the city. On my way to the course I was driving along the Belmont Road, when I saw police cars racing up the road. They pulled up outside the home of Martin McBirney, a magistrate, who sat each week in Bangor court. One of the officers told me that Martin had been shot dead. I was horrified and very upset. I had given evidence before him on many occasions and had sometimes taken coffee with him after court finished. He was a well-known academic and highly acclaimed writer and was happy to share his views on socialist and political issues. He was a man I much admired and liked.

Chapter 4 ∾

I AM PROMOTED TO DETECTIVE SERGEANT: STRABANE, LONDONDERRY AND WEST BELFAST

In October 1974, with the rank of Detective Sergeant, I was posted to Strabane. Weeks before my move, a documentary on BBC national television had suggested that the town was an IRA citadel and that the rule of law did not exist. It was a depressing place with high unemployment and a polarised community. The police and army were peripheral figures. Most shops refused to serve them.

The geographical position of the town on the border with Donegal in the Irish Republic failed to provide any advantage in terms of trade or business. Paramilitaries from Northern Ireland stayed in Donegal; they were untroubled by the Irish security forces and could cross the border into towns on the Northern side to bomb, shoot and cause mayhem.

My own office was small and with a squeeze accommodated two desks, a couple of chairs and a filing cabinet; I was sharing it with five detective constables and a typist. On my first night, several vehicles were hijacked and set on fire by rioters, and a booby-trap bomb in a garage injured three soldiers on patrol. I spent several hours talking to the resident Special Branch officers and was amazed at the amount of high-quality intelligence they had on suspects; I wondered why more success against the paramilitaries had not been achieved. They identified the proximity of the border as the main security issue and suggested that some of my predecessors, CID officers who had been sent there from Belfast and other faraway places, had little interest in the problems of the area and showed little inclination to take action. They were delighted when I declared that arrests would begin the following morning.

Over the coming months, the small contingent of CID officers charged nineteen paramilitaries with a variety of serious offences, including murder, attempted murder, bombings, shootings and hijackings. It was an example of Special Branch, CID, uniformed police and the military working in perfect harmony. Morale increased within the group and reports from senior officers suggested that many people in the town were also delighted.

Each evening we made the hazardous journey to our accommodation at Browning Drive in Londonderry. The complex of portacabins was completely defenceless against paramilitary attack, protected merely by a wire fence. Because of health and safety issues, the living quarters would not have been deemed suitable today. But they were clean and comfortable. There was great companionship among the residents, and the atmosphere there was wonderful. Some of these officers were killed in the course of duty; many more would die, officially from natural causes; but I believe these were aggravated by the conditions of the job—such as working long hours, high stress levels and the use of radio-communication devices. These colleagues have left me with a treasure chest of memories and friendships.

One of the most interesting cases in my thirty years' service involved an explosion at the British Legion Hall in January 1975. Two armed men planted a bomb in the hall while elderly people were playing whist. Everyone fled except an old, partially sighted man who, in the confusion, was left behind. He was rescued by police before the bomb exploded. In April, Special Branch named Willie Gallagher, an IRA activist on the run in County Donegal, as one of the bombers. He was expected to sign at the Labour Exchange in Strabane on the morning of 23 April 1975. I planned an arrest operation. A Special Branch sergeant hid in an observation van parked nearby to make a positive identification; the army took up positions further along the road. Gallagher was about to enter the Exchange when he was warned about the presence of the army. I grabbed him as he was about to run off, and I put a gun to his head. I later interviewed him with other detectives. He verbally admitted his part in the bombing. At his trial, he alleged that the admissions had been concocted. Two of the elderly whist players who had earlier identified him as one of the bombers now declared that he was not involved in the incident. The judge decided that they had been intimidated and accepted my evidence that Gallagher had admitted the offence.

In May 1976, Gallagher and an accomplice were sentenced to long terms of imprisonment. He continued to plead his innocence and went on hunger strike. His father stood against Roy Mason, the Northern Ireland Secretary of State, in a Westminster election in Barnsley.

The story took another twist in September 1978 when BBC national television broadcast a dramatic reconstruction of the arrest and interview of Gallagher. The character who played me was a stout, bald chain-smoker—none of which remotely resembled me. The programme depicted Gallagher as an innocent man who had been wrongfully convicted.

Years later, I met Gallagher at Castlereagh police office, where he was being interviewed about his part in a bomb attack on Robinson's Bar in Patrick Street, Strabane—a favourite drinking place for off-duty police. Many people were injured in the blast. He was sentenced to twenty-one years' imprisonment for this. We spoke for a few moments. It was a warm and friendly exchange. He apologised for any trouble he had caused me.

Gallagher continued his paramilitary career and later became a prominent member of the INLA. Strange to say, I always felt sympathy for him. He was a product of a provincial, economically deprived background. The IRA was traditionally strong in the area and he was recruited at a young age. His father was a decent man, a good father who was heartbroken at his son's involvement in the IRA: he told me he blamed army harassment of his son for it.

Strabane was a difficult posting with its own special pressures, not least for the soldiers. Due to a chronic lack of accommodation, they were forced to bunk down in the back of the station. They were always on stand-by, not permitted out of their uniforms except for a shower or to go to the toilet. Not surprisingly, some soldiers buckled. On one occasion a young soldier threatened people with a firearm in Sion Mills. It was obvious from the circumstances that he was distressed and suffering mental problems. I suggested to the military authorities that they should have him examined by a psychiatrist. A legal adviser declined the suggestion. I told the major in charge that I was going to take the soldier to Londonderry for interview. He said he would not allow this. As I and other detectives attempted to drive out of the station with the suspect, a number of soldiers blocked the way and pointed their rifles at us. The major said they would shoot if we tried to drive through them. I took the threat seriously and reversed the car. The matter was only resolved some hours later after negotiations between very senior police officers and military in Londonderry. The soldier, who should have been referred for medical treatment, was sentenced to five years in jail.

On one occasion, I was in the Special Branch office with a sergeant-major in the local company; we were having a beer. The sergeant-major said, 'Watch this,' and dropped his can onto the roof of a sangar just below the window. He shouted to the soldier on guard duty to get the f****** tin off the roof. The soldier set down his rifle and climbed onto the roof of the sangar. The sergeant-major demanded to know why he had left his rifle unattended. The soldier was later fined £70—a very substantial sum in those days.

The quality of the troops was variable, from the undisciplined to the heroic. I was full of admiration for one particular captain in charge of a Quick Response Unit of eight soldiers. As soon as a serious incident was reported, this unit would rush straight to the scene. Several paramilitaries were detained and many weapons recovered as a result. These were among the bravest soldiers I ever met; they should have been honoured for their valour.

A peculiar form of relaxation for us was going out on salmon poaching patrols after midnight. We wore dark clothing and darkened our faces when there was a full moon. The army provided us with plastic buckets filled with stones to throw at the poachers, who operated from the Donegal side of the border and laid illegal nets across the river. It was our only form of deterrence short of shooting at them. The river was only twenty to thirty yards wide at this point and formed a crucial part of the route for spawning salmon. I remember an official from Foyle Fisheries telling me that up to 25,000 spawning salmon needed to reach the weir at Sion Mills in order to restock the whole Foyle system; at an advanced stage in the season, only twenty-five had been recorded. The IRA was a major player in, and beneficiary of, this poaching.

The police had an arrangement with the Foyle Fisheries that

salmon caught in recovered nets could be kept and the nets handed over to the Fisheries Board. It was a dangerous and probably foolhardy enterprise in an area where the IRA was very active; but most of the men were happy to do the patrol to get access to the salmon. My motivation was different: I was an animal welfare activist and a vegetarian and was appalled at the sight of beautiful salmon, twenty to twenty-five pounds in weight, entangled and drowned in poachers' nets.

On one occasion, we set up an observation post in the ruins of Senator Jack Barnhill's house (he had been brutally murdered by the official IRA in 1972) and witnessed men carrying sacks from the river just as dawn broke. We arrested them and found them to be in possession of 600 lbs of salmon.

Later that year, I was posted to Rosemount, Londonderry. The city was a dangerous, volatile place where any period of relative calm could be shattered without warning. Intensive and prolonged rioting, shootings and bombings were regular occurrences. Many nights we were trapped in the station—it was too dangerous to venture out. Some of the killings I investigated had a surreal quality about them: for example, a young girl was shot dead by a male companion playing a form of Russian roulette. When I interviewed him, he alleged that the fatal shot had come from a nearby housing estate. An examination of the house showed that the windows had been closed and had not been penetrated by a bullet; a post-mortem examination confirmed that the girl had been shot at close range. He later admitted the offence and was convicted of manslaughter.

On another occasion, a convicted paramilitary, recently released from jail, was shot and killed while travelling on a bus as it passed a military sentry post. The soldier on duty, who had suffered some sort of mental aberration, alleged that he saw a gunman on the roof of a nearby garage and opened fire; in addition to killing the passenger he wounded two pedestrians as the bus crossed his line of fire. When restrained by colleagues, he cried, 'I'm cracking! I'm cracking!' He was subsequently sentenced to five years' imprisonment.

Other killings showed the callous cunning of the IRA. On 18 December 1975 two young soldiers were on duty in a sangar at Bank Place beside the historic city walls. It was later established that a child aged seven or eight approached the soldiers and offered them sweets. The soldiers stepped out of the sangar and spoke to the child. While they were distracted in this way, a man lowered a bomb onto the sangar roof. A short time later, the device exploded and mutilated the soldiers. A detective inspector and myself, unable to drive to the location because the explosion had brought tea-time traffic to a standstill, started to walk to the scene. It was raining heavily and I was disquieted when he decided to take cover under a shop canopy. I left him and hurried on. The scene of the explosion was in total darkness. I remember thinking how inappropriate the Christmas carols in a nearby shop sounded. The area could not be examined properly for some time until the army arrived with powerful searchlights. The following day, after the post-mortem, I helped the mortuary attendant embalm the bodies. It was my way of showing respect for the two young men who had been so cruelly betrayed by the exploitation of a young child.

In May 1975, during an IRA ceasefire, Constable Paul Gray was shot dead on the city walls by a sniper. I and other colleagues who were close by raced to the scene, having heard that a police officer had been shot. When I arrived, I was horrified to see women and youths trying to pull the body off the stretcher. I was devastated when I realised it was Paul. He was a resident at the Browning Drive complex, a lovely young man, a rascal who liked to make a nuisance of himself; he was exceedingly popular. We were in mourning, and senior officers decreed that the bar should stay open all night. Many of us were there until 6 a.m.

In November 1975, I interviewed one of the two suspects in the killing. Both men made admissions and were subsequently convicted at Belfast City Commission, Crumlin Road, where all paramilitary cases were heard. One received a life sentence, the other seven years.

Early the following year, I was preparing to give evidence at the Commission involving some accused men from Londonderry. They had been charged with a rocket and gun attack on an army base in the city. The presiding judge asked me if I thought the killing of a Special Branch officer in the city that morning was in any way connected with the case being heard. This was my first notification that something terrible had happened and I had to ask him who had been killed. I was devastated to learn that it was Paddy McNulty, a brave and honourable man and a good friend. He had been shot by IRA gunmen when he left his car in for a service. I had met Paddy on my first night in Londonderry. He took me for a drink in a pub in William Street—a

dangerous location and out of bounds for police. Paddy was well
known to the owner and customers and we were well received. Before
we left the premises, well after midnight, several men checked the street
to make sure it was safe for us to leave. I was pleased that Bishop
Edward Daly condemned the killing at Paddy's funeral Mass.

The murder of Reserve Constable Linda Baggley plunged everyone
connected with policing into abject despair. She was a lovely nineteen-
year-old girl, shy and well-respected, and was shot by the IRA in the
Waterside in May 1976, close to the spot where her father had been
killed, also by the IRA, in 1974. Later in the year, as a result of Special
Branch intelligence, a number of suspects were arrested and
interviewed by detectives from North Region Crime Squad, of which I
was by then a member. Four local activists were convicted of Linda's
murder and received life sentences. One of them was among thirty-
eight prisoners to escape from the Maze Prison in 1983. The following
year he drowned while trying to escape a confrontation with SAS
soldiers.

The death of any colleague from Browning Drive felt like a family
bereavement and caused deep anguish. We lived and socialised together
in our little oasis; inevitably we were constantly reminded of that
colleague's absence by an empty bed, at mealtimes in the canteen and
during recreation. Constable James Heaney was killed by the IRA when
off-duty and visiting his widowed mother in Andersonstown. He
worried about his safety, but the urge to be a dutiful son was strong.
When news of his death reached Londonderry, I wrote to his mother
and told her that James had been a good friend and a valued colleague.
I signed the letter 'Kevin'. Some weeks later, she came to the city in
search of the writer of the letter. When we met, she embraced me and
through her tears explained how much comfort my sentiments had
brought her.

In April 1977, two further friends, John McCracken and Kenneth
Sheehan, also residents of Browning Drive, were shot dead by members
of an IRA unit which had been terrorising security personnel in south
Derry for some time. Many UDR soldiers had also been killed. John
'Badger' McCracken was a fine footballer and had played with me in
the Londonderry divisional team. The IRA unit included Francis
Hughes and Dominic McGlinchey. In March 1978 Hughes was
wounded and captured after a shoot-out with undercover soldiers. I

later interviewed him about a number of killings. He was sentenced to a long term in prison. In May 1981, he was the second of ten republican hunger strikers to die in the Maze.

In February 1994, McGlinchey, by then a member of the INLA (Irish National Liberation Army), was shot dead in Drogheda by former associates. His wife, Mary, had been killed by the same faction in 1987. A third gunman involved in the shooting of John and Kenneth was convicted of a number of serious incidents in south Derry and was sentenced to life imprisonment.

It would be dishonest of me to imply that all the citizens of Londonderry supported the on-going violence. Many concerned members of the public, representatives of the business community, clergy and some politicians maintained contact with senior police figures, including the legendary Frank Lagan and Maurice Johnstone, who appreciated the importance of good community relations. Many potentially volatile and dangerous situations were quietly diffused, while rumour and misunderstandings were clarified and corrected. There was also much evidence of parental disapproval and criticism of paramilitaries. Unfortunately this was not enough to keep some children from getting involved. In one incident, a fifteen-year-old student threw a hand-grenade from the nearby technical college and injured three soldiers building a security wall at the back of Strand Road station.

In a follow-up search of the college, a second device was recovered. The student was arrested and interviewed by me. He admitted his involvement in the incident and was subsequently sentenced to a long term of imprisonment. His heartbroken parents, who were on holiday at the time of the bombing, spoke to me on their return. Despite their loving and protective concern, they had not beeen able to prevent their son from becoming involved with the paramilitaries.

Londonderry was an abnormal and complex environment. Often policing procedures, such as identification parades, could not be arranged because of public reluctance to participate. The only alternative was an informal parade, where witnesses (invariably army or police) were brought to a room to view the lone suspect. The procedure was flawed and unsatisfactory and was unpopular with the judiciary. I used the process after a number of men were arrested leaving the scene of a rocket and gun attack on Fort George army camp.

A suspect ran off and was not located for several days. The only witnesses to his escape were army personnel. While I was preparing the confrontation with the suspect, I saw soldiers passing his photograph around. They all identified him as the man who had fled after the attack. Although I was certain that he was one of the attackers, I brought the issue of the photograph to the attention of the Director of Public Prosecutions. He rightly declined to prosecute.

Civil witnesses to incidents rarely contacted the police. One exception was a brave citizen whose action saved the life of a police officer. One afternoon he was driving into the city and passed two officers on patrol. He recognised one of them as an old school friend. Further along the road, he spotted two gunmen in an alleyway; he assumed they were about to mount an ambush. He turned his car and drove back to warn his friend. Other police were summoned to the area and arrested the suspects. A loaded Magnum revolver was recovered. I interviewed one of the suspects, who admitted that his intention had been to shoot the male police officer and steal his weapon. (Back then, female officers were not armed.) He was subsequently sentenced to fifteen years in prison.

I genuinely believe that the RUC did their utmost to provide a service to the community in Londonderry. On a daily basis, we investigated burglaries, thefts and car crime in every part of the city, including the Bogside and Creggan. I was always received with a handshake and an offer of refreshment. One afternoon a colleague and I visited a house in the Bogside, an IRA stronghold. As we prepared to leave the area half an hour later, we learned to our consternation that every road had been blocked by women. (I later discovered that they were protesting against breaks in the electricity supply.) Our anxiety increased when they refused to let us pass. We considered requesting urgent assistance from the station, but decided that tactful diplomacy was a better option. I invited a mature woman over to the car and quietly informed her that we were CID officers and had been on a call to a burglary in the area. She spoke to the other women and they immediately cleared a passage for us.

The contribution of the army in the city at this time has not been fairly represented nor sufficiently appreciated. There were major problems concerning their acceptability, coming so soon after the divisive issues of Internment, Operation Motorman and Bloody

Sunday. It is true that on occasions they used indiscriminate and excessive force, which caused resentment and alienation. However, due to the frequency of bombings, shootings and rioting which, on occasion, lasted several days, I believe that without their support the police (due to lack of resources, manpower, etc.) could not have continued to function in areas where the IRA were strongly entrenched, and the city might well have descended into anarchy. I saw army technical officers defusing bombs with great courage and disregard for their own safety. The Special Investigation Branch (the army equivalent of CID) was professional and extremely efficient. They traced soldiers who had finished their tour of duty in Northern Ireland and had been posted to locations throughout the world; they recorded statements and located exhibits for investigation files, fed us, provided transport and afforded protection when required.

I still wonder how the business community, schools, hospitals and law-abiding citizens coped with the upheaval. I am immensely pleased to hear of the current rejuvenation in the city. Today it is a thriving, expanding and prosperous place, a 'must see' destination for tourists. My brother Paul served there as a uniformed sergeant in the Neighbourhood Policing Unit during the 1990s until his untimely death in 2004. He loved the city and the people in it and always defended them against criticism. At his retirement function, many leading figures in business, local political dignitaries and citizens paid tribute to him and the police for their contribution to the city's renaissance.

In December 1976 I was transferred to Springfield Road in west Belfast. The working environment was similar in many ways to that of Londonderry. Both were dangerous areas where extreme violence could erupt without warning. Republican and loyalist paramilitaries were ruthlessly active and appeared to have substantial support in their local communities. Entering and leaving the area was a hazardous and stressful experience. Several police officers and army personnel were shot doing so. My new boss, Detective Chief Inspector Leo McBrien, had not been there long before he was seriously wounded at traffic lights at the junction of Falls Road and Grosvenor Road close to Springfield Road police station.

In March 1977, I was assigned to a special detective unit under the command of Detective Chief Inspector George Caskey to investigate the relationship between Sinn Féin and the IRA. Publicly, they claimed to be quite separate, sharing only a common political objective. Special Branch knew differently. It had information linking Sinn Féin to the military strategy of the IRA. One instance of this involved telex messages accepting responsibility for bombings and shootings sent to media outlets from the Sinn Féin press centre, Falls Road. One particular message was circulated minutes before a bomb in Belfast city centre had exploded.

It was also apparent that Sinn Féin was using its advice centres to usurp the functions of the RUC by recording and investigating crime in republican areas. Offenders were kneecapped, beaten or forced to leave home.

The aim of Mr Caskey's investigation was to compile evidence for an offence of conspiracy (i.e., a secret plan or agreement to carry out an illegal or harmful act, especially with political motivation), to be brought against senior figures in Sinn Féin.

Raids on republican premises and the homes of activists in December 1977 and April 1978 led to the seizure of several thousand items, including telex machines, minutes of meetings and strategy documents.

There was a great deal of concern within the RUC and the Northern Ireland Office when plans detailing Sinn Féin's intention to establish a 'people's police' and 'people's courts' were uncovered. A list was found containing the names of a number of alleged offenders. Twenty-five of them had already been severely punished. This suggested that Sinn Féin's policing policy was being implemented.

In April and May 1978, I took part with hundreds of other police in a major search and arrest operation. A number of prominent Sinn Féin activists were detained. Over the next week, I interviewed three suspects. They were all intelligent, articulate and sincere believers in Sinn Féin's vision. But they fell a long way short of convincing me that republican violence was either necessary or morally justified.

The investigation collapsed in September 1978 when the Lord Chief Justice, Lord Lowry, ruled that speculation about a suspect's involvement in criminality was no substitute for evidence in a court of law. Influenced by his ruling, the Director of Public Prosecutions ordered the Chief Constable to withdraw charges against a further seven defendants.

The failure of the investigation allowed Sinn Féin to strengthen its influence over Catholic areas. 'Anti-social behaviour' was outlawed and over the next two decades the IRA used guns, baseball bats, nails and iron bars to inflict appalling injuries. Many victims were disfigured and maimed. Paramilitary operations increased and racketeering and extortion flourished; the official transport system was largely replaced by republican-run black taxis; hundreds of pubs, the traditional meeting place for the local community, were forced out of business and replaced by republican drinking clubs.

In my view, the greatest crime of all was to create two generations of young people incapable of differentiating between right and wrong behaviour. Loyalist paramilitaries did the same.

While many paramilitary attacks were directed against the security forces, much of the violence was essentially sectarian. At an Easter republican commemoration parade in April 1977 a bomb exploded in Beechmount Avenue as Official IRA members prepared to march to the republican plot in Milltown Cemetery. A ten-year-old boy was killed and several other people injured. The Officials blamed the Provisional IRA, who had left the same location an hour earlier. Members of the two groups clashed at the cemetery and shots were fired. As the tension increased, the young boy's uncle was shot dead by the Provisionals on the Springfield Road. I attended both incidents but had difficulty in establishing the facts or locating reliable witnesses. High-grade intelligence obtained by Special Branch over the ensuing weeks clarified the situation and indicated that members of the UVF had been responsible for the bombing.

Not long afterwards, detectives at Tennent Street in the Shankill area identified a number of individuals who were believed to have killed as many as nineteen Catholics. Several of the victims had been kidnapped, tortured and stabbed. The persons responsible became known as the 'Shankill Butchers'. I had unwittingly encountered some of them while investigating the kneecapping of a man outside the Lawnbrook Social Club—a loyalist drinking club situated in the interface between the Springfield and Shankill areas. The ground around the club had no lighting and the interior was dimly lit and cheaply furnished. I was unnerved by the eerie and sinister atmosphere of the place. In time it was established that people were abducted and taken there, tortured and killed. The man who was kneecapped was later identified as a prominent member of the notorious 'Butchers'. He had been kneecapped following a violent and alcohol-fuelled altercation with other gang members.

In May 1977 members of the gang were arrested by detectives from Tennent Street. I was invited to interview six of them about murders in west Belfast. Four of them were subsequently convicted of the bombing in Beechmount Avenue and received long prison sentences.

In west Belfast, sectarian killings were not confined to loyalists. The shooting of a 64-year-old Protestant man at Ainsworth Avenue was not publicly claimed by the Provisionals, but a firearm recovered some time later was forensically proven to have been used in the incident and other IRA attacks. I considered various possible motives for the killing, but found none, other than that the victim was randomly selected because he lived in a Protestant area.

In July 1977 an escalation of a simmering internal IRA feud between the Provisionals and Officials left four men dead, many injured and houses destroyed in republican areas of Belfast. On 27 July I attended twenty-one serious incidents, including the killing of Thomas Tolan, a prominent IRA figure in Ballymurphy. I interviewed several members of the official IRA who had been involved in these incidents. Some received long prison sentences.

Despite this internal feuding, the IRA maintained its campaign of violence with attacks on the security forces and an on-going bombing campaign against commercial targets throughout Northern Ireland. Near the end of June, a well-planned gun attack on the army at North Howard Street resulted in the death of two soldiers and the wounding of an army padre.

Tyre tracks at the scene indicated that a Mini had been used as the getaway vehicle—a clever ploy by the gunmen who rightly assumed that the security forces would be on the lookout for something more powerful. As always in such cases, I was not able to locate any civilian witnesses. The forensic examination of the scene and the results of the post-mortems on the deceased soldiers merely revealed the make of weapons used and the number of shots fired. However, high-grade intelligence obtained in early August by Special Branch identified the persons involved. Three adult gunmen and seven juvenile lookouts were arrested and interviewed. One adult was subsequently convicted of the murders and sentenced to life imprisonment; several juveniles were ordered to be detained in juvenile detention centres.

Everyday life in this densely populated area went on amidst the violence. I, like other police officers, attempted to provide some sort of policing service to the people who wanted it; as in Londonderry we investigated the whole spectrum of crime. I became increasingly aware of widespread alienation among young people. I was shocked by their level of anti-social behaviour: drug and alcohol abuse and glue-sniffing were widespread, and the residents of local housing estates were plagued by unruly behaviour, with youths driving at speed in stolen or unlicensed vehicles. These social problems did not get sufficient coverage in the media, as paramilitary violence continued to dominate the headlines. In one particularly sad case which I investigated, a young, drunken father broke into a gas meter in his home, while smoking a cigarette. This caused a fire which engulfed the house and killed his two young children.

Chapter 5

I MOVE TO HEADQUARTERS CRIME SQUAD

In early February 1978, I moved to the Headquarters Crime Squad and was placed in charge of one of ten units of detectives which investigated paramilitary crime throughout Northern Ireland. Most of the squad members were known to me, including its head, Detective Chief Superintendent Bill Mooney. The week after I joined, a bomb exploded at La Mon House, a hotel and restaurant complex on the outskirts of south Belfast. I was one of dozens of detectives assigned to the investigation. It was horrifying and condemned by many people, including the Pope.

The IRA had attached two blast incendiary devices made up of explosives attached to cans of petrol. It caused a huge fire-ball which raced through the building. Twelve people died in the blast and many others were seriously injured. Some victims were burned beyond recognition and had to be identified from dental records. None of us who witnessed the scene in the early morning daylight will ever forget it.

The IRA knew how lethal this type of device was: they had used it in more than one hundred attacks on commercial premises. They must have known that the La Mon was a thriving and popular complex. At least three hundred people were attending various functions on the night of the explosion. How could they have been so reckless? The bomb exploded without warning, despite IRA claims to the contrary. It would appear that it was a random attack on an economic and tourist target as part of their campaign to destroy the Northern Ireland economy. In September 1981, a west Belfast man pleaded guilty to twelve counts of manslaughter and explosives offences. He was sentenced to life imprisonment. A second man was acquitted.

The squad frequently re-opened and solved murder cases. One such incident involved the killing of Thomas Paisley, a milkman from County Antrim. On 29 September 1972, four members of the UVF attacked and robbed the elderly occupants of a farmhouse at Straid Road, Ballyclare. Thomas Paisley knew the couple well. When he arrived at the farmhouse in his milk cart, he realised what was happening and grappled with one of the robbers. He was shot and killed. In May 1978, I interviewed Victor Loughlin about the killing and he admitted his involvement. At his trial, he pleaded guilty to charges of manslaughter and robbery and was sentenced to ten years' imprisonment. Three other men were convicted of the same offence.

On 17 June 1978, the IRA ambushed a police car at a crossroads outside Camlough, Co. Armagh. Constable Hugh McConnell died instantly and his companion, Constable William Turbitt, was abducted. The IRA announced soon afterwards that they were interrogating him. I had known Hugh through his involvement with the RUC soccer team. He was a quiet, lovely guy, a skilful player and first eleven regular. When reports came through of the incident, I was working with other Crime Squad officers in Castlereagh police office. We were told to go immediately to Palace Barracks, Holywood, where a helicopter was waiting to take us to Bessbrook and on to Forkhill. We joined dozens of uniformed officers who were flooding into the area in the search for Constable Turbitt. By the end of a very hot day, we were exhausted and lay overnight in the backyard of the station. At first light, the search resumed.

It was not long before we got the startling news that Father Hugh Murphy, a Catholic priest based in Ahoghill, Co. Antrim, had been kidnapped by two masked and armed men at 7.30 a.m. He had been abducted from the parochial house in his dressing-gown and slippers, tied up and blindfolded. He was taken to the home of the McCaughey family on the outskirts of the village and locked in a shed with a coal bag over his head. It later transpired that he had been kidnapped to ensure the release of Constable Turbitt.

I had met Father Murphy many years ago when I lived in Newtownabbey. He was a well-known cleric, respected by both sides of the community. A former chaplain in the Royal Navy, he had been honoured with an OBE by the Queen in a ceremony in Buckingham Palace in 1974.

When I told other officers his story, their mood darkened at this development. Some of them were moved to tears later in the day when they heard Mrs Turbitt, the wife of our missing colleague, make an impassioned radio and television appeal for the release of Father Murphy and her husband. The Rev. Ian Paisley broadcast a similar message.

Later that evening, we learned that Father Murphy had been released safe and well. Sadly there was no news of Constable Turbitt. It was too much to hope that the Provisional IRA would respond to Mrs Turbitt's impassioned plea. Constable Turbitt's remains were not recovered until 9 July 1978. A post-mortem mercifully revealed that he had died at the same time as Constable McConnell.

For some time, police believed that the kidnapping of Father Murphy was the work of loyalist paramilitaries. The investigation took a dramatic and shocking turn three months later when it was discovered that at least two police officers had been involved. Late in the afternoon of 15 September 1978, I and other members of the Crime Squad were told to report to Castlereagh police office. One of the first people I met was Detective Superintendent Frank Murray. He was clearly agitated. We went to the canteen for a coffee. He told me that a group of uniformed police officers attached to Armagh station had planned to kill Detective Chief Inspector Maurice Neilly, the head of CID in the region, that very evening by placing a booby-trap bomb under his car. I was stunned. Maurice was a hugely popular officer whose skill as an investigative detective was universally acknowledged. I had worked with him in the past and liked and respected him very much. Apparently he had discovered that a number of local police had taken part in serious terrorist attacks in the area. Frank told me to speak to no one until he and Chief Superintendent Bill Mooney had an opportunity to fully brief detectives.

I joined a number of specially selected officers, all of whom I knew. Our remit was to interview these rogue officers. Teams of four detectives were assigned to each prisoner. Several times during the day, we met to discuss progress.

During the next six days, I interviewed Constable Ian Mitchell and

Constable Lawrence McClure. They were not difficult subjects and in time both admitted their involvement in a bomb and gun attack on the Rock Bar, outside Keady, on 5 June 1978. They said they were accompanied by Constable William McCaughey, who was being questioned by other detectives in a nearby room. In due course, McCaughey admitted his part in the incident.

On the night in question, they had stolen a car and travelled to the bar. They placed a 10 lb gelignite bomb by the entrance and fired a number of shots through the window. McCaughey shot an elderly man as he tried to flee. They then left the area in the stolen car and burned it some distance away. A colleague took them back to Armagh station in an unmarked police car.

McCaughey also described his part in the murder of William Strathearn, a Catholic man with seven young children, who owned a grocer's shop in McCaughey's home village of Ahoghill. Mr Strathearn was shot dead on 19 April 1977. It appears that McCaughey, who held strongly anti-Catholic views, believed local gossip about Mr Strathearn's alleged involvement with firearms and explosives. There was no foundation to this malicious rumour.

McCaughey took an unlicensed Colt .45 from his home and joined Sergeant John Weir and two prominent UVF men from Lurgan: Robin Jackson, known as 'The Jackal', and R.J. Kerr. They drove to the grocer's shop and arrived shortly after 2 a.m. The two policemen remained in the car while Jackson banged on the shop door. When Mr Strathearn spoke to him from an upstairs window, Jackson addressed him by his Christian name and said he needed aspirin for a sick child. When he opened the door, Jackson shot him twice in the head. After the shooting, McCaughey parted company with his three companions and went to the family home on the outskirts of Ahoghill. He buried the gun in a field on the farm.

In April 1980, McCaughey appeared at Belfast City Commission with Sergeant John Weir. Both denied the charges against them, including the murder of Mr Strathearn. Later in the trial, they changed their plea to one of guilty. Both were sentenced to life imprisonment.

In a second trial, in July 1980, McCaughey and Sergeant Gary Armstrong pleaded guilty to the kidnapping of Father Murphy. McCaughey also pleaded guilty to a charge of robbery and involvement in the gun and bomb attack at the Rock Bar. Ian Mitchell and Lawrence

McClure pleaded guilty to their part in the attack. Constable David Wilson also accepted in court that he had withheld information about the incident. McCaughey's father, a Presbyterian elder, pleaded guilty to a charge of withholding information about Father Murphy's abduction. He and Wilson received one-year suspended sentences. Armstrong, Mitchell and McClure received two-year suspended sentences; and McCaughey was imprisoned for a further seven years.

In his summing up, Lord Chief Justice Lord Lowry said: 'It is a matter of admiration that the RUC has resisted the temptation to resort to violence when friends, colleagues and neighbours have been killed.' In dealing with the six police defendants in this lenient way, he seems to have been influenced by the defence counsel's submission that the officers, while working in Armagh, faced a daily risk of attack from bombs and bullets. He suggested that they were before the court because of a feeling of frustration that ordinary policing methods had proved ineffective.

I cannot understand nor accept the conclusions reached by Lord Lowry. The guns used in the Rock Bar attack had earlier been used to kill Brian, John and Anthony Reavey on 4 January 1976. This suggests a deep and prolonged involvement between some of these officers and a notorious UVF killer gang operating in the area during this period. A 10 lb gelignite bomb was successfully detonated outside the Rock Bar, which suggests two possibilities: either the police got the bomb from the UVF, or one of them was competent at handling and assembling explosive devices.

I was not entirely surprised by the actions of these officers. In 1976, I had played a football match for the police at Strand Road, Londonderry, against a team from Armagh. We had changed in dormitories in Armagh station. Huge Ulster flags and other loyalist paraphernalia were inappropriately displayed on the walls. They should have been removed by senior ranks. It was evidence of a serious religious bias. The imposition of long prison sentences would have been a more appropriate way of dealing with these people.

On his release, Weir made allegations about the involvement of RUC officers and UDR members in the murders of Catholics and the 1974 bombings in Monaghan and Dublin. I have read Weir's 3 February 1999 affidavit in support of Sean McPhilemy's book *The Committee.*[5] I cannot refute all of Weir's allegations, but am inclined to believe they are not true. I knew these officers personally and am convinced that they would not have acted illegally vis-à-vis loyalist paramilitaries. Moreover, I am certain that all the known information connecting the rogue officers to serious crime was put to them during the six days of interview in 1978. The management team of Bill Mooney and Frank Murray were men of the utmost integrity and the fact that they picked their most experienced detectives to conduct the interviews of the suspect police officers showed their determination to get the full truth of the matter.

These rogue officers betrayed the trust and honour of other officers working in Armagh, one of the most dangerous areas for policing in the world in the decades spanning 1970–1990. Innumerable acts of heroism saved lives on a daily basis and were deserving of greater recognition and appreciation. They provided a much-needed service on behalf of law and order.

When I moved to Dungannon in June 1980, I worked with Maurice Neilly on a number of investigations and often socialised with him and other detectives from Armagh at Gough Barracks where I had quarters. It was one of the few places in the area that was safe for local police to socialise. Maurice later joined Special Branch on promotion. Sadly, he was in the Chinook helicopter which crashed in Scotland, on 2 June 1994, killing all on board.

The year 1979 saw no reduction in paramilitary violence: 113 people died violently and 1,292 bombs and incendiary devices were planted by republicans and loyalists. Between June and August, my unit at Headquarters Crime Squad researched IRA incidents involving the use of explosive devices in the greater Belfast area.

I remember 27 August as if it were yesterday. I met the research team at Castlereagh and spent the latter part of the morning working with explosives experts at the forensic laboratory. The day dawned clear and warm in Mullaghmore, Co. Sligo, where Queen Elizabeth II's cousin, Lord Louis Mountbatten, and members of his extended family were on holiday. At 11.30 a.m., he and a fishing party boarded his 29-foot-long boat, *Shadow V*. They planned to recover lobster pots he had laid the previous day. Although Garda officers were not on board, they maintained visual and radio contact from a clifftop on the shore. At 11.45 a.m., when the boat was roughly half a mile from the harbour and two hundred yards offshore, it was blown to pieces by a 50 lb bomb.

The device was detonated by a radio signal set off by IRA men positioned further along the shore. Everyone on board was thrown into the water by the force of the blast. Lord Mountbatten, Lady Patricia Brabourne (his daughter's mother-in-law), Nicholas Knatchbull (his fourteen-year-old grandson) and Paul Maxwell (a fifteen-year-old boatman hired for the summer) were killed. Three other family members survived the blast but were seriously injured. A post-mortem showed that Lord Mountbatten had died not from the blast but from drowning.

Garda and forensic investigators later established that the IRA had planted the bomb the previous night while the boat was moored in the harbour. The cabin was locked but they were able to hide the device among fishing tackle, ropes and lobster pots placed in the locker in the cockpit. Shortly after the explosion, Thomas McMahon, an expert bomb-maker and one of the IRA men who planted the device, was arrested by Gardaí seventy miles away. Forensic experts proved that sand particles, flecks of green paint and traces of nitro-glycerine found on his clothing linked him to Mullaghmore harbour, the boat and the bomb.

In November 1979 he was sentenced to life imprisonment. He was released under the terms of the Good Friday Agreement after serving some twenty years in jail. A second accused, Francis McGirl, was acquitted. In 1995, McGirl was killed when a tractor he was driving overturned, crushing him underneath.

The killing of Lord Mountbatten stunned the nation and people around the world. My initial shock quickly turned to anger. I spent much of the afternoon listening to news reports on the incident. Just after 5.15 p.m., I got a telephone call that deepened my gloom: four soldiers were reportedly dead after being caught in an explosion in Warrenpoint. My unit was placed on stand-by. Fifteen minutes later, I received a second telephone call reporting that six soldiers had died. We were ordered to get to Warrenpoint as quickly as possible. We travelled to the scene in two green Cortinas with registrations of some historical significance: NOI 1690 and NOI 1691.

We went to a roundabout on the Warrenpoint-Newry by-pass adjacent to the northern shore of Strangford Lough and met up with Detective Chief Superintendent Bill Mooney. He appointed Detective Inspector Eric Anderson as the senior investigator and myself as the scene exhibits officer.

A number of facts were established during conversations with police and fire crews at the scene: six soldiers travelling in a five-ton vehicle had been killed by an explosive device hidden under bales of barley straw in a trailer left at a lay-by a hundred yards from the roundabout. When army reinforcements arrived, they took cover around a gatehouse attached to Narrow Water Castle estate two hundred yards away. Half an hour after the first explosion, a 600 lb bomb, hidden inside the gatehouse, exploded, killing a further twelve soldiers.

The scene was one of utter devastation, surreal against the beautiful and tranquil background of low hills, the lough and mature trees. Mutilated and burnt bodies were scattered over a wide area. Debris from the bombed vehicles littered the road. The gatehouse, which had been constructed of granite blocks, had been blown apart, leaving a deep crater.

Our first priority was to mark and photograph the position of bodies, vehicles and other debris that might be of forensic importance. I joined uniformed police and soldiers in a minute search of the area. A helicopter was used to dislodge human remains from nearby trees. I delivered the bodies and body parts to the mortuary at Daisy Hill Hospital in Newry. They were then taken to Foster Green Hospital mortuary for post-mortem examination.

Over the next five days, I recorded the work done by forensic experts, mappers and photographers. Eighteen soldiers had died in the two explosions. In an exchange of fire between the bombers and soldiers, a civilian standing on the southern shore of the lough was shot dead. I recovered the rifles of all soldiers who attended or were involved in the incident and took them to a forensic laboratory for examination. The results of these tests were forwarded to the Garda Síochána.

Within two days, the investigation team established that an 800 lb bomb constructed of homemade explosives had been concealed on a trailer laden with bales of barley straw. The trailer had been abandoned the previous afternoon. A significant forensic breakthrough was made when part of a McGregor radio-controlled device used to detonate the bomb was found near the site of the first explosion. This device was similar to the one used to kill Lord Mountbatten and his party.

The IRA had first experimented with radio-controlled devices in 1972, using systems employed by model-plane and -boat enthusiasts.

During trials, IRA explosives experts discovered that the operational capability of this device was hampered by the length of time it took the electrical circuit to close. This meant that detonation was not instantaneous and was affected by the time it took a servo mechanism to move from one point to another, which could take seconds. This meant a loss of accuracy, particularly when aimed at moving vehicles some distance away. The IRA engineering department realised that a direct signal from a hand-held transmitter, like a CB radio, to a compatible frequency receiver, such as a McGregor, would ensure almost simultaneous detonation and guarantee greater accuracy and reliability. By 1979, they had perfected the process.

Special Branch, MI5 and Army Intelligence were aware of these technological advances and worked hard to develop counter-measures. For a time, they kept pace with IRA technology and fitted devices on most vehicles to counteract the signals. The development of the McGregor system gave the IRA a temporary advantage.

The police almost caught up with one of the IRA bomb-making engineers after he attempted to purchase ten transmitters from a toyshop in Belfast. The IRA learned a lesson and decided not to take further chances close to home. Instead, they looked to England and the Continent, particularly Amsterdam, to purchase the equipment.

The more sophisticated McGregor device meant that IRA volunteers could safely transport explosives over a long distance without fear of detonation. Local supporters researched the movement of police and army on routes across Northern Ireland. From the mid-1970s, many devices caused a large number of fatalities and injuries among the security forces. Few alterations were made to the mechanism right up to the IRA ceasefire in 1994. Their motto seemed to be, 'If it's not broken, don't try to fix it'. On 17 April 1979, four police officers were killed by a 1,000 lb bomb detonated by a radio signal outside Bessbrook. As late as 7 March 1993, a McGregor device was used in an explosion in Main Street, Bangor.

From the IRA point of view, the Warrenpoint explosions which caused so many casualties were due to intelligence gathering and meticulous planning. For years, they had scrutinised army and police responses to bombing and shooting incidents, particularly when these were directed against their colleagues. They researched where reinforcements came from and how long it took them to arrive at an incident. In the case of Warrenpoint, they knew that a response would come from Newry and Bessbrook. They also anticipated that reinforcements would take up defensive positions around the gatehouse and a moat in the lough. Five days earlier, they had packed 600 lbs of explosives into the gatehouse. This, the second of the two explosions, was detonated by an electrical timer, similar to the device that almost killed Margaret Thatcher in Brighton in 1984. The timers were effective up to forty-two days.

The trailer used to transport the first bomb was a twin-axle 261 tandem trailer manufactured by York Trailers in England in 1962. Our research showed that it had been bought and sold five times before ending up in the hands of the IRA in South Armagh.

The morning after the deaths, we were told by local detectives that two men had been arrested by Gardaí. They were travelling on a Suzuki motorcycle and were stopped at a checkpoint in Omeath several miles from the detonation point, which had been located in a field on a hillside on the southern shore inside the Republic. We could see a huge amount of Garda activity in the field from our side of the estuary. The Garda refused a request that our forensic experts should join them in the examination. Three days later, after the matter was referred to our Headquarters, we were granted access. The Garda search had finished. The undergrowth had been scythed down and the ground disturbed in other ways as part of their examination. Our forensic experts saw no value in doing any work at the site.

Over the coming weeks, we learned that a substantial forensic case incriminating the men had developed. A transmitter used to detonate the bomb had been found discarded near the field. The Suzuki 100 motorcycle, which the men were riding when arrested, was seen by two elderly women from Liverpool. They had rented a cottage in the area beside a disused railway line not far from the detonation point. They noticed that the registration plate was missing and that a hole had been cut into the seat. This hole was used to transport the transmitter en route to the firing-point. Traces of ammonium nitrate, often used in explosive devices, and firearm residues were found on the hands and clothing of both men. Lemonade bottles and a cigarette butt later identified as a Major (a brand manufactured by the Carrolls' Tobacco group in Dundalk)—the type smoked by one of the men—were found in the field. Ferns similar in appearance to the ones growing in the field were found in the clothing of both suspects. In 1995, a botanist proved that the fern specimens were of the same biological strain.

The two elderly ladies made detailed statements to the Gardaí describing what they had seen. When asked to sign the documents, however, they refused, hinting that they had been intimidated. Both men were released from custody after being charged with motoring offences (mechanical defects, no registration plate, and no insurance).

In the months that followed, senior officers from the RUC, including Detective Chief Superintendent Mooney and Detective Inspector Anderson, met with senior Garda officers in Dublin on four occasions. They put four possible scenarios to the Garda in the hope of getting access to the suspects: (a) the Garda should re-arrest the two men and question them on our behalf about the explosions at Warrenpoint; (b) the Garda would interview them with RUC officers present; (c) the RUC would question them with Garda officers present; and finally, (d) the Garda would question them with the RUC present in another room so that matters could be clarified if necessary. All the proposals were rejected.

During the fourth and final meeting, on 8 January 1980, senior Garda officers announced that they had been instructed by the Taoiseach, Charles Haughey, to treat the deaths at Warrenpoint as a political incident and refuse assistance to the RUC investigators. Most of the soldiers killed at Warrenpoint were members of the Parachute Regiment, which had been involved in the fatal shooting of thirteen people in Londonderry in January 1972 ('Bloody Sunday'). This was a bitter blow to the RUC investigation team and caused much ill-feeling.

Through local contacts, we were given an unofficial copy of the forensic report, but were denied the full, official version until the case was re-opened by the RUC in 1994.

We made one last attempt to arrest the suspects: Eric Anderson was made aware that Brendan Burns and an associate (who cannot be named for legal reasons) intended to cross a narrow strip of countryside into Northern Ireland along the Fermanagh border with the Irish Republic on their way to court to answer the motoring charges. At our request, the Welsh Guards set up a covert operation at the crossing-point with the intention of intercepting the two men. Unbelievably, the soldiers fell asleep and the two suspects passed through undetected.

The RUC never managed to prosecute either of these men in connection with Warrenpoint. In 1983, Brendan Burns was arrested by Gardaí on suspicion of being involved in an explosion which killed five soldiers at Camlough, Co. Armagh, in May 1981. They were killed when a massive 1,000 lb bomb hidden in a culvert was detonated by a radio-controlled signal.

This was one of a series of major bombings highlighting the government's failure to compromise with republican prisoners on the 'dirty protest' and the hunger strike. On 21 April, Margaret Thatcher in an interview in Saudi Arabia declared, 'We are not prepared to consider special category status for certain groups of people serving sentences for crime. Crime is crime, it is not political.'

The Camlough incident happened not far from the home of Raymond McCreesh, who was on hunger strike at the time and close to death. He died two days later. Burns was held in custody while an extradition warrant was prepared by the RUC. He was released two years later when the warrant was declared invalid by judges in the Dublin High Court. On 29 February 1988, he and a companion were killed when a bomb they were handling exploded.

I worked on the Warrenpoint investigation team for four months and, like everyone else, became increasingly disillusioned by our inability to progress in the inquiry. That day of tragedy, 27 August 1979, could and should, by the same token, have been a day of triumph for the Garda Síochána. They had arrested suspects after two of the most highly publicised incidents of the Troubles; but political considerations were obviously more important than justice for the deceased and their families.

In 1994, the second suspect was arrested and convicted of involvement in a mortar attack on an army watch-tower in Drummond, South Armagh. The motor-cycle and other exhibits, including the cigarette butt connected to Warrenpoint, were made available by the Garda to the RUC investigation team. Consideration was given to a DNA examination of the butt, but a suitable sample could not be obtained. The two elderly ladies who had seen the motorcycle had long since died; but a Crown DPP prosecutor in Belfast accepted that the Garda officer who took their statements could legally give evidence of their content. The same prosecutor felt that there was a strong forensic and circumstantial evidential case against the surviving suspect. However, the decision was taken not to prosecute. The IRA ceasefire had just been declared and it is possible that a prosecution was not considered to be in the public interest.

One of the great mysteries of the early part of the Troubles was the events surrounding the disappearance of Herr Thomas Niedermayer, the managing director of Grundig, a German electrical company which had a plant in Dunmurry. He was also the Honorary German Consul. At approximately 11 p.m. on 27 December 1973, two men called at his home in Glengoland Gardens in Andersonstown and persuaded him to go out to the street on the pretext that his car had been damaged in an accident. The men overpowered him and forced him into a car. It was the last time his family would see him alive. Some days later, Grundig received a ransom demand; despite concerns expressed by the German Chancellor, Willy Brandt, the British and Irish governments refused to negotiate with the kidnappers. The RUC had no idea who was behind the kidnapping. Special Branch tasked their informants within republican and loyalist groups to find out. Any information obtained was vague and of no real value. Despite extensive search operations, which included excavating areas in isolated parts of North Antrim, no trace of Herr Niedermayer was found. A unit of the Headquarters Crime Squad led by Detective Sergeant Alan Simpson reviewed the case over many years, assessing any new information that came to light.

In March 1980, information suggesting that Herr Niedermayer might be buried in a wooded area at Colin Glen on the outskirts of west Belfast was thought to be sufficiently strong to justify a dig. A body was discovered in a shallow grave. Forensic experts carefully removed vegetation and earth and the skeletal remains. It was quickly established that this was the body of a male person. His hands had been tied behind his back and his legs bound. The post-mortem was not able to establish an exact cause of death. Three possibilities were considered: one of two skull fractures, a heart attack, or asphyxiation.

Steps were taken to make a positive identification: a process known as cranio-facial reconstruction was used for the first time in Northern Ireland. Herr Niedermayer's family provided a photograph taken not long before his disappearance. A scan was made to obtain an outline of the skull geometry. A clay reconstruction was made of the skull recovered from the shallow grave. Markers were used to position the eyes and nose while layers of modelling clay were applied. This process continued until the geometry of the skull was similar to that of the photograph. Dental records were also checked and the remains of items of clothing recovered from the corpse were shown to the family. In this way, a positive identification of Herr Niedermayer's body was made.

Over the years, several suspects were interviewed. Eventually, John Bradley admitted his involvement in the kidnapping and, for the first time since Herr Niedermayer's disappearance in 1973, details emerged of the incident. The German industrialist had been held in an upstairs bedroom of a house at Hillhead Crescent, a short distance from where he was abducted. He was forced to lie on a mattress in a locked room, guarded by members of the IRA. On the third day of his captivity, he attempted to escape but was forcibly restrained. He was held down while his hands and feet were tied. When he tried to call out, one of the men hit him over the head with a Browning pistol and pushed his face into the mattress. He suddenly stopped struggling and went limp. The following evening, Bradley and two other men took the body to Colin Glen under cover of darkness and buried it. Bradley insisted that no one intended to hurt or kill Herr Niedermayer, that his death was accidental and occurred during their attempts to subdue him.

In April 1980, further arrests were made. I interviewed Eugene McManus, Adjutant of the IRA Belfast Brigade. He told me that the IRA intended to exchange Herr Niedermayer for the Price Sisters, Marian and Dolours, who were being held in connection with bomb attacks in London in March 1973. McManus was paid £200 to clean the house and have it redecorated.

On 16 February 1981, he and Bradley appeared at Belfast Magistrates' Court. The prosecution accepted Bradley's plea to a charge of kidnapping. He was sentenced to twenty years in prison. McManus pleaded guilty to charges of assisting offenders and membership of the IRA. He was sentenced to five years in prison.

The story of the Niedermayer family took a final, tragic turn in June 1990, when the body of his widow, Ingerborg, was found on a beach in Greystones, Co. Wicklow, a week after she arrived in Ireland from Germany. She had drowned. The Grundig factory in Dunmurry closed and one planned for Newry, intended to create 1,500 jobs, was cancelled.

Chapter 6 ∾

I AM PROMOTED TO DETECTIVE INSPECTOR AND MOVE TO DUNGANNON

In June 1980, I was promoted to the rank of Detective Inspector and moved to Dungannon in County Tyrone, a historic market and textile manufacturing town. It was an area of mixed religion, but tensions between the communities increased during the 1970s as a result of an upsurge in paramilitary activity. The IRA was strong in local estates and surrounding areas and had been responsible for many bombing and shooting incidents. Loyalist gangs from Portadown and nearby towns had committed many gruesome sectarian murders, creating a climate of fear and suspicion. My new bosses were Detective Chief Inspector Eric Anderson and Detective Superintendent Frank Murray. Eric and I had worked together in the past.

Frank was a charismatic figure with iconic status within the RUC. On 7 July 1976, he and a colleague, Detective Sergeant Davy Davidson, were given the location of an arms hide in the countryside outside Portadown by an informant who was considered reliable. In fact, the informant was about to betray them and lead them into a deadly trap. Guns in the hide had been booby-trapped as part of an elaborate plan to kill Frank, and were primed to explode when disturbed. As Frank lifted one of the weapons, it exploded. He suffered horrific injuries, losing an eye, arm, leg and parts of four fingers. Davy suffered serious injuries to his stomach, legs and upper body. He crawled three quarters of a mile across rough ground in darkness to raise the alarm. Both men were hospitalised for a long period of time. After a lengthy recuperation

Davy returned to duty and served many years in Belfast.

Frank was released after seven months of treatment. Within weeks he was out mowing his lawn and agitating for a return to work. Despite his injuries, he insisted on going back to operational CID duty. He worked in Portadown for a couple of years before moving to Dungannon about the same time as myself. He had lost none of his drive or leadership qualities. As a decision-maker, he was incisive, fearless and gifted; as a leader, he expected total commitment and absolute loyalty. During the next couple of years, my respect for him grew; so did the bond of friendship and trust between us.

I had first met him in late 1974 at Victoria Barracks, Strand Road, Londonderry. I was working as a detective sergeant in Strabane and had come to the city to interview a prisoner about an IRA bombing. Frank burst into the CID office, pointed a finger at me and told me he needed a helicopter urgently. Before I could reply, he rushed out of the room. Other detectives present laughed heartily and helped me make the arrangements. When I informed Frank that the army helicopter was waiting for him at the nearby Ebrington Barracks, he told me to drive him to the camp. I replied that it was my first time in the city and that I had no idea how to get there. He ordered me into the car and, under his direction, we got to the helicopter pad. When I left the camp, I was hopelessly lost and ended up in Limavady, seventeen miles away.

The next time we met was at Frank's farewell function at Portadown prior to our joint move to Dungannon. At one point in the evening, he drew me aside and told me that he was determined to re-open a number of incidents involving the UVF in Dungannon—in particular the murders of Peter and Jane McKearney. This crime seemed to have some personal significance for him, but he did not elaborate.

Soon after our arrival in Dungannon, we reviewed current and past crimes committed by republican and loyalist paramilitaries. One loyalist gang in particular, based in Portadown, was led by a number of seasoned killers, including Robin Jackson ('The Jackal'). Rank and file members were recruited from a wide area, including Lurgan and Dungannon. Many attacks by this group resulted in multiple deaths, including the shooting of six members of two families, the Reaveys and O'Dowds, in two separate attacks at Whitecross and Gilford on 4 January 1976; the killing of three Catholic men in a darts club near

Bleary on 27 April 1975; and the murder of three members of the Miami Show Band on the Banbridge–Newry Road on 31 July 1975.

During research into these atrocities, one name stood out: Garnet Busby, a 27-year-old bread-server from Dungannon. The previous year, he had been interviewed about a number of killings in Dungannon and nearby Moy village, but had been released because of lack of evidence. I decided to re-interview him and spent several days briefing detectives about him and his associates. On 8 December 1980, he was arrested and taken to interview rooms at Gough Barracks in Armagh. We had statements from witnesses to a number of serious incidents, but had no identification, forensic or pathological evidence to incriminate him. We needed admissions, either verbal or written, to charge him, otherwise he would be released for a second time.

In the early stages of the interviews, he denied his involvement, as he had done the previous year. However, within a couple of hours we were more hopeful: he seemed less defiant and callous than before. He became pensive and appeared to listen to what we said. For the first session after lunch, I chose as my partner Detective Constable Don Smith, a gentle giant of a man who had shown considerable promise during his brief period in CID, having lately joined from Uniform Branch. Within an hour, I could see that Busby was a troubled soul, deep in thought. It was increasingly obvious that he wanted to get something off his chest. He was silent for a few moments and then, tears filling his eyes, he admitted his involvement in the murders of six people.

The first incident he described involved the murder of pensioners Peter McKearney and his wife Jane at their farmhouse outside Moy village on 23 October 1975. He was one of two UVF gunmen who arrived at the quiet farmhouse; they shot Jane eleven times as she answered the door. The gunmen stepped over her body and shot Peter eighteen times as he rushed to her assistance.

Unfortunately, this elderly couple bore the same surname as a prominent republican family in the area; according to Busby, they were shot in the mistaken belief that there was a family connection. It was a pitiless, brutal killing and caused widespread shock. But the leadership of the UVF gang was neither remorseful nor embarrassed by their blunder: within six days, they had killed a twenty-year-old Catholic youth in Lurgan.

The second incident incriminating Busby was a car bomb attack on a public house, the Hillcrest Bar, situated in a Catholic part of Dungannon. Shortly after 8 p.m. on St Patrick's Night, 1976, a green Austin 1100, containing a bomb, was left by Busby and another UVF man outside the bar. Ignoring the fact that children were playing close by, Busby and his companion left the scene in a vehicle stolen earlier in Portadown. No attempt was made to give a warning. A short time later, the bomb exploded, causing damage over a wide area. Two children, James McCaughey and Patrick Barnard, both thirteen years of age, were killed in the blast. Andrew Small, who had been walking past the bar with his wife, was also killed. A customer in the bar, Joseph Kelly, was the fourth person to die.

I went looking for Frank to tell him about Busby's admissions. He interrupted me and earnestly asked about the McKearney case. I told him that Busby had admitted his involvement. Frank was delighted and embraced me. I never found out why this meant so much to him.

Busby was charged with the six murders and remanded in custody. In 1981, he appeared at Belfast Commission and pleaded guilty to all six. He was sentenced to six life sentences, to run concurrently. The trial judge accepted that he was remorseful and did not stipulate a minimum term to be served.

Not long after I arrived in Dungannon, I was taken on a fact-finding tour by two young detectives. We eventually arrived in Coalisland, six miles from Dungannon. My first impressions were of a town in need of regeneration and financial investment, much like Strabane. The local police station was an ugly, functional building surrounded by high, heavily fortified concrete walls and iron security gates. I was introduced to several officers, but the man I wanted to meet was Constable Sam McClean, reputedly a walking encyclopaedia of knowledge of the local area. I found him to be a reserved, stern man and I knew that we would never be close friends. When he did talk to me, he was direct, almost sarcastic. He said he had seen many CID officers come to the area and leave without making an impression. He pointedly asked me what I was going to do about an IRA gunman, Seamus Dillon, whom he had seen in the town in the previous couple of weeks. (It was not uncommon for known killers to walk about Northern Ireland quite openly, knowing in practice that the police lacked sufficient evidence to prosecute them.)

Before I could respond, he declared that this man had killed Constable William Logan in the town in 1972 and that nothing had been done about it. I told him that I would research the case as a matter of some urgency. When I was leaving, he remarked sarcastically, 'See you next year...'

Despite our first raw exchanges, I grew to respect his forthright manner. He made an invaluable contribution to many CID investigations and saved us many hours of researching suspects. He was a forerunner of today's community police officer, whose role is seen as essential to good relations with the public. He was, of course, right about Dillon.

On 24 November 1980, I ordered Dillon's arrest. I and other detectives interviewed him at Gough police office over three days. He denied his involvement and seemed determined and hostile. We concentrated our questioning on the murder of Constable Logan. This seemed to hold his attention. He eventually indicated his willingness to talk. He said his involvement with the IRA had led to his participation in many terrorist incidents. He was constantly on the move, running and hiding. The stress was horrific. It was obvious that he was a ruthless and dangerous gunman and bomber. He had been involved in so many incidents that he had difficulty remembering exact details and dates. However, his recollection of the events leading to the death of Constable Logan was precise.

On 14 March 1972, he was one of two gunmen who ambushed a joint RUC/army patrol with sub-machine-guns on the Brackaville Road outside Coalisland. Almost fifty shots were fired at the security forces' vehicles. Constable Logan, driving a police Land Rover, was seriously injured. He was taken to the South Tyrone Hospital in Dungannon, but quickly moved to the Royal Victoria Hospital in Belfast, as his condition worsened. Within four hours of the shooting, he was dead.

Dillon also outlined his part in two other murders: the killing of Private John Rudman by IRA snipers hiding in the grounds of Edendork Chapel, and the murder of William Hughes outside the parochial house at Coagh. Dillon was one of two gunmen who fired shots at a blue Ford Escort parked at the parochial house, believing it to be a police car. The vehicle was struck by twenty-nine bullets. William Hughes was killed and his daughter seriously wounded.

In 1982, Dillon appeared at Belfast Crown Court and pleaded guilty to charges of killing Constable Logan and Mr Hughes. He was acquitted of the murder of Private Rudman. He was sentenced to life imprisonment. In 1994, he was released on licence. Three years later, he was shot dead by LVF gunmen outside the Glengannon Hotel in Dungannon, where he worked as a doorman. He was not the intended target. The gunmen fired a number of shots in the direction of people standing at the entrance to the hotel. Two other doormen and a young waiter were seriously wounded.

Constable Sam McClean was originally from Donegal and made frequent trips to see his parents at their farm. He had bought an eight-acre spread close to the family home with the intention of retiring there. On 2 June 1987, two IRA gunmen shot him dead as he worked on a relative's farm. It was a sad end for a man who had served the RUC and policing with such courage and dedication.

One of the most highly publicised shootings of the period was an attempt on the lives of Bernadette McAliskey and her husband Michael by the UDA in 1981. During the 1970s, Bernadette Devlin (as she was then known) became a well-known voice in radical street politics in Northern Ireland. She was an outspoken and articulate critic of the unionist establishment, the RUC, the British Army and the involvement of Britain in Northern Ireland. On 17 April 1969, aged twenty-one, she was elected to the Westminster Parliament as member for Mid-Ulster—the youngest woman in history to secure a seat at Westminster. In a parliamentary debate on the events of Bloody Sunday in Londonderry on 30 January 1972, she famously slapped the face of the Home Secretary, Reginald Maudling. He was making a speech in support of the paratroopers who shot dead thirteen people on that fateful day. During the late 1970s, she took an active role in the protest by republican prisoners against the removal of political status. In 1979, she was a prominent member of the National H Block/Armagh Committee, which campaigned vigorously to generate worldwide publicity for the prisoners' demands.

Militant elements in the UDA, under the control of John McMichael, were disturbed by the potential propaganda value of the group and decided to take action. Their first victim was John Turnly, shot dead in Carnlough on 4 June 1980. A couple of weeks later, on 26 June, Miriam Daly, Queen's University lecturer, was murdered at her home in west Belfast. She had publicly represented the views of INLA prisoners on the committee.

The prime target for McMichael's team was Bernadette McAliskey, the most prominent figure on the committee. In January 1981, a UDA hit team picked her as their next target. Through local UDA contacts in County Tyrone, they learned that she, her husband and two young children lived in an isolated cottage at the end of a long lane on the outskirts of Coalisland. Reconnaissance work on a route to and from the cottage was carried out by Raymond Smallwoods, a van driver and active gunman. It is known that he drove his works van several times to the McAliskey household and made a detailed route map of the location.

Detective Superintendent Murray was given intelligence about a possible attack on Mrs McAliskey. He deliberated whether he should tell her. After considering various courses of action, he decided that she was unlikely to agree to a protective presence of police or army at her home. Instead, Frank placed a unit of covert soldiers in a copse close to the cottage. He knew that Michael McAliskey was a greyhound enthusiast and kept dogs in a pen beside his home. The soldiers were made aware of this fact and were told to position themselves at least five hundred metres from the cottage to avoid detection.

The early hours of 16 January 1981 were bitterly cold. Freezing temperatures and snow showers made the night-time vigil unpleasant for the soldiers. Just before dawn, at approximately 8 a.m., they heard a car turn into the laneway and travel towards the McAliskey home. In the darkness, they hurried through the trees to investigate. Before they could establish what was happening and intercept the occupants of the Hillman Avenger car, three UDA men, Raymond Smallwoods, Andrew Watson and Thomas Graham, had alighted from the vehicle. Smallwoods threw a rope over the telephone wire outside the cottage and severed the connection. He was about to smash in the door with a sledge-hammer when, to his surprise, he discovered that it was not securely locked. He pushed it open with little difficulty. Watson and Graham, armed with hand-guns, fired a number of shots at Michael and Bernadette as soon as they gained entry. Michael was hit by five bullets; Bernadette was shot seven times as she dressed her two children. She bravely pushed them away from her just before she was shot. As the three UDA attackers ran from the house, they were confronted by the soldiers, who had emerged from the trees. They were immediately disarmed and forced to lie on the ground at gunpoint.

The soldiers were shocked by what they saw in the cottage and summoned urgent assistance. Michael and Bernadette received first aid treatment before being flown by army helicopter to the secure wing of Musgrave Park Hospital in Belfast. The three prisoners were eventually removed from the scene and taken to the police office at Gough Barracks for interview.

I remained with other detectives at the McAliskey cottage for some time while a forensic examination was carried out. I then travelled to Mahon Road Camp in Portadown to interview the military personnel who had apprehended the gunmen.

Over the next number of days, I visited the McAliskeys in hospital and recorded statements outlining their horrific ordeal. I found them pleasant and cooperative. Remarkably, I saw no evidence of bitterness against the men who had attempted to kill them and who had placed their children in mortal danger. They were appreciative of the treatment and kindness shown to them by the military medical staff. Lieutenant Colonel McFarlane, the surgeon who treated them, and the soldiers who rendered first aid after the shooting, undoubtedly saved their lives. In appreciation, Bernadette presented the colonel with a Tyrone Crystal bowl. He told me afterwards that it was one of his most precious possessions.

The interview of the three suspects progressed satisfactorily. We were made aware that they were a select assassination team chosen by John McMichael and that their loss would be a major blow to the UDA. They admitted their involvement in the shooting and other serious incidents in Belfast. On 20 January 1981, I charged the three accused with the attempted murder of Bernadette and Michael McAliskey. They were remanded in custody.

The arrest of this particular team undoubtedly saved Catholic lives because it forced McMichael to call a halt to further attacks on high-profile figures. They had already selected their next target, Michael Farrell, the prominent civil rights activist.

Unfortunately, the attack on the McAliskeys was to lead to retaliation by the IRA and resulted in the deaths of a number of Protestants. Strategists within Sinn Féin and the IRA had become paranoid about the frequency of UDA/UVF attacks on high-profile republicans. They decided that a speedy and ruthless response was the most likely way of slowing or ending the murder campaign. Five days after the shooting of the McAliskeys, up to eleven IRA gunmen smashed their way into the 230-year-old Tynan Abbey on the Armagh-Monaghan border and shot dead 86-year-old Sir Norman Stronge, a former Speaker of the Stormont parliament for a quarter of a century, and his 48-year-old son, James, a merchant banker and Unionist member of the former Northern Ireland Assembly. They planted a number of incendiary devices which burned the abbey to the ground.

Officers in an armoured police vehicle tried to block the escape of the gunmen's cars. Hundreds of shots were fired at the police vehicle from high-velocity rifles, but fortunately none penetrated the reinforced metal panelling or glass. Had they fired through the thinner panels on the roof of the vehicle, the officers would have been killed.

It is believed that several of the gunmen who took part in this attack were later shot dead by the SAS during an IRA bomb and gun attack on Loughgall police station on 8 May 1987. Eight IRA gunmen were killed in this incident.

Some historians and political commentators have alleged collusion between the security forces and the UDA in the shooting of Bernadette and Michael McAliskey. Questions have been asked as to why undercover soldiers were used, why they were not positioned closer to the cottage and why they did not intercept the gunmen before the McAliskeys were shot. I have tried to explain in some detail the circumstances of the incident. As one of the senior CID investigators, I am satisfied that the decisions made by the police and the army were a genuine attempt to protect the McAliskeys and that nothing else could have been done to prevent the UDA attempt on their lives. It was one of a number of brutal and shameful attacks carried out by loyalist and republican assassins during this period.

Smallwoods, Watson and Graham were sentenced to fifteen years in prison. After sentence, they turned to the McAliskeys and gave them a clenched fist salute—a last act of defiance before they were led away to prison.

The next time I saw Raymond Smallwoods was on 11 July 1994 in a mortuary. Earlier in the day, he had been shot by IRA gunmen outside his home at Donard Drive, Lisburn, and died on his way to Lagan Valley Hospital. Thomas Graham, on his release from prison, returned to his violent ways. He was charged in connection with the attempted murder of a Catholic in a caravan outside Lisburn and returned to prison (for witholding information). Andrew Watson appears to have severed his links with the UDA.

During the following months, I visited the McAliskeys at their new home in Coalisland and was impressed by their determination to get better for the sake of their children.

On 14 March 1981 at 8.00 a.m., Detective Chief Inspector McBurney hammered on my bedroom door at Gough Barracks and told me to get dressed. Within minutes, I was in an army helicopter alongside him and Frank Murray on our way to Fermanagh. Frank told me that the SAS had captured an active service unit of the IRA. It was believed that one of the four men caught was Seamus McIlwaine, who was right at the top of the RUC's Most Wanted list. The men had been captured in an isolated farmhouse and surrendered only after the SAS threatened to storm the building. Rifles and ammunition were recovered. It is believed that the men were on a mission to kill a member of the UDR who lived nearby.

My first impression of McIlwaine was of a slight, insignificant man, but he was undoubtedly a ruthless, calculating killer who had been responsible for many deaths in County Fermanagh. He lived across the border in Cavan and Monaghan and only came North on active service missions. The countryside along the border is sparsely populated, so IRA gunmen had plenty of opportunity to attack their victims in isolated areas. Intelligence was provided by republican/nationalist sympathisers, often people living in the vicinity of the intended targets.

I interviewed McIlwaine with other detectives at the police office in Gough Barracks. He was quiet and sullen, showed no sign of nerves and stared at us intently. We referred to many killings that had taken place in recent years in Fermanagh. He seemed unmoved and said nothing. We then discussed in great detail the circumstances of his arrest and the evidence from SAS soldiers that would be put before a court. He obviously knew that he would be going to jail for a long time. Eventually he calmly—and almost as an act of defiance—described his part in two murders. He said that he was one of two gunmen who shot Alexander Abercrombie, a part-time corporal in the UDR. Mr Abercrombie was shot dead as he sat on his tractor at his remote farm near Kinawley, about five miles from the border.

The second shooting resulted in the death of full-time Reserve

Constable Ernest Johnston, who died outside his home at Lurace, five miles from Rosslea. McIlwaine was one of two gunmen who fired at least fifteen shots. Mr Johnston was hit in the head and chest. On 11 February 1980, he had been injured when an 800 lb landmine, hidden in a culvert under the Lisnaskea-Rosslea Road, exploded. Two RUC officers, Constable Winston Howe and Constable Joseph Rose, were killed. Mr Johnston was off work for many months after the incident.

I was one of the officers who investigated that explosion and I am convinced that McIlwaine was involved. In a similar incident, a local woman, Sylvia Crowe, was killed on the same stretch of road on 17 July 1979; I believe McIlwaine was involved in that as well.

His arrest and that of the other members of the unit must be viewed against the devastating effects of a series of murders in County Fermanagh in the latter part of the 1970s. I got to know Ken Maginnis, an ex-major in the UDR and prominent member of the Unionist Party, at this time. I found him to be a man of the highest integrity. He researched all of these killings and believed that there was a sectarian element to them. In his view, they were aimed at Protestants who owned farms in the border region. Many Protestant families had abandoned their farms because of the fear of attack.

One of the worst cases of the targeting of Protestants involved the Graham family, who had a working farm in the area. Thomas Ronnie Graham was a lance-corporal in the UDR. On 5 June 1981, I went to the scene of his shooting. He was killed by the IRA as he delivered coal to a house near Lisnaskea. It was later established that a thirteen-year-old boy had moved weapons for the gunmen. In 1986, aged eighteen, he was jailed for seven years.

Ronnie's sister, Hilary, also a member of the UDR, was seriously injured by a car crashing at speed through a UDR checkpoint. It is believed that the injuries sustained contributed to her death. Another brother, Cecil, was shot dead by the IRA while visiting his wife and five-week-old child at her parents' house in Donagh. The Graham family were shocked and saddened that not one Catholic neighbour offered condolences. On 1 February 1985 Jimmy Graham, another brother, was shot dead by the IRA on a school bus at St Mary's Primary, Derrylin, as he waited to take children to a swimming lesson. Ken's moving account of this shocking story confirmed for me his suspicions that nothing less than ethnic cleansing was involved.

McIlwaine and his co-accused appeared at Belfast Commission and were convicted of a series of offences. McIlwaine, convicted of two murders, was sentenced to life imprisonment, with the judge's recommendation that he should serve at least thirty years. His career took another dramatic twist on 25 September 1983, when he was one of thirty-eight republican prisoners who escaped from the Maze Prison. A prison warden died of a heart attack after being stabbed by a chisel and another was shot and wounded in the breakout. McIlwaine remained on the run until 26 April 1986, when he was shot dead by the SAS as he prepared to work on an 800 lb landmine hidden in a culvert near Rosslea.

The number of attacks on the security forces fell dramatically after the death of McIlwaine. Relations between Catholics and Protestants, however, have remained strained to this day. It will take many generations to erase these memories and suspicions that Catholic neighbours and friends had colluded with the IRA.

On 5 May 1981, I was on the M1 motorway and passing Milltown Cemetery on my way to work in Dungannon when I heard an early morning news bulletin that Bobby Sands, the Provisional IRA hunger striker, had died. Although his death was anticipated because of a deterioration in his health the previous day, I was shocked by the news. Like many people, I had expected an eleventh-hour resolution to the dispute, or some form of medical intervention to save him.

The dispute over prisoners' demands for political status had begun with the 'blanket protest' when prisoners refused to wear the clothing issued by the prison authorities (which would have meant accepting criminal status). Instead, they covered themselves in blankets as a symbol of protest. The position of both sides hardened and the protest escalated: prisoners who refused regulation prisoner garb were denied access to toilet and shower facilities. In response, the prisoners embarked on a 'dirty protest', smearing their excrement on the walls of their cells.

The campaign received widespread publicity throughout the world. Attitudes in Northern Ireland were largely influenced by people's political beliefs. Those who supported the republican or nationalist causes blamed the government and prison authorities for the impasse; unionists believed it was another attempt by the IRA to undermine the rule of law and extract concessions.

As a serving police officer, I had seen too much of the pain, suffering and sense of loss caused by paramilitary violence. I had clear views on the issue of political status: no violent act leading to murder, injury to the person or the widespread destruction of property could be justified by the claim that it was done in the furtherance of a political cause.

Every fair-minded person will accept that for decades there had been institutionalised discrimination and injustice against the Catholic population, but nothing could possibly justify the horrifying brutality of the republican campaign. Loyalist paramilitaries and their apologists who sought to justify a violent response as a way of safeguarding the unionist and Protestant population were equally devoid of moral legitimacy.

The moral basis for the prison protest was weakened in June 1980 when the European Commission on Human Rights ruled, in a case brought by four republican prisoners on the 'dirty protest', that under international law there could not be a finding in favour of political status, and that conditions in Northern Ireland prisons connected to the 'dirty protest' were self-inflicted. The same year, Amnesty International refused to support the aims of the protest or the demand for political status. These findings strengthened my view. From the republican perspective, the hunger strikers were undoubtedly brave, self-sacrificing activists who sincerely believed in their cause. But in conscience, I could not condone the acts of brutality which were a consequence of these beliefs.

The first hunger strike of the protest began on 27 October 1980, when seven republican prisoners refused food and declared that they would fast to death. On 12 December 1980, six UDA prisoners joined the fast. Within days, a further thirty republican prisoners were refusing food. Behind the scenes, discussions between the prisoners and the government were taking place. There was a perception that progress had been made and the strike was called off. When the wording of a document containing the government's interpretation of the prisoners' demands was fully analysed by leaders of the protest, however, it was obvious that a satisfactory agreement had not been reached: their demands had not been met.

There was a widespread belief among the Northern Ireland population (including myself) that the prisoners had capitulated. It came as something of a shock when Bobby Sands became the first prisoner to embark on a new hunger strike on 1 March 1981. I had no reason to believe that it would end in his tragic death; I believed that attempts would be made to resolve the dispute. His death on 5 May 1981 changed everything.

By the time I reached Dungannon that day, I was fearful and apprehensive. I knew his death would lead to a huge emotional response among republicans and nationalists. Inevitably, it would lead to widespread public disorder and a violent response by the IRA— followed by an equally brutal retaliation by loyalist paramilitaries. I felt no sympathy at the news of his death, nor did I rejoice: I knew there could be no winners. Bitter divisions would become more entrenched and people would suffer. By the end of the month, 101 people had died; there were 1,140 shooting incidents and 530 bombs had been planted.

I vividly recall being in the Prison Officers' social club in the Maze Prison on the day Frank Maguire, the Catholic independent nationalist MP for South Fermanagh and Tyrone, died. I was managing a police soccer team from Dungannon which had played a match against the prison officers earlier in the day. We were having a sandwich and drink when a TV news flash announced Mr Maguire's death. My team and I were totally shocked by the reaction of some of the prison officers who cheered and shouted sectarian abuse at the screen; it caused disquiet among us and we left as soon as we could.

It had been assumed that Frank's brother, Noel, would stand in his place. Subtle pressure was brought to bear on him, however, causing him to withdraw in favour of hunger striker Bobby Sands. At one level, this was a stroke of propaganda genius, injecting a hugely emotive element into the contest for Catholics; but it caused immense resentment among Protestants who had borne the brunt of IRA violence in Fermanagh. Police authorities expected trouble on election day. I and other officers were detailed to travel in unmarked police cars around polling stations as a precaution. In the event, the election passed off peacefully, but the fact that Sands was elected did little to heal divisions in the community; instead it set them back for decades.

I also recall being surprised and disappointed that senior figures in the Catholic Church, including Cardinal O'Fiaich, publicly criticised the British government for its failure to compromise on the issue of political status for the prisoners on 'dirty protest' and hunger strike.

Had they confined their involvement to welfare issues surrounding the prisoners and the concerns of the families, their public statements would not have been misinterpreted as support for the campaign. It permitted opponents of republicanism to conjure up the myth of a 'pan-nationalist front', justifying a violent response by loyalists, which resulted in the deaths of more Catholics.

Church figures aligned themselves with Charles Haughey, the Taoiseach, in again trying to raise the matter at the European Court of Human Rights. Haughey seemed to have forgotten that De Valera, when leader of the Fianna Fáil Party and head of government in 1940, had refused to grant political status to republican prisoners and did nothing to stop two inmates, Tony Darcy and Jack McNeela, from dying on hunger strike. In 1946, Sean McCaughey, the chief of staff of the IRA, also died on hunger strike.

The second hunger striker to die was Francis Hughes from Bellaghy. He died on 12 May 1981 after refusing food for fifty-nine days. I knew something about Hughes and the activities which had resulted in his imprisonment. He and a small number of close friends, including Dominic McGlinchey, had terrorised South Derry over a five-year period from the mid-1970s. They were responsible for many gun and bombing attacks on UDR soldiers, police and prison officers, causing at least twelve deaths. They enjoyed widespread support among the local Catholic community, where the republican and nationalist tradition was historically strong. Many people supplied them with safe accommodation, food and transport. They were also given accurate, up-to-date intelligence on the addresses and movements of local members of the security forces. The methods used by Hughes and McGlinchey were ruthless and showed a total disregard for life. They jeopardised the lives of women and children in their pursuit of targets.

Hughes was a skilled bomb-maker and specialised in making simple but lethal booby-trap devices. I investigated some of his operations and interviewed him prior to his conviction. Having seen at first hand the consequence of his attacks, news of his death made no impact on me. I am sure that relatives of his victims felt relief and some satisfaction that he was dead. My thoughts were with them on that day.

Memories flooded back of various incidents involving Hughes and McGlinchey. On 22 December 1976, they attached a two-pound booby-trap bomb to the underside of a car belonging to Samuel Armour, a member of the RUC Reserve, who lived at Curragh Road, Maghera, with his wife and children. The bomb exploded and killed Mr Armour around breakfast time as he drove from his home. Normally he took his children to school in the car; but that particular morning marked the beginning of the Christmas holidays. Some people might argue that Hughes knew the children would not be attending school that morning and planted the bomb in the knowledge that this was so. However, a second incident two years later suggests that the welfare of the children was not a consideration.

During the early hours of 8 February 1978, Hughes and McGlinchey secured a similarly constructed booby-trap bomb to the underside of a Ford Escort parked in the driveway of a house belonging to William Gordon of Grove Terrace, Maghera. He was a well-known and popular resident of the small country town. He was also a part-time member of the UDR. The locals who provided intelligence on Mr Gordon to Hughes and McGlinchey must have known that he used the car to drive his two young children, Lesley, aged ten years, and Richard, aged seven years, to school each morning. On the fateful morning of 8 February, Mr Gordon made a security check of the boot and underside of his car but failed to notice the bomb. As the car moved out of the driveway, the bomb exploded. Mr Gordon and Lesley were killed and Richard suffered horrific injuries to his lower body. I am convinced that Hughes, when he planted the device, knew that the children would be in the vehicle, but ignored the fact in his determination to kill Mr Gordon.

Further evidence of the callousness of these two men was evident in a gun attack in March of the previous year. They ambushed a lorry being driven by Mr McMullan, a member of the RUC Reserve. In spite of the vehicle being struck by a number of high-velocity shots fired from rifles, Mr McMullan managed to drive off and escape with minor injuries. The three IRA gunmen, Hughes, McGlinchey and Fintan Scullin, drove to the McMullan household at Culnafay Road, Toomebridge, and fired thirty shots through the windows and doors. Hester McMullan, aged seventy-seven years, the mother of seven children, including the RUCR officer attacked earlier, was fatally wounded. Her 81-year-old husband and one of her daughters narrowly escaped death. Why did Hughes and co. attack the house when they knew that their preferred target was not present? Is it possible that they had a sectarian motive? Mrs McMullan and all the targets killed during their reign of terror were Protestants.

Some years later, in November 1983, gunmen led by McGlinchey (who had by now defected to the INLA) fired shots from automatic weapons into a Pentecostal church during an evening service at Darkley in County Armagh. Three male church elders were killed and seven worshippers were injured. No one can deny a sectarian motive to this attack.

Hughes's reign of terror ended on the night of 16 March 1978 when he and McGlinchey were challenged by two undercover soldiers from the Parachute Regiment on observation duty outside a house at Ranaghan Road, near Maghera. In an exchange of fire, Lance-Corporal David Jones was killed and his companion, Lance-Corporal Kevin Smyth, was wounded. Smyth managed to return fire and shot Hughes in the left thigh. It was a serious wound and led to a heavy loss of blood.

As the IRA men fled, it soon became obvious that Hughes could not travel fast enough to escape. McGlinchey decided to leave him and ran off into the darkness. Hughes managed to stagger and crawl across a couple of fields. Reinforcements were summoned by Lance-Corporal Smyth and an extensive search of the area began. In the darkness, Hughes managed to crawl across a road close to where soldiers were standing and hide under a thorn bush several hundred yards away. Fourteen hours later, he was discovered after a tracker dog and soldiers followed the trail of blood. Hughes surrendered without a fight. He was flown by army helicopter to Musgrave Park Hospital, where he was detained in secure accommodation and treated for his injuries. Surgeons operated on his leg and fitted a pin to his shattered thigh bone. The following day, he received further surgery to relieve haemorrhaging.

In preparation for his formal interview, I and other detectives were sent to South Derry to review a number of incidents where his involvement was suspected. Three months later, I was a member of the team which interviewed him at Castlereagh police office. Hughes had recovered sufficiently well to be interviewed, but was still in considerable discomfort and walked with a pronounced limp. Detective Chief Superintendent Mooney, the head of the Crime Squad of which I was then a member, gave strict instructions on how the interviews were to be conducted. They were to be of short duration and were to stop immediately if Hughes complained of discomfort or pain in his leg. In the event of such a complaint, Hughes was to be returned to his cell and a doctor informed. He was also provided with a soft cushion and chair on which to rest his leg during questioning. Every fifteen minutes, he was to be permitted to walk in an adjacent corridor and offered a supporting arm if required.

We questioned him for several days about serious incidents in South Derry, including twelve murders. As expected, he did not make any admissions; in fact, he hardly spoke during the interviews. However, there was strong evidence to link him to the shooting attack on Lance-Corporals Jones and Smyth. He was charged with murder, attempted murder and several firearms offences and remanded in custody.

In 1979, he appeared at Belfast City Commission and was sentenced to life imprisonment with a recommendation from the judge that he serve a minimum of twenty years in jail. I was not surprised that he joined the hunger strike: republicanism was in his blood and he was a committed and determined member of the IRA. He died on 12 May 1981.

McGlinchey's fortunes took a turn for the worse on 17 March 1984 when he was arrested by the Gardaí after a shoot-out in the Irish Republic. The RUC successfully applied for his extradition on a charge of murdering Mrs McMullan. He became the first republican to be extradited to face terrorist charges in Northern Ireland. He received a life sentence after being convicted of the murder. However, he won an appeal against his sentence when three judges ruled that a fingerprint found on a car at Mrs McMullan's home could have been placed there at a time before or after the murder. McGlinchey was shot dead in 1994 in an INLA feud. His wife, Mary, who assisted him in some of his killings, had been murdered by the same faction seven years earlier, on 1 February 1987 as she bathed her children.

Mrs McMullan's family got some justice for the killing of their mother: in January 1979, I interviewed Fintan Scullin about the incident. He admitted his involvement and was subsequently sentenced to life imprisonment.

My knowledge of these violent and tragic incidents in South Derry influenced my attitude to the hunger strike. Every prisoner involved had been convicted of very serious, violent offences and I saw no reason why their deeds should be exonerated by the manner of their dying.

Chapter 7 ∾

I JOIN THE ANTI-
RACKETEERING SQUAD

A Special Branch dossier suggested that the development of racketeering in Northern Ireland was linked to the outbreak of sectarian violence in 1969. The two dominant paramilitary groups, the IRA and the UVF, were, like everyone else, shocked by the scale of the violence and found that they could not fully protect their respective communities. They lacked volunteers, weapons and money. Senior figures in both organisations, particularly the IRA, quickly formulated strategies aimed at meeting their long-term goals: the IRA's ultimate aim was to drive the British out of Ireland; the UVF's to remain British and to resist these ambitions. The leadership of both groups realised that a regular supply of money was essential—for the purchase of weapons and explosives. Finance was also essential to meet the needs of volunteers and their families. Donations from Irish Americans through groups such as Noraid were significant, but not sufficient to bankroll the IRA.

By the early 1980s, the government was aware that Gerry Adams and his supporters in Sinn Féin and the IRA were interested in pursuing a political dimension as part of their strategy. However, it was also known that many republican activists believed that an intensification of military action in Northern Ireland and on the mainland would be more harmful to British interests. Some security analysts had identified the important connection between the fund-raising activities of paramilitary groups and their ability to sustain a prolonged violent campaign. They advised government that the matter should be addressed with some urgency.

Northern Ireland ministers and the RUC believed they had made progress in tackling paramilitary violence. However, it was accepted that the preoccupation with civil disorder meant that other aspects of policing had not been adequately addressed. A subculture of criminal activity had become established, particularly in areas where the influence of paramilitary groups was strong.

In response to complaints from community representatives and members of the business establishment, the RUC created the Anti-Racketeering Squad (C19) in September 1982. I was one of a group of twenty detectives tasked with identifying and quantifying criminal activities which financed paramilitary violence. It was a daunting prospect and no one had a clear understanding of how to proceed. None of us had experience of financial investigations, but we had all been CID officers for a long time and understood the structures and tactics of paramilitary groups. Our brief was straightforward: to investigate sources of paramilitary finance; to estimate the size and value of each enterprise; to identify procedures which would enable police and government agencies to close down illegal schemes; to present evidence to government so that legislation could be drawn up to bring racketeering to an end.

During the first few weeks, squad members studied information from many sources, including the intelligence services (MI5), governmental departments, political analysts and victims of paramilitary extortion. Within a relatively short period of time, we had a general appreciation of the situation and had drawn up a plan to tackle it.

Racketeering was a lucrative and ruthless business. It affected a staggering number of companies and small businesses. Some of the biggest companies, with large workforces, were paying protection money; small shopkeepers, taxi drivers, pizza delivery boys, undertakers and market traders were also forced to hand over hard-earned cash. The climate of fear and uncertainty stopped people resisting these gangsters or reporting the problem to the police.

One Catholic taxi driver I knew well was forced to take relatives of loyalist prisoners from Bangor to the Maze Prison five days a week, for months on end, without payment. He was obliged to work excessive hours at night to earn a wage for his own family. He was too terrified to make a complaint; so I was forced to resort to unorthodox methods to resolve the matter. I discussed the problem with an associate who knew Andy Tyrie, head of the UDA. Within days, a leading loyalist from Bangor was summoned to Shankill Road Headquarters and told to end the intimidation. My friend had no further problems from loyalist thugs.

Paramilitary enforcers were able to operate unmolested for many years and were open and direct in their dealings with the business community. They merely announced that they represented a particular paramilitary group and expected their victims to capitulate. They seldom used violence to secure the required response. When necessary, they secretly researched the family background of any businessman who threatened resistance. They then presented him with details of his home and children, sometimes accompanied by photographs taken outside school, as a way of reinforcing their threat.

With such criminal activity an endemic part of life, it came as no surprise to us that local criminals exploited the situation. A sizable percentage of money collected was used by hoodlums to pay for a decadent lifestyle, drink, gambling and fancy cars. When money was handed into local paramilitary commanders, it was used to ensure the efficient running of the organisation. Each group had four main operational priorities: to purchase munitions (weapons and explosives); to finance operatives on the run from the authorities; to make donations to families of members in prison; and to pay for a propaganda and information service, such as that run by Sinn Féin.

There were marked differences between the effectiveness and profitability of schemes run by republican and loyalist paramilitaries. Republican groups were better organised and had in place accounting and investment procedures. Vast sums of money poured into their coffers each year. Along the border, smuggling was viewed as a romantic pastime and was celebrated as a way of robbing the British Exchequer; it was run as such by the IRA godfathers. Republicans ruthlessly exploited differentials and subsidies between Northern Ireland and the Republic and smuggled grain, livestock, cigarettes and machinery. This generated millions of pounds during the 1970s: e.g. one lorry laden with grain crossed the border six times in one day, qualifying for a payment of a subsidy each time.

In areas away from the border, the IRA made vast sums of money from the construction industry, social clubs, taxis and extortion. The methods used were sophisticated and well-planned. They avoided schemes which would alienate the Catholic working class, where Sinn Féin was trying to broaden its support. In the building trade, the IRA sought to employ supporters, activists and ex-prisoners. The workers were facilitated, enabling them to leave the site and claim unemployment benefit. My Uncle Vincent, who was an expert bricklayer, could not get regular work on these sites because of his connection to me and was forced to emigrate to Australia with his family. He confided this to me the evening before he left. I was shocked and deeply saddened.

Many taxi drivers were supporters or ex-prisoners and provided a regular and reliable transport service in Catholic working-class areas. A number of social clubs were established in areas where the IRA was influential. The hijacking of lorries transporting large quantities of alcohol and cigarettes was a regular occurrence. In time, agreements were reached with breweries to refurbish the clubs and supply consignments of drink at a competitive rate in return for the safe passage of their produce. Public houses were attacked, burned and bombed out of existence to increase the turnover in the social clubs. It is believed that more than 250 pubs closed down during this period. The aim of the IRA was to increase its financial portfolio by making its enterprises popular with its support base. It was successful on all counts.

The Official IRA also made a fortune out of similar enterprises. It was probably the first group to appreciate the importance of money-laundering, that is, converting illegal money into business investments which, for all intents and purposes, appeared legitimate. Like the Provisional IRA, it employed accountants, investment brokers, estate agents and legal experts to manage its finances. Eventually records were produced and made available to the Inland Revenue so that tax liability and VAT returns could be made on business enterprises that appeared legitimate.

Loyalist rackets tended to be less complicated and relied much more on intimidation and fear. They opened pubs and clubs and ran a black taxi service but looked to the construction industry as their main source of income. Like republicans, they saw opportunities to make money out of the Housing Executive's huge rebuilding programme to replace thousands of slum houses demolished from 1975 onwards. They established a number of bogus security firms and offered their 'services' to building contractors and business firms throughout Northern Ireland. Any firm which refused to pay encountered serious problems of vandalism, arson and theft.

The most startling revelation was the level of collusion between paramilitary groups in many rackets, particularly in the construction industry. On the republican side, the Provisionals, the Official IRA and the INLA co-existed in some areas. They disliked each other intensely, but after the 1975 feud between the Provisional and Official IRA which claimed ten lives, they did their best to avoid further major conflict. During major reconstruction programmes in the Falls Road, Short Strand and Markets areas, financial expediency took precedence over political/ideological differences.

More surprisingly, the cooperation between these three groups and the loyalist UDA and UVF was widespread. I could not believe the emerging picture. Like most people of my age, I remembered the communal violence and hatred of 1969 and 1970; the hundreds of brutal sectarian murders on both sides; the public condemnation of each other and the bitterness engendered by parades and their different political aspirations.

Few rank and file members of these groups knew much about these arrangements; and of those who did many bitterly disapproved. Against their wishes, senior management recognised the necessity of such cooperation in the small confines of Northern Ireland.

An understanding by squad members of these complex issues made us appreciate the enormity of our task. The decision was made to concentrate on the construction industry because of the availability of records and documents held by the Housing Executive and because it appeared to be the most lucrative source of income for the various paramilitary groups.

During the period from 1971 to 1982, the Housing Executive was placed in an invidious position. It was tasked by government to build thousands of new homes in deprived working-class districts, the very place where republican and loyalist paramilitary groups were strongest. The Housing Executive premises had been bombed on several occasions, machinery and property had frequently been destroyed on construction sites and intimidation of Housing Executive workers was a daily occurrence. Senior management knew that the building programme could only proceed with the approval of paramilitary warlords. It is not surprising that the Executive and government turned a blind eye to arrangements with paramilitaries which guaranteed the continuation of the building programme and the safety of their workforce.

While the Executive and other government departments did their best to provide documents and accounts, it soon became apparent that many of their employees were alarmed at the prospect of working with the RUC. In many instances, staff at Social Security offices refused to cooperate and threatened strike action. The government quickly resolved the problem by making available to the squad a select group of Inland Revenue financial experts based in London. I spent a considerable amount of time in England briefing them on the Northern Ireland situation. In time, they prepared a financial strategy which helped us access necessary documents from government departments, businesses and financial institutions. They spent time with us in Northern Ireland working as advisers and helping us in many practical ways.

Within two years, we had charged 180 suspects with frauds totalling £55 million. Companies and banks were forced to tighten procedures, which made it more difficult for gangsters to make use of their services. We had discovered that one bank in central Belfast cashed cheques to the value of £40,000 and £50,000 for individuals who had no accounts with them. The money from these cheques was used to pay a workforce involved in the tax exemption fraud. On another occasion, a senior director of one of the biggest construction firms was detained by squad members after a surveillance operation photographed him handing £25,000 in cash to a major fraud suspect.

Early in the inquiry, I was given a letter written by a prominent figure in the construction industry in which he described in detail various scams on building sites. I interviewed him with my old friend, David Morwood. He had made complaints about such goings-on in the past to government and senior members of the RUC but said that he had got no satisfaction. He gave us a disturbing insight into problems facing the industry.

He highlighted the abuse of tax-exemption documents, extortion, bogus security firms and the wholesale abuse of Social Security benefits, as the principal areas of concern. He controversially alleged that most construction firms, banks and even government departments knew about these issues, but turned a blind eye in the belief that compromise was the only way to get houses built. The man, anxious for his own safety, refused to give specific details on any individual or group or to meet us again. We left him with the assurance that this time something was going to be done.

We submitted a report on this meeting to senior officers and after consultation with them were given clearance to investigate his complaints. We quickly identified the illegal use of tax-exemption documents as the most lucrative source of finance for republican groups.

The scheme was simple and open to wholesale abuse. Most large construction firms retained a small specialist workforce, such as foremen and quantity surveyors. When they secured a major contract, they sub-contracted much of the work to holders of tax certificates (i.e., firms or individuals who had been operating for a minimum of three years in the building industry) who then supplied the required number of bricklayers, plasterers, joiners and labourers. This process exempted the large construction firm from payment of tax; the liability rested with the sub-contractor. The main contractor, at the end of each week, would pay an untaxed sum of money received from the Housing Executive to the certificate holder who, in turn, would use this to pay his workforce.

Republicans made use of a number of tax certificates made out in the name of fictitious individuals or companies who subsequently could not be traced by Inland Revenue at the end of the financial year. Some legitimate holders of tax certificates (for example in England) were prepared to sell them for several thousand pounds and subsequently, when approached by Inland Revenue for tax owed on some building work in Northern Ireland, could claim that (a) they knew nothing of this/had never been to Northern Ireland or (b) that the document in question had been stolen. The main contractor was obliged to examine and verify the legitimacy of these certificates. Many of them merely went through the motions and accepted documents, knowing them to be fraudulent. In this way, vast sums of money, totalling millions of pounds, were paid out to certificate holders and tax liability was evaded.

The Inland Revenue in London supplied us with a monthly print-out showing monies paid on tax-exemption certificates. By examining these records, we were able to identify certificates that had been sold or stolen. By calculating the amounts paid on the certificates and the firms using them, we were able to pinpoint current misuse.

One such case involved a pig farmer from Ballymoney. When interviewed by David Morwood and myself, he admitted that he had worked with the IRA in using his documents on sites they controlled in Belfast and Co. Antrim. By presenting himself to the construction firms, he satisfied their legal liability by verifying the legitimacy of the documents. Over a period of eighteen months, £2.5 million was paid on the documents of this full-time farmer. The IRA used most of this money to pay the workforce. The tax liability to the Inland Revenue was approximately £800,000; but the actual billing process took up to eighteen months, at which point the pig-farmer alleged that his tax-exemption certificate had been stolen. In many instances, the Inland Revenue back then would simply write off the tax owed as being too trivial to justify the time and effort needed to bring legal proceedings. However, in this particular case, the pig farmer's admission to us that he had worked with the IRA led to a prosecution on charges of fraud and two and a half years in jail. For his pains, the IRA paid him £15,000 and pocketed the remainder of the £800,000.

Hundreds of these certificates were being abused, many of them from England. David and myself interviewed English certificate holders in Southampton, London and Birmingham, who had sold their documents for £2,000. These people knew nothing about Northern Ireland or the IRA and were shocked to hear that their documents had ended up in Belfast. With the help of the Inland Revenue, we tightened up procedures for holders and firms and succeeded in dramatically reducing the extent of criminal misuse.

When we turned our attention to loyalist protection rackets, one name in particular stood out: Jimmy Craig, a UDA thug and gangster. Craig had been a gangster from an early age. During the 1970s, he served a prison sentence for armed robbery. While in prison he struck up friendships with members of the Official and Provisional IRA. On his release, he secured the permission of the UDA leadership to maintain these contacts. The IRA groupings and INLA had a good reason to foster a working relationship with Craig. It was financially beneficial to both sides in west Belfast, where a huge housing regeneration programme was in full swing. Republicans were able to extend the tax-exemption fraud to public sector housing sites in loyalist areas, because Craig was in a position to guarantee the safety of Catholic workers. In return, he was permitted to establish loyalist protection rackets on sites bordering nationalist districts and sometimes into areas where Protestants could not normally operate safely.

Unknown to his UDA bosses, Craig was also an important source of intelligence to republicans concerning loyalist paramilitaries, particularly members of loyalist killer gangs active during this period.

As early as October 1982, Craig and his two close associates, Billy Quee and Artie Fee, were the main targets of the squad. A number of confidential complaints by construction companies and businesses in various parts of Belfast, Newtownabbey, Carrickfergus, Lisburn and Holywood indicated that they were extorting money from up to one hundred businesses. Every complaint painted the same picture: Craig and his gang would approach the firm and pointedly tell them that they would not be allowed to operate their business if they did not pay protection money. Their manner was straight to the point with no niceties. Violence was not used nor were guns produced. Craig relied on the menace of the UDA name and his own reputation. Everyone knew that he kept much of the extorted money to pay for his decadent and seedy lifestyle of foreign holidays, extensive dining and fancy women. The UDA leadership tolerated this behaviour for many years because the group established itself as the biggest contributor to UDA finances.

One night I went to the Europa Hotel with friends after a Barry McGuigan fight. We had difficulty getting access to the hotel because of the large crowd. We had even more difficulty finding a table and getting service from busy waiters. I had to pay one waiter £5 to get attention. Just then I noticed Craig and his entourage seated around a circular table in the middle of the room like visiting heads of state. He had a waiter detailed to provide exclusive service to his party.

We soon had a thick dossier on the activities of Craig and his gang. During a number of surveillance operations, we took photographs of him visiting firms throughout the greater Belfast area. Follow-up visits to staff members confirmed that he had demanded money with menace. In every instance, the firm refused to press charges.

On one occasion, squad members got information that he was extorting money from bookmakers at Dunmore Stadium, a greyhound track in north Belfast. I went to a meeting at the track with a colleague on Saturday, 25 August 1984, to see what was going on. I saw Craig and Fee walking about with two bleached blondes in matching white leather suits, fringes and white boots. They looked as if they owned the place. My colleague and I observed his group and Tommy 'Tucker' Little, the west Belfast brigadier of the UDA and a well-known extortionist, place bets with bookmakers before the first three races. No money was offered in payment. Before the fourth race, I introduced myself to one of the bookmakers, a man I knew from Coalisland, and asked him why this had happened. He looked shocked and, without replying, he and a number of others closed their pitches and left the stadium. Within minutes, word had reached Craig; he came into the betting area to investigate. He spotted me and my colleague and slowly and menacingly walked past without speaking. By the end of the evening, I had plenty of suspicion but no evidence.

The fortunes of the squad seemed to take an upturn when, within a short period of time, three businessmen declared that they would stand firm against the extortionists and help us prosecute them in court. I would dearly like to name these fearless and honourable men, but for their safety, sadly it is not possible. To me they should be numbered among the real heroes of the Troubles.

Two of the men had been approached and threatened by Craig and his gang. They had bravely refused his extortionist demands and declined his offer of 'protection'. Craig took these refusals as a personal insult and was determined to teach them a lesson. He appeared several times at their places of business and threatened them. He telephoned their place of work and home at all times of the day and night and made it known that he was in possession of intimate details of their families. A business partner of one of the men found a booby-trap bomb attached to his car.

Despite feeling isolated and under threat, both men made statements of complaint against Craig, Quee and Fee which enabled us to charge them. All three suspects were arrested and interviewed at Castlereagh police office.

During my questioning of Craig, he was talkative and confident. I never felt that there was any likelihood of him making admissions.

Early in the interview, he smirked and declared that he knew a lot about me. He was aware that I was a Catholic and went to Trinity College. He knew the name of my partner, where I lived and details of the car I drove. For a few seconds, I could not conceal my shock. The smile on his face told me that he was enjoying the moment. When I reflected on the exchange, I deduced that some of the information had been given to him by an ex-student of Trinity who held strong loyalist views.

After investigating the case for several months, we submitted a file to the Director of Public Prosecutions. His office decided that there was sufficient evidence to support blackmail charges against the three accused. Our witnesses agreed to give evidence, despite the realisation that their identities would almost certainly be known to the three men. They asked that their appearance be disguised during the hearing. It was agreed that they could wear anoraks with the hoods raised and sit in a position in the court where their faces could not be seen.

On 25 March 1985, a preliminary inquiry was scheduled at Belfast Magistrates' Court to enable a resident magistrate to assess the weight of evidence against the three accused and decide whether they should be returned to Belfast Commission for trial. When the three accused entered the court handcuffed to prison officers, I was shocked and dismayed to see that they were wearing masks. Whoever in the Prison Service sanctioned this ought to be ashamed of themselves. It was obvious to me that the Prison Service had failed in its duty. The magistrate ordered the masks to be removed. The accused then shouted out the names of the witnesses and my own name. Within minutes, the courtroom had descended into chaos; the DPP representative and the magistrate had no option but to abandon proceedings. It was a devastating blow to the two courageous witnesses, the squad and the judicial process in Northern Ireland.

We had well-earned and overdue success with our third witness. He and his wife in 1985 took over a public house in Queen's Square in the centre of Belfast. During their first week of business, four men (who had no connection with Craig) entered the bar and it soon became obvious that they were not paying customers. Two of them boldly announced that they were members of the UDA; the other two claimed membership of the UVF. They quickly explained the purpose of their visit: the publican would have to make an initial payment to them of £7,000 plus further 'donations' on a regular basis. The publican asked what would happen if he did not pay. He was told that he would be forced out of business.

The following morning, the publican contacted the squad. I invited him and his wife to the office to discuss the problem. We were immediately struck by their determination not to pay and their resolve to have the blackmailers brought to court. The publican's wife was incensed by the cheek of the four men and told her husband that he had her full support for whatever course of action he decided to follow. He told us that the four men had given him a couple of days to consider their offer and had left a contact telephone number.

We gingerly explained the process that we would have to follow in order to bring the men to court. They would have to face the men in public and describe in open court the events that occurred after the men entered the bar. The couple seemed unfazed by this prospect and repeated their resolve to resist the demands. We then explained the dangers and security considerations that would follow. It was made clear to them that police officers could not be placed outside their premises on a daily basis. We also referred to security issues about their home and their children at school. They said that they would reflect overnight on all that we had discussed and contact us with their decision. At nine o'clock the following morning, the publican telephoned and said that he and his wife would cooperate fully with us and do what was necessary to ensure the arrest and prosecution of the four men.

We spent the remainder of the day devising a strategy that would guarantee a successful outcome. It was obvious that we needed to lure the blackmailers to a location that suited us. It had to be spacious so that undercover police officers could blend easily with other customers. We also needed premises where background music would not interfere with the recording of verbal exchanges between the publican and the blackmailers. After much deliberation, we chose the first floor lounge of the Europa Hotel. It was a perfect location and satisfied our requirements. The publican was told to telephone the contact number and arrange the meeting. The men responded positively, obviously believing that their demands were going to be met.

On the agreed day, we placed male and female undercover officers in the lounge, positioned so that they were not facing the table where the rendezvous was to take place. This would reduce the possibility of eye contact with any of the 'spotters' whom the blackmailers, for security reasons, might locate in the lounge. Other police personnel carrying concealed cameras were positioned near the hotel entrance in Great Victoria Street, in the hotel foyer and in the first floor lounge. A concealed microphone was taped to the publican's chest. All the communication devices were then connected to a control room in the back of the surveillance van parked a short distance from the hotel.

The four men obligingly arrived punctually for the meeting. Their easy manner suggested that they were confident of the outcome. The publican skilfully encouraged all four to contribute to the discussion. They set out details of the financial package they expected to be paid. Some minutes into the conversation, the publican hinted that he was not certain that he should pay the money. The atmosphere changed immediately and the men aggressively repeated their earlier threat that he would be put out of business.

The detective sergeant in the control room was at this point satisfied that all the legal elements required to secure a successful prosecution for blackmail had been met (an unwarranted demand with menaces). He gave the order to restrain and arrest the suspects. They were shell-shocked when surrounded and handcuffed. They were then taken to Castlereagh police office for interview. The evidence against them was overwhelming and left them with no option but to admit their guilt. They were remanded in custody while the prosecution file was prepared.

The following year, they appeared at Belfast City Commission and pleaded guilty to a charge of blackmail. Two of them were sentenced to eight years in prison and the other two to nine years each. This was a pleasing outcome for the squad, but many complications remained: our witness could not continue to operate the public house in Queen's Square because of possible dangers to his life and the likelihood of the premises being burned down or bombed. These were real possibilities, because in the early Seventies, a bus driver had been shot dead in the east of the city the day before he was scheduled to give evidence against IRA hijackers.

The publican sold the bar and the family home and moved into a police witness protection programme. This required the family to change their name and live in secure accommodation under twenty-four-hour police protection. It was a huge price to pay in the pursuit of justice. They were the first witnesses to join the scheme. Several 'super-grasses' had previously been given similar protection but had been taken to secret locations outside Northern Ireland.

The publican's family wanted to remain close to Belfast to reduce as much as possible the disruption to their children's lives. Once I had agreed a budget with Headquarters, I took the family to view a number of houses. They selected rented accommodation on the outskirts of Moira and lived there for some time. Two armed officers working eight-hour shifts were positioned in the house. During family trips for shopping or the cinema, they were accompanied by one of the armed officers; the other remained at the house. The children were escorted to and from their new schools.

Their welfare and safety was kept under constant review. After several months, they were forced to move on security grounds after undesirables were spotted in the locality. They took up residence in a house in south Belfast and were happy there for some months, until safety concerns again forced them to move. They settled in a house in the Malone area which was convenient to schools but made them vulnerable to attack. It was a difficult and trying time for them, particularly the children. Occasionally they fell out with individuals in the protection unit, which meant replacing the officers.

The family is still living under an assumed identity and seems to be prospering. To this day, I feel an enormous debt of gratitude to them. I respect and admire them for their courage and sacrifice. They enabled the Anti-Racketeering Squad to register our first successful prosecution against paramilitary extortionists. Dozens more convictions would follow. With each success, the confidence of the business community to resist increased. The problem of extortion still exists, but not on the scale seen in the 1970s and 1980s, when the integrity of the whole business community in Northern Ireland was under threat.

In 1985, I enjoyed two notable highlights: in March, I was promoted to the rank of Detective Chief Inspector within the squad; in June, I was selected to accompany the Chief Constable (Sir John Hermon) and Ronnie Flanagan (then a Chief Inspector) to a weekend conference at Cumberland Lodge in The Great Park at Windsor. The subject for discussion was 'Police and Politics: the Dilemma'. Notable dignitaries of the period, including Sir Cyril Philips, Lord Harris of Greenwich, Sir Philip Knights and Robert Kilroy-Silk, made presentations. It was intellectually demanding, but the weekend produced many wonderful moments. On Saturday, I queued for a buffet lunch with Sir John Hermon. He quietly described the other participants as a 'stuffy crowd' and whispered, 'Watch this!' In a raised voice and with a wink of the eye, he asked: 'What's it like to be a Fenian in the RUC?' People around looked stunned. In a manufactured, posh English accent, I replied: 'Delightful, Sir John, quite splendid.' It was a lovely moment. I laugh every time it comes to mind.

In the afternoon, we watched Prince Charles play polo. At half-time, I helped other spectators replace divots dug out by the ponies' hooves—and wondered what the residents of North Queen Street back home would make of it all.

On Sunday morning, many of us went to the service in the Royal Chapel. Members of the royal family were in residence and also attended. As we stood on the lawn after the service, a royal official called Sir John forward to meet the royal party. I was thrilled when Sir John beckoned Ronnie Flanagan and myself to join him. He introduced us to the Queen, the Duke of Edinburgh and other family members.

During the latter part of 1986 and into 1987, the fight against loyalist extortion intensified. A number of complainants from the business community reported an increase in UDA and UVF extortion. At least four men made allegations against Craig and indicated a willingness to assist the squad. Our previous attempts to convict him had failed miserably, so it was obvious that a change in tactics was necessary. We wanted to secure evidence that did not rely entirely on contact between him and his victims. In each of the four reported cases, senior personnel in the firms permitted us to place undercover policemen as substitutes in the negotiations with the blackmailers.

After an initial approach, Craig always gave the firms a short period of time to consider his terms, which were aggressively delivered and beyond negotiation. Failure to accept his 'protection' inevitably led to serious problems of theft, criminal damage and intimidation of workers.

The officer meeting Craig was wired for sound; during the night, prior to the meeting, concealed cameras and recording devices were installed in the office where the transaction was to take place. I tasked Special Branch's elite surveillance team (E4A) to follow Craig to the premises and E4's uniformed support team (Headquarters Mobile

Support Unit) to make the arrest once evidence of blackmail was secured.

The planning of these operations required a great deal of time and energy, but we were hopeful of a positive outcome. On each of the four occasions, Craig and his cronies turned up and spoke to our undercover officer. Unlike the previous meeting with the firms' representatives when he had been aggressive and demanding, he was pleasant and accommodating. Where before he had demanded money and expected complete capitulation during the first encounter, his offer of 'protection' was now optional and could be refused without penalty. On each occasion, he left the meeting without incriminating himself.

Squad members accepted that the failure of the first operation might have been the result of bad luck; the failure of the second caused real concern; the collapse of the third convinced me that Craig had been forewarned of our plan; the failure of the fourth convinced me that he was an informant.

One night shortly after this, I was socialising in a public house in Holywood. I met a Special Branch officer I had known and liked for many years. I gave him details of a car I knew Craig was using and asked him to find out all he could about it. The following morning I received a telephone call from an irate Special Branch superintendent attached to the Source Handling Unit. I had worked with this officer in 1975 and 1976 when we were both part of a regional crime squad based in Londonderry. He told me in no uncertain terms that I was not to task any of his men again without his authority. Before I could reply, he slammed the phone down. This call was confirmation to me that Craig was an informant. I have no idea whether it was for RUC Special Branch or MI5. The superintendent was tragically killed along with twenty-four other intelligence officers when the Chinook helicopter in which he was a passenger crashed on the Mull of Kintyre on 2 June 1994.

If I am correct in my belief, it is a shameful indictment of the authorities. It means that the Anti-Racketeering Squad was repeatedly betrayed each time we mounted an operation against Craig. It was hard to believe that all our effort, planning and the expense incurred was a waste of time.

Morale within the squad was undermined and our reputation within the business community was damaged. Even more unacceptable was the betrayal of the four brave witnesses and their companies. Craig and his gang continued to extort money and terrorise Northern Ireland society for many years to come.

In January 1987, I attended a meeting of senior press officers at RUC Headquarters. They introduced me to Clive Entwhistle, an experienced investigative journalist with Central Television's *Cook Report*. During this period, it was a hugely popular series with a large viewing public. Journalists working undercover exposed the illegal and violent activities of major criminals, such as drug dealers and fraudsters. Roger Cook, the programme's front man, in a dramatic climax, would confront the criminal bosses on camera. Mr Entwhistle explained that he was in Belfast to research the criminal activities of paramilitaries.

I was told that my involvement in the proposed exposé had been approved by the Chief Constable, who saw the programme as an opportunity to highlight the link between racketeering and paramilitary violence. During a two-hour presentation, I described in detail the most lucrative schemes operated by the various paramilitary groups. We agreed that the programme would show misuse of tax-exemption documents by republicans and extortion practices employed by loyalists.

The tax-exemption case selected for broadcasting involved a man called 'Black Bob' and Official IRA associates. This was a straightforward example showing how the scheme worked. The case had been dealt with at the Crown Court in December 1985. The second issue featured Jim Craig and Eddie Sayers, two prominent UDA members and infamous racketeers.

I approached 'Black Bob' and persuaded him to take part in the programme. He agreed to do so, on condition that he was given an opportunity to differentiate between the motives of the Official and Provisional IRA in misusing tax-exemption documents. The Officials did so in support of a strategy of peace and reconciliation; while the Provisional IRA used monies from the scheme to further their military campaign. He also asked that his appearance and voice be disguised and his name be withheld. This was agreed by the programme makers.

Sadly all these promises were broken. Twenty minutes into the broadcast, he telephoned me and accused me of betraying him. He never spoke to me again and was forced by his paramilitary associates to live in Wales. He died a couple of years later.

During the three months it took to make the programme, I

provided Clive Entwhistle with useful background information, statistics and profiles of major suspects. He was a determined and exceedingly brave man. Within a few weeks of his arrival, the UDA heard that he was researching their activities and harassed and threatened him repeatedly. He survived one frightening experience and was lucky to escape serious injury or worse. I told him that Craig, Quee, McMichael and other prominent loyalist figures were scheduled to attend the wedding reception of one of Craig's right-hand men in the Buffs' Club in north Belfast. Entwhistle and his camera crew parked in a car a short distance from the club at the appointed time. Unfortunately, Entwhistle left the car to get closer to the arriving guests. He was spotted and recognised by a group including Craig and McMichael. They caught up with him before he had an opportunity to escape in the fleeing staff car. He was punched a number of times and told to get out of Belfast. McMichael told him they would have 'finished him off', but did not want to spoil the wedding celebrations.

With the assistance of squad members, Cook set up a meeting with Eddie Sayers, the UDA brigadier for the west of Ulster. While we provided security cover, Cook met Sayers in a car in Omagh. He posed as a businessman seeking to open a factory in Northern Ireland. Sayers, using his front cover, 'Borderline Security', attempted to extort money to enable this to happen. He was later jailed for the blackmail attempt. The programme successfully exposed the debased behaviour and decadent lifestyle of many of the self-appointed leaders of the UDA and caused huge embarrassment to the organisation.

Because of the programme's betrayal of 'Black Bob' after I had given him my assurance of total confidentiality, I felt unable to offer any further services to the *Cook Report*. I was not involved in a later programme called 'Blood Money' televised in June 1989 which wrongly claimed that the community centre at Conway Mill in Belfast was raising funds for the IRA. The Mill directors later brought a successful civil action against Central Television.

The status quo and the relationship between Craig and republican groups was threatened on 12 July 1986 when Brian Leonard, a Catholic worker on a building site in Snugville Street, off the Shankill Road, was shot dead by UVF gunmen. The IRA was furious and summoned Craig to a meeting. He made inquiries on the Shankill and quickly established that the attack had been carried out on the orders of John Bingham, a senior member of the UVF. The killing was an attempt by Bingham to establish his own racketeering credentials, as a rival to Craig's gang. The solution for Craig was simple: he passed information about Bingham's address and movements to the IRA; he also told them that Bingham had taken part in recent murders of Catholics. On 14 September 1986, Bingham was shot dead by the IRA at his home in Ballysillan Crescent, north Belfast.

Another victim of Craig's double-dealing was William 'Frenchie' Marchant, an iconic figure within loyalism. It is believed that he was a member of the UVF team that bombed Dublin in 1974. He was already known to the IRA, having been charged with fifty-one terrorist offences after being named by the UVF 'super-grass', Joe Bennett, in 1984. On 28 April 1987, he was shot dead by the IRA as he walked to a rendezvous with Craig.

Craig's fate was finally sealed after the IRA killed John McMichael, the UDA's deputy leader and main tactician, in a booby-trap bomb attack at his home in Lisburn. It was widely known that McMichael had suspicions about Craig's involvement in the killing of several prominent loyalists and had ordered him to end his involvement with republicans. An internal investigation by the UFF indicated that McMichael had in fact been killed as a result of information passed to republicans by Craig.

It is ironic that Craig's demise and eventual death was at the hands of members of his own organisation. On the evening of 15 October 1988, he was shot dead by two UFF gunmen in The Bunch of Grapes bar on the Beersbridge Road in east Belfast. A UFF statement alleged that he was 'executed for treason'. Billy Quee, his close associate, had been shot dead a month earlier by IPLO gunmen. Artie Fee, the third member of the group, was sentenced to ten years in prison on blackmail charges.

My tenure in the Anti-Racketeering Squad was weakened by revelations made by me in a tax-exemption fraud case at Belfast Crown Court on 10 February 1987. One of the accused, an Englishman from Southampton, had sold a certificate legitimately obtained by him from the Inland Revenue. The certificate was brought to Northern Ireland and subsequently misused on building sites in Ballymurphy, west Belfast. Two Belfast men, Francis Duffy and Bernard McKeaveney, who had got hold of these documents, submitted them to local contractors on behalf of the INLA. In court, the two accused, through their barrister, alleged that the INLA had threatened to kneecap them if they did not cooperate. I did not necessarily believe this allegation but was not in a position to refute the claim. In giving my evidence, I reluctantly accepted that the possibility of the men being kneecapped existed. Building contractors had paid Duffy and McKeaveney £600,000 for work done. Their failure to pay income tax meant that the Inland Revenue had incurred a loss of almost £200,000. The two men were paid approximately £500–£700 for making the documents available. The remainder of the £200,000 owed to Inland Revenue ended up in the coffers of the INLA.

In most cases detected by the squad since 1982, the defendants pleaded guilty in court. This meant that the prosecutor was not required to present a comprehensive picture of the methods used in that particular type of fraud. As a result, press reporting of proceedings contained little more than references to the accused, the amount of money fraudulently obtained and the sentences imposed.

The trial involving Duffy and McKeaveney in the initial stages appeared to be following the same pattern. They pleaded guilty to charges of false accounting, handling stolen property (the tax-exemption certificate) and conspiracy to cheat the Inland Revenue. They were sentenced to two years in prison. The English accused also pleaded guilty and was fined £1,000. However, the trial judge, Lord Justice Nicholson, was disturbed by various aspects of the case and requested further information on how the fraud worked. He was particularly concerned by the involvement of the INLA. Prior to questioning me, he informed the DPP prosecutor that some of the issues he intended to raise might cause me some disquiet and make me feel less than qualified to respond. He made it clear that I was 'compelled' to answer.

In reply to a question about the involvement of paramilitary organisations, I told him that the Provisional IRA, Official IRA, INLA, UVF and UDA were deeply implicated in building-site fraud. When asked where these sites were located, I explained that the problem was commonplace on construction projects throughout Northern Ireland, particularly in working-class areas where the Housing Executive was engaged in a major housing regeneration programme. I confirmed that the criminal practices were worth millions of pounds to paramilitary groups and represented a huge loss to the Inland Revenue and the Exchequer.

Had Lord Justice Nicholson finished his probing at this point, I would have been relieved. Instead, he turned his focus to the supervisory responsibilities of construction firms and governmental departments. He asked me who in authority knew about the frauds. In reply to a series of probing questions, I told him that most construction firms and many senior officials in the Housing Executive knew what was happening. I explained that for them it was a matter of expediency: they believed the quota of houses they were obliged to build could only be realised with the cooperation of local hoodlums and paramilitary gang masters.

My anxiety increased when he switched his attention to accounting practices in the Housing Executive, the Northern Ireland Office and the Central Exchequer. He was aware of my unease and again indicated that I was 'compelled' to answer. I confirmed his suspicions that the accountants allocating taxpayers' money to building and roads projects in Northern Ireland were aware of the arrangements with paramilitaries.[6]

Lord Justice Nicholson thanked me for my assistance and asked the DPP representative to contact the Chief Constable and make it clear that he had required me to answer his questions. He stated that for this reason I should not be criticised or penalised in any way by the RUC.

On the way home, I bought the evening edition of the *Belfast Telegraph*. The case had made front-page headline news. Lord Justice Nicholson was quoted as saying that millions of pounds of taxpayers' money had been made available to terrorist organisations to buy guns to kill and explosives to destroy large parts of Northern Ireland.

The atmosphere in the squad room the following morning was tense. People seemed almost afraid to talk to me. My boss, who completely ignored me, was busy sending out several of my colleagues to recover footage of TV news bulletins and newspaper cuttings from several sources.

Later in the morning, he disappeared—presumably to discuss his findings with the Chief Constable and senior staff at Headquarters. Neither he nor any other superior ever discussed my revelations in this court case with me. I knew I was doomed and that my membership of CI9 was soon to end. Later that day, a friend showed me the document taken to Headquarters. It was part of the transcript of the trial. The first word at the top of the page was 'continued'. It did not contain the preliminary remarks of Lord Justice Nicholson when he said I was 'compelled' to answer his questions. It was merely a copy of the questions put to me and my replies. This may have been an oversight, but I am inclined to believe that my revelations had already meant my days in the squad were numbered.

Two months later, I was transferred out of the squad—no fuss, no emotional farewells. I was disappointed, but not surprised. A few days later, I discussed my change in fortunes with a solicitor friend, who was a close associate of Lord Justice Nicholson. He wanted to raise my predicament with the judge. I told him it would not serve any useful purpose.

I am certain that the trial judge was right to highlight the details of paramilitary involvement in construction frauds: millions of pounds of taxpayers' money were being siphoned off to finance brutal campaigns waged by republicans and loyalists. The business community was being held to ransom; and governmental departments, charged with responsibility for replacing derelict housing and an inadequate road system, were forced to negotiate with paramilitary gangsters to secure their cooperation so that projects could be completed and the safety of their employees guaranteed.

Court transcripts held by the judicial archivist will contain an accurate record of the actual proceedings.

Chapter 8 ∿

ON THE MOVE AGAIN!
SERIOUS CRIME
SQUAD/DRUGS SQUAD

After my abrupt departure from the Anti-Racketeering Squad, I was appointed head of the Serious Crime Squad for fourteen months. It dealt with non-paramilitary crime and its brief extended to the whole of Northern Ireland. A couple of investigations will suffice to give a flavour of our work.

A mixture of good quality investigative work and surveillance led to the capture of two professional criminals, Beattie and Lavelle. They had stolen more than £1 million worth of goods from two English salesmen who had travelled to Northern Ireland to sell jewellery. An accomplice in England had supplied information about their itinerary. Their cars were broken into while they held business meetings or went for refreshments.

Over a period of several months, we watched the thieves stalk the reps at several locations, including Larne, Belfast, Dungannon, Bangor and Portadown. Each sighting and suspicious act formed one part of the jigsaw—of limited evidential value on their own, but when put together with several similar incidents, strong enough to secure a conviction for conspiracy to steal. The men were eventually detained and imprisoned for terms in excess of five years.

In May 1987, a blackmail letter arrived at the Baker Street London headquarters of Marks and Spencer containing a threat to the group and a demand for £350,000. The letter gave instructions for the handover of the money. It was to take place in front of the City Hall in Belfast. The money was to be placed in two sports bags, one of which had to carry the logo of Liverpool Football Club. We discussed the matter at length with the police in London and the senior management of Marks and Spencer. They promised to cooperate with us in whatever strategy we decided on for the arrest of the culprits. It was agreed that an undercover police officer would carry the money, instead of the store manager as stipulated by the blackmailers. Other officers were positioned in and around the grounds of City Hall and in the upper floors of nearby buildings. Hundreds of photographs were taken of anyone in the vicinity of the rendezvous point.

After a considerable wait, a man approached the undercover officer. The code phrase was: 'Do you know where Marks and Spencers is?' The officer was then to point in the direction of the store. As soon as the man took the bags, we planned to move in and make the arrest. However, the man panicked, got the code words all wrong and left without taking the money. We followed him discreetly for some time, but did not make an arrest.

Two hours later, the operation was suspended. Would the blackmailers make further contact? Things took a bizarre turn the following day when a male caller telephoned a local journalist working for *The Sun* newspaper. He asked for £30,000 in return for details of an aborted blackmail plot. I met the journalist and agreed a plan of action. The following evening, he met the caller in the Crown Bar in Belfast to discuss the story. We had undercover officers standing close by to listen in on their conversation. As soon as it was apparent that the story related to Marks and Spencer, the decision was taken to arrest the man. He was detained following a car and foot pursuit after leaving the building. Further arrests followed. I interviewed one of the suspects at Castlereagh police office. He directed us to a shop in Smithfield Market, where we recovered a typewriter which a forensic expert confirmed had been used to type the blackmail letter to Baker Street. A number of people were charged with offences, including attempted blackmail, and sentenced to various terms of imprisonment, one of eight years.

In June 1988, I was transferred to the Drugs Squad at Donegall Pass, Belfast. I had been approached about the position some weeks previously by the head of CID. I hesitated before accepting the post because I was not certain I knew enough about drugs to do an effective job. He told me that my experience as a detective would see me through because most of the work in the Drugs Squad was similar to normal detective work—intelligence gathering, surveillance, interviewing suspects and presenting evidence in court.

On my first day I was still apprehensive but was soon reassured by the warm greeting I received from squad members, many of whom I had worked with in the past. They explained that Northern Ireland had a developing drugs problem. On a sliding scale of 1–5, it sat around 3, lower than most cities in the rest of the UK, and certainly not like Dublin with its heroin epidemic in inner-city estates. Belfast had a small number of addicts, but the demand for heroin, although readily available, was small. Cannabis, LSD and ecstasy were the drugs of choice. The 'rave' scene which was sweeping Britain was also starting to happen here.

In 1990, we made our first seizure of ecstasy: 2,500 tablets in a house in south Belfast. Intelligence had suggested that the suspect was connected to the INLA, so I enlisted the help of the Headquarters Mobile Support Unit, which specialised in rapid response situations/gaining entry to houses where there was a danger of armed conflict. As they made a dramatic and speedy entry into the property, the 'Welcome' sign on the front hall doormat caused some hilarity.

Ecstasy was a drug associated with a 'rave' dance youth culture. In 1990, approximately 40,000 doses were seized in Britain, compared to a staggering 252,000 in 1991. By the middle of the decade, it was estimated that at least two million young people were taking ecstasy every weekend. 'Raves' sprang up all over Northern Ireland; owners of many clubs kept pace with the changes and provided the facilities required. These included the trafficking of ecstasy on and around the premises. The drug appeared mainly in tablet form and was produced in a variety of colours, shapes and sizes. It was popular because in many cases it increased self-confidence and trust and was referred to as the 'peace drug'.

The 'rave' involved prolonged and energetic dancing. Reports from undercover officers put into a number of premises painted a picture of loud music, poor ventilation and congestion. Sometimes unscrupulous management turned the water off in the toilets and sold tap water in bottles at an exorbitant price. Health and safety rules were frequently flouted and the danger from fires and stampede was very real.

We took decisive action against a number of premises: licence holders in Portrush and Banbridge were prosecuted. I was asked to address various district councils concerned about breaches of safety regulations at premises in their areas. They took the matter very seriously; scrutiny of premises and licensing was tightened.

I knew from my time in the Anti-Racketeering Squad that loyalist and republican paramilitaries were determined to make trafficking in drugs a major source of income. The Provisional IRA did its best to stop volunteers from becoming directly involved. In Gerry Adams, they sought to improve their public image and strengthen their political influence through an emerging peace process. They feared that their position would be weakened in Ireland and the USA if a link was made with trafficking.

Some years previously, they had been embarrassed by a Sinn Féin councillor and IRA activist, Hugh Brady, who was arrested while in possession of a small amount of cannabis. He was immediately disowned by the republican movement and humiliated in his own area. The IRA had no ethical concerns about making money from trafficking. Dealers not connected to the organisation were allowed to operate at home and abroad as long as they paid a tariff.

Other paramilitary groups had no concerns about the public consequences of being implicated in trafficking. By the late 1980s, trafficking was a major and lucrative source of income for the INLA, UVF, UFF and Red Hand Commando. Some members of these groups strongly disapproved of this activity but were ignored by rank and file members who saw no conflict of interest in diverting funds to pay for a luxurious and decadent lifestyle.

I quickly realised that the RUC needed to improve its response to the problem. A small number of detectives in the specialist Drugs Squad could not keep the lid on the situation. Every officer in every department potentially had a part to play. The first priority for the organisation remained the containment of paramilitary violence; but like other people, I was disturbed by the emergence of organised criminal gangs who were making huge sums of money through smuggling, extortion and trading in illicit drugs, cigarettes and alcohol.

The squad lacked sophisticated equipment: radio communications were ineffective, surveillance vehicles were not rotated on a regular basis to avoid identification, equipment for searches and undercover work was inadequate. Money was scarce and payments to informers ludicrously low—it was nonsensical to expect someone to risk their personal safety for a few hundred pounds when they could make ten times that amount in dealing drugs.

All this was a far cry from the portrayal of drug cops on TV and in films. High-speed chases using powerful cars, speedboats and helicopters seldom happened. In reality, RUC Drugs Squad officers do carry guns, break down doors in early morning raids and sometimes intercept vehicles carrying drugs. Most of the time, however, their work is uneventful and mundane. Endless hours are spent following suspects, doing ordinary things and sitting outside premises while making little discernible progress. Human rights legislation and rules governing searches, seizure of property, arrest of suspects and charging with criminal offences require the actions of the squad to be proportionate and legal.

The situation improved after Special Branch, the recognised experts in gathering and analysing evidence, agreed to provide training courses in surveillance and the handling of informants for squad members. From this point on, we had a reputation for professionalism and reliability. Week-long drug-familiarisation courses were held for uniformed officers to establish a network of knowledge of drugs in every area of Northern Ireland. We updated the Force policy on drug misuse and solvent abuse. Payment to informants was increased, but remained smaller than the amounts paid by Special Branch. After some persuasion, we were provided with two telephone intercepts—far fewer than the number available to Special Branch. Members of the squad lectured to anyone interested in the subject of drug misuse, including civil servants, educationalists, medical staff and voluntary organisations.

In October 1991, I appeared on *The Gerry Kelly Show* on Ulster TV to discuss the topical issue of ecstasy and LSD. Gerry became a close friend and on many occasions was helpful in promoting health issues surrounding drug misuse.

The Northern Ireland Office continued to monitor the situation and held quarterly meetings at Stormont. The conferences were attended by various governmental departments, pharmaceutical experts, HM Customs, the RUC Drugs Squad and voluntary organisations. I also represented the RUC at a number of conferences in England. This ensured that we were part of the UK policing effort to combat drugs. I learned that organised crime and international trafficking involved major criminals throughout the island of Ireland. These people had access to major drug suppliers in Holland and Spain and were fully exploiting the international banking system.

In September 1990 I was invited to speak on the subject of paramilitary involvement in drug trafficking at the Scottish National Drugs Conference. I explained how trafficking provided income for the purchase of weapons and to make payments to activists and the families of men in prison. The talk was well received and was a major topic of discussion over dinner. The organisers were delighted by the response and invited me back in seven years' time to update the situation. By 1997, when I returned to the Conference, the political situation in Northern Ireland had changed and the perceived enemies of peace and democracy were now at the heart of a developing peace process. My declaration[7] that paramilitary gangsterism was booming caused much consternation among senior officials in the Northern Ireland Office and among senior officers in my own organisation and was to cause me much personal anguish; it ultimately contributed to my downfall.

Earlier in 1990, I attended a month-long course run by the DEA (Drug Enforcement Agency) in Washington DC. Delegates from twenty other countries encompassing South America, Europe, the USSR, Asia and Australasia took part. The DEA were wonderful hosts and made the course interesting and informative.

The course was part of the DEA's local strategy for monitoring the production and supply of illicit drugs. An international network of agents already existed and the course was designed to improve the working relationship between them and foreign enforcement agencies like the RUC.

Our host's financial outlay for the course was substantial. They paid the airfares of all participants, full board in a $180 per night luxurious hotel and conference fees. They also gave us $1,800 spending money. For some delegates, particularly from Asia, this sum of money was equivalent to six months' wages. During the month-long stay, they spent little on entertainment or luxuries. Instead they bought clothing and other goods for their families. For Europeans like myself, and Australasians, the money was used to pay for trips to New York and evenings of entertainment at clubs and sporting events.

On each weekday, DEA experts lectured us on a range of topics, including the production and supply methods used by international traffickers; the difficulties facing governments and enforcement agencies in areas of production, such as Afghanistan, Lebanon and Colombia; health and social issues caused by addiction; organised crime and money-laundering within the global banking system; the involvement of dishonest government officials, accountants, bankers and solicitors in laundering money; and the financing of terrorist organisations through trafficking, such as FARC guerrillas in Colombia.

The highlight of the course was a morning spent with drugs squad officers from Miami. They explained how they tackled ruthless criminals and drug dealers on a daily basis. This often involved violent confrontation. Millions of dollars worth of drugs, money and vehicles were seized from gangsters each year. They emphasised the importance of high-grade intelligence, meticulous planning and trust within their group. They also showed a video compilation of operations that had gone wrong through bad luck or the unpredictable behaviour of the dealers. It brought home to us the real dangers which enforcement officers working undercover had to face on a daily basis. The 1980s TV series *Miami Vice* was a vivid and accurate depiction of this.

The most disturbing issues highlighted during the course were the consequences of addiction for individuals, families, neighbourhoods and the whole of society. It was a sobering thought that the producers of heroin in Afghanistan and Pakistan, cocaine in Colombia and cannabis in Lebanon and Morocco could have such a devastating effect on Western society. Washington DC was a case in point: we were told that eighty children each month were being abandoned in the city by parents addicted to drugs.

I made many lasting friendships with delegates. The two Russian representatives fascinated everyone. The older of the two was a KGB officer who spoke no English; his companion had to translate during lectures. They were wonderful company and became great friends. On a number of nights we visited a club in Blues Alley, where world-class jazz musicians played. One night a party of African-Americans sat next to us. They had wonderful style: the women wore fur coats and were draped in gold; the men wore white suits and huge Stetson hats. They loved their jazz. They were speechless when I identified our party as being from Ireland, Holland, Denmark, Yugoslavia, the USSR, Australia and the Philippines. One of them playfully asked if we were connected with the Tower of Babel. Later in the evening, he took us in his white stretch-limousine to another club. As dawn broke, he gave us a guided tour of historical monuments. Back at the hotel, the Russian lads presented our hosts with bottles of Russian vodka, which were promptly opened and for the next couple of hours memories of Cold War times gave way to the warmth of human solidarity. It took the 'united nations' and several night porters to transport our African-American comrades back to their stretch-limousine.

The conclusion of the course was marked by a formal dinner. Guests included senior DEA officials, who had flown up specially from Colombia, and senior embassy officials from the participating countries. I was asked to make a speech of thanks on behalf of the delegates. I returned to Northern Ireland thinking that some of the people I had met would not be out of place in a Hollywood blockbuster movie. In 1995, I met one of the Russians at a conference in England; he told me that the KGB colonel had been thrown out of a twenty-third storey window during the overthrow of the Communist regime.

On my return, I discovered that a number of robberies and break-ins had happened at chemist shops in Belfast and that a large quantity of prescription drugs, including Diazepam and Temazepam, had been stolen. These drugs are used in treating a variety of complaints, including insomnia, depression and anxiety. They are particularly dangerous if taken with alcohol or dissolved and injected. There was little demand for these drugs on the black market in Northern Ireland, so it was likely that they were destined for Dublin. I travelled South and met members of the Irish Drugs Squad. We shared intelligence on possible suspects. Informants on both sides of the border eventually identified the persons involved. Surveillance was concentrated on these suspects. During follow-up searches, most of the stolen drugs were recovered.

Stephen Pollock, a well-known drug addict, frequently appeared during these operations. He was arrested but denied involvement. In late 1990, we discovered that Pollock was under threat from the INLA because of a lost consignment of drugs. Surveillance had confirmed that he was dealing to both loyalist and republican paramilitaries.

In January 1991, Pollock and his friend, Renwick Dennison, were seen boarding a plane for London. About a week later, I was invited by the Metropolitan Police to provide an undercover officer for a UFF trafficking operation in London. In this operation, a man was arrested and a substantial amount of ecstasy was recovered. It was not possible to establish whether Pollock and Dennison were involved. A short time later we learned through informers and telephone intercepts that dealers in Northern Ireland were expecting a large consignment of cannabis. I passed this information to NCIS (the National Criminal Intelligence Service), the organisation responsible for collating intelligence on serious crime throughout the UK. A few days later, a detective inspector from No. 9 Regional Crime Squad in England met me in Belfast. He had information about a large importation of cannabis from Spain and that Pollock, Dennison and another Belfast man, Thomas McCreery, were involved. I told the detective inspector that McCreery had been a notorious gunman in the UDA and had gone to England after being shot six times for dealing drugs with republicans. We believed that he was working with major drug dealers in Spain. A concentrated surveillance operation identified a house in Kent that was being used by Pollock and his gang. A number of suspects were photographed entering and leaving the address. Undercover officers watched the drugs being delivered to the house and, as dawn broke, stun-grenades were fired through a bedroom window to subdue the occupants. One million pounds worth of cannabis and a firearm were recovered.

On 30 May, a detective sergeant from the squad accompanied me to London to analyse the operation. We were unexpectedly taken to a murder investigation team and were told that some of the Northern Ireland men in custody were suspected of being involved in two shooting incidents in which one man had been killed and another seriously wounded. The dead man, David Norris, was an informer and 'super-grass' and had been giving evidence against a number of major traffickers. It was believed that a contract had been placed with a loyalist paramilitary gunman in Belfast to kill Norris and prevent him from giving evidence. The second man was shot for allegedly ripping off dealers in a huge transaction. The trial against four men, including a Belfast loyalist, mysteriously collapsed; but at a second trial in July 1992, Dennison and an Englishman, Stuart Warren, were sentenced to life imprisonment for attempted murder.

Drug misuse among serving soldiers became a problem at this stage. It was obviously potentially dangerous to the public and embarrassing to the military authorities. In one incident, ten soldiers were detained after failing drug tests; during searches of their private quarters small amounts of cannabis were recovered. In a second incident, a number of soldiers who frequented nightclubs in Bangor were found to have taken LSD. The army's SIB (Special Investigation Branch) invited us to assist them in the investigation. The culprits were prosecuted in a civil court, then court-martialled and dismissed from the army. From this point, the army recognised the importance of random drug-testing.

It was during this period that my health suddenly deteriorated: I suffered a stroke and was diagnosed with a serious blood condition, Polycythaemia Rubre Vera. In layman's terms, I was producing too much blood and therefore too many red cells. At an early point in my treatment, I was told that I could expect to live for a maximum of six years. The news did not bother me; but I wondered if I had been unfortunate, or whether my lifestyle of working long hours, heavy drinking and too little sleep had contributed to my condition. From the start of my career, I had lived to work, usually averaging more than 250 hours per month. During busy periods this rose to 300 and more. The work was undoubtedly stressful and at times dangerous; on occasions I found it a convenient excuse for bouts of heavy drinking. I avoided deep analysis of this issue: why release demons when I could easily convince myself that this was happening through no fault of my own?

In March 1992 I left the Drugs Squad and moved on promotion with the rank of Detective Superintendent to Grosvenor Road, as the most senior CID officer in Belfast and Lisburn. I am satisfied that the hierarchy of the RUC did their best to support the Drugs Squad, but the depressing statistics of paramilitary violence, which included 410 deaths, 1,903 bombing incidents and 2,665 shootings, determined their priorities.

Chapter 9 ✎

BACK WITH REGIONAL CID

Since the start of the Troubles in 1968, west Belfast had been a challenging area for policing. It was one of the chosen battlegrounds for republican and loyalist paramilitaries. The IRA attacked the security forces with bombs, rockets and guns. Businesses were destroyed by arsonists and bombers; vehicles and buses were hijacked in frequent street disorder. The proximity of this predominantly Catholic area to the Protestant Shankill area led to repeated sectarian clashes and murders and in time forced the government to erect security barriers.

I had worked in the area in 1976 just after Sir Kenneth Newman, the Chief Constable, had pledged his support for a ministerial document for policing called 'The Way Ahead'. The paper set out a long-term strategy for the downgrading of the army's role in favour of the primacy of the RUC. Two objectives were seen as essential to success: a speedy and effective confrontation with the paramilitaries, and progress on the development of community relations by adopting a system of policing which considered the needs and feelings of local people.

By 1992, when I returned to the area as a detective superintendent, the first part of the equation had been partially met: thousands of paramilitary activists had been imprisoned, tons of explosives and hundreds of weapons had been seized. The second part of the plan had failed to materialise: the RUC was less popular with Catholics than at any time in the past. The legacy of the army curfew of 1971 and internment had been exacerbated by the emotional response to the 'dirty protest', the deaths of the hunger strikers and murderous attacks by loyalists. Support for the Provisional IRA appeared as strong as ever and Sinn Féin was enjoying unprecedented electoral success.

Sir Hugh Annesley, the Chief Constable since June 1989, had publicly declared his vision of policing: he looked forward to a time when the RUC could stop using armoured Land Rovers and work towards a general community-based policing service.

In late 1991, an upsurge in republican and loyalist violence made this vision seem a far-off dream: forty-one people were murdered and one hundred seriously injured in a six-month period; both sides had discovered new ways of attacking each other: the IRA detonated a bomb in the dining-hall of Crumlin Road prison and killed two loyalist prisoners; the UFF threw a hand-grenade at Catholic supporters of Cliftonville during a football match at Windsor Park; two soldiers were killed in an IRA bomb attack at Musgrave Park Hospital.

The west Belfast I encountered in 1992 showed little evidence of community harmony. Many terrible things had happened since 1976: both sides had shamelessly engaged in sectarian killings and many police officers and soldiers had been killed or seriously injured. House takeovers and the hijacking of vehicles were commonplace, and were often the prelude to an attack on the security forces in the area, or a bombing mission into Belfast city centre. Hundreds of businesses had been bombed out of existence, including many public houses, which were seen as competition to republican and loyalist drinking clubs. Buses were frequently targeted by rioters and arsonists. This led to the withdrawal of services and increased trade for paramilitary-run black taxis. Extortion, intimidation, vehicle theft, joy-riding, alcohol and drug misuse were just some of the problems affecting the lives of law-abiding people. Young people deemed by paramilitary punishment squads to be involved in 'anti-social behaviour' were kneecapped, beaten with baseball bats or sticks with protruding nails, and, in many cases, forced to leave the district. The legacy of this relentless violence over many years was one of suffering and enduring loss that left a sense of injustice and grievance.

The type of policing applied to the area was not what had originally been envisaged. Heavily armed officers patrolled on foot and in vehicles, often with military support. Mobile Support Units, known as 'The Blues', patrolled west Belfast and assisted in house searches, arrest operations and the policing of public order disturbances. The system of patrolling was skilfully organised to afford as much protection as possible to officers. It could provide speedy support and quickly extricate them from any situation regarded as too dangerous. CID investigators operated as best they could, but relied heavily on uniformed police and army protection. Police in west Belfast worked closely with their counterparts, 'The Blacks', who patrolled Ardoyne, Shankill, part of the Antrim Road and the New Lodge areas.

Mobile Support Units faced dangers every day, but their specialist training and bravery made them formidable. They were the bravest officers I worked with during my thirty years of service. I remember one night in 1995 when serious rioting took place in nationalist areas. An IRA sniper shot at one of these men; the bullet penetrated his riot helmet, ricocheted and exited by the side. He was shocked but unharmed. He returned to Antrim Road station, reported the incident and was on the street again within half an hour. That same evening, a Land Rover with members of 'The Blacks' on board was struck by an RPG rocket. The rear of the vehicle was badly damaged, but no one was injured. They pursued and arrested a number of men who were believed to have fired the rocket.

Every crime report was analysed and, when possible, double-checked in case we were being drawn into an ambush. In any case where there was a doubt, the scene of the reported incident was not visited for some hours or days. Many police officers and soldiers were killed responding to reported incidents: in 1971, Constable Stanley Corry and Detective Constable William Russell were shot dead while investigating a burglary at a boutique in Andersonstown. On 2 May 1991, Sergeant Stephen Gillespie died when a rocket hit his Land Rover on the Springfield Road.

Policing works best when it has the trust and support of the local community. When cooperation is withheld, as was the case in west Belfast, the police have to function as best they can. However, the ability to provide an efficient and effective service is greatly impaired. They rely on the public to provide information on crime and criminals and to give evidence in court. When this does not happen, the police are forced to rely on intelligence gathering, surveillance and telephone intercepts to catch suspects. Most police forces in the world use these techniques, but in Northern Ireland they are seen by some as controversial and unethical. Since the start of the Troubles, the RUC has applied these tactics to recover explosives and firearms and arrest suspects involved in serious crime.

Evidence including fingerprints, DNA, footprints, paint fragments, glass particles and hair strands was routinely collected and presented in court by forensic scientists. Paramilitary groups recognised the dangers of forensic evidence and took steps to reduce the risk of detection. After incidents, they discarded clothing, vehicles, firearms and anything else that might link them to the crime. They washed up in safe houses to remove incriminating residues from explosives and firearms. The combined weaknesses in these areas of criminal investigation forced the RUC to rely heavily on admissions from suspects.

Between 1970 and 1988, almost 12,000 people were convicted of involvement in paramilitary offences. During the fifteen-year period after 1970, the success of this process caused great difficulties for republican and loyalist paramilitaries. Paramilitary organisations, particularly the Provisional IRA, trained volunteers in ways of counteracting interviewing techniques. They produced 'The Green Book', a copy of which was given to every member. It set out the IRA constitution, aims, objectives and disciplinary code. In General Order No. 5, part 2, a volunteer under arrest was instructed to remain silent and refuse to give any account of his or her movements, activities or associates.

Prisoners were given, as a right, access to a solicitor who, in keeping with his or her legal responsibilities, advised clients not to incriminate themselves. Eventually, allegations from influential public figures and human rights groups of mistreatment of prisoners forced the government and the RUC to implement strict codes of practice and new legal restraints on how prisoners were treated while in custody. In time, this reduced the reliance on confessions from suspects.

Sometimes, public statements by community representatives, politicians and clergy during times of heightened tension or after some heinous incident undermined the credibility of the police and increased public mistrust. One instance of this occurred after the murder of two Catholic workmen in Kennedy Way. Father Denis Faul publicly accused the police of being 'grossly negligent' in the way they went about safeguarding Catholic areas. He asked, 'Is there a real wish on the part of the authorities to protect Catholic areas at this time?' He also said there must not be 'double standards' on the part of the authorities. He was quite entitled to highlight the anguish and fear undoubtedly felt by Catholics, but some of his words appeared inappropriate and insensitive. Less than seventy-two hours earlier, the IRA had planted a bomb inside Frizzell's fish shop on the Shankill Road which killed nine Protestants. It had been intended for the leadership of the UFF who had been meeting earlier in premises above the shop.

During my first week in Grosvenor Road, two UFF men, Alan Skey and Paul McNeilly, were arrested in an early morning operation on the outskirts of west Belfast. They were found in possession of a sawn-off shotgun and cartridges. The case gave me an opportunity to appraise myself of my new responsibilities as a superintendent in dealing with paramilitary prisoners held at Castlereagh police office. I was obliged to inquire as to why they were in custody and to ensure that their detention was lawful. All prisoners were entitled to see a doctor. If the right of access to a solicitor was denied by me, I had to make certain that the decision was made in accordance with legislation. I was expected to brief interviewing officers and supervise the conduct of interviews. All documentation connected to the prisoner had to be in order. Access to prisoners was strictly controlled by uniformed officers, and no one was allowed into the cell block area without their approval. Prisoners were escorted to and from the interview room by uniformed officers. Interviews were limited to periods which allowed prisoners to rest and have meals. In the event of a complaint by a prisoner, a senior uniformed officer had to be informed. All interview rooms were fitted with visual recording equipment enabling a uniformed chief inspector in an adjoining room to monitor proceedings. I also had to give written permission for any clothing to be removed from prisoners for forensic examination, as well as finger-prints, buccal swabs, nail-scrapings and hair. I spent a great deal of time in the police office at Castlereagh over the next three years.

On 24 March 1992, my very first day at Grosvenor Road, the IRA left a huge car bomb containing 1,100 lbs of home-made explosives in Pakenham Street, at the rear of the Donegall Pass police station. A warning was given and people were safely evacuated from the area. The bomb exploded, causing considerable damage to private houses, business premises and the police station. Local detectives and Special Branch believed that the device had been planted by an IRA unit from west Belfast, my new area of responsibility.

I travelled across town to inspect the damage at my old place of work. I had a fondness for the building and had pleasant memories of my time spent there. Two friends, Ray (a Crime Prevention sergeant) and Arthur (a long-serving, uniformed beat constable) met me on the street. They had seen the aftermath of previous bombings in this part of south Belfast and were philosophical about the latest incident. They were pleased to see me and invited me in for a drink. We gingerly picked our way through the rubble and found the remains of Ray's office in the lower reaches of the building. We dusted down three chairs and spent a couple of pleasant hours reminiscing. On the street outside, Alan Hay (a building engineer) heard voices. Thinking that people were still trapped inside, he shouted down in panic. He knew me well and was delighted to hear that everything was fine. He declined an invitation to join us.

The preliminary findings of the Ammunition Technical Officer and forensic experts indicated that the explosives and detonating device used were similar in construction to a number of bombs which had destroyed parts of Belfast city centre over the previous six months.

The following morning, I discussed these attacks with Special Branch officers from west Belfast. They told me they had been 'doing work' on a number of suspects and premises and were hopeful of taking decisive action in the near future. I had worked with Special Branch long enough to know that further probing was inappropriate. It was obvious that they were carrying out surveillance and using technical aids to monitor the activities of suspects. The security of their undercover officers was an absolute priority and information about on-going operations was restricted to essential personnel. I did not fit that category.

I had not long to wait for news of a dramatic breakthrough. When it happened, it proved to be one of the most significant setbacks for the IRA during the period. In the early hours of 16 April 1992, the duty inspector at Headquarters phoned me at my home and told me that two suspects had been arrested in possession of explosives at Pembrook Loop, Poleglass, on the outskirts of west Belfast. I travelled to Woodburn police station, not far from where the arrests were made. I was told that E4A, Special Branch's elite surveillance unit, had watched suspicious items being loaded into a stolen Peugeot taxi the previous evening. The two men involved had featured in previous sightings and were believed to be part of the bombing team. Undercover officers followed the car until they were able to direct two Headquarters Mobile

Support Unit armoured cars into a position to intercept. In a dramatic climax to the pursuit, the IRA suspects attempted to escape by driving over a steep grassy bank. The car spun out of control and landed on the roof of a pursuing police vehicle. Luckily, no police officer was killed or injured. Scott Gary Monaghan from Locan Street and Stephen Jameson from Nansen Street, both west Belfast, were arrested; 50 lbs of explosives were found during a search of the boot. Jameson was taken to Castlereagh police office for interview; Monaghan, who had been injured in the crash, was taken to the secure military wing of Musgrave Park Hospital. I spent most of the night piecing together details of the operation.

Just after 9 a.m., I chaired a conference with detectives who were about to interview Jameson. I outlined details of the arrest operation and the background to the recent bombings in Belfast. I then went to Musgrave Park Hospital to speak with medical staff who were treating Monaghan. His injuries were not serious, but the doctor in charge imposed strict guidelines for the frequency and duration of questioning: the staff at the hospital had the power to stop an interview at any time if the medical condition of Monaghan worsened; Monaghan could also terminate an interview if he felt pain or discomfort. It was therefore essential that I selected two experienced and dependable officers to question him. I chose Detective Sergeant Jimmy Myles and Detective Constable Jack Bohill, who had been investigating serious crime for many years. I knew they could be relied on to carry out my strict instructions and work within the parameters set down by the medical staff.

I stayed with them for a short period during their first meeting with Monaghan. He was friendly and relaxed and we had high hopes that the interview would be productive. By mid-afternoon, I was called back to the hospital by Jimmy Myles. He told me that Monaghan had admitted he had made bombs which had caused millions of pounds worth of damage in Belfast city centre.

Monaghan was an interesting character. He told us how, as a youth growing up in Glasgow, he had been a member of a republican flute band. He came to live in Belfast in 1988, met and married a girl from west Belfast and went to live in Locan Street. In 1990, he worked as a security guard at Castle Court shopping centre, one of the biggest malls in Belfast. Here he helped plant incendiary devices which caused considerable damage to the complex. He was made redundant soon afterwards. He admitted planting further incendiary devices at shopping centres in other parts of Belfast, as well as Ballymena, Portadown and Newtownards.

The importance of his capture became more apparent when he admitted his part in the bomb-making process. He described in detail how he had made thirty coffee jar bombs, a lethal weapon when thrown or dropped on members of the police and army as they drove past. We were hopeful that he might be one of the IRA's engineering department responsible for the major bombing campaign in the city centre. By the evening, we were making significant inroads.

He described his part in the booby-trapping of a car owned by a UDR soldier at Kyle Street on 3 January 1992. He said he had made bombs for a number of attacks: an explosion at Botanic Avenue on 2 February 1992, which caused widespread damage; a 450 lb bomb at Adelaide Street on 15 February, which caused millions of pounds worth of damage; a 250 lb bomb in the same street before repair work had been completed. He was one of an IRA unit preparing 1,500 lbs of homemade explosives at Broom Park Heights, Twinbrook, found after a surveillance operation by Special Branch and army undercover soldiers. He had helped make the 1,100 lb bomb which wrecked the area around Donegall Pass police station in March. He had also mixed explosives for a 500 lb bomb left outside Castlereagh police station on 13 April which was defused by the army.

Like many people, I had been caught up in the traffic chaos which followed these bombings. I was frustrated and angry at the widespread destruction caused to the commercial heart of Belfast. It was hard to believe that this young man lying before me in a hospital bed with his baby face and ready smile could have been one of the architects of such mayhem.

Monaghan quickly recovered from his injuries and was charged with a number of offences under the Explosive Substances Act of 1883. On 14 September 1993, he and Jameson appeared at Belfast Crown Court and pleaded guilty to a catalogue of charges. He was sentenced to fifteen years in prison and a total of 989 years concurrent terms. Defence barristers told the trial judge that he had severed his links with the IRA and was feeling genuine remorse for his part in the bombing campaign.

His arrest was a major blow to the IRA and slowed down their attacks in Belfast for a time. It was not long, however, before they had filled the void.

Since 1990, the UFF in the Shankill area had been very active and posed a serious threat to Catholics in west Belfast. Under the leadership of Johnny Adair, C Company seemed to attract an endless supply of young, militant volunteers. They had killed several people in north and west Belfast and were the main target of police and army surveillance. The police had several major successes against them, none bigger than the capture of Adair's most active killing unit, 'The Dream Team'. Special Branch learned that they intended to kill a Provisional IRA commander in west Belfast. At 7 a.m. on 17 July 1992, five UFF members in two cars were stopped by police outside Finaghy railway station, less than a mile from the home of their target. They were interviewed at Castlereagh police office and later charged with conspiracy to murder and firearm offences. At Belfast Crown Court, Andrew Watson, the driver of the scout car, was sentenced to ten years' imprisonment; Matthew McCormick, who was driving the three gunmen in the following car, was sentenced to fourteen years; the three intended assassins, Sam 'Skelly' McCrory, Thomas Potts and Jackie Thompson, were each sentenced to sixteen years.

Sadly, every success seemed to be accompanied by terrible tragedy. Shortly before 9 a.m. on 28 April 1992, security gates at Lanark Way on one of the routes connecting the Falls and Shankill Road were opened to enable the movement of traffic between the two districts. It had been closed during the night to prevent clashes between rival groups and to stop incursions by loyalist murder gangs. Soon after this, two men on a red Suzuki motorcycle drove through and parked near a shop on the Springfield Road. The pillion passenger entered the shop and shot Philomena Hanna. After she fell to the floor, he shot her several times more.

When a shooting like this is reported, it is natural to assume that a male has been shot. I was shocked and disgusted at what I found. A lovely woman, horribly disfigured by bullets to her head and upper body, lay motionless in a pool of blood. I immediately considered that the UFF of C Company were responsible. I imagined the killers safely back on the Shankill Road enjoying their notoriety and celebrating their kill with Adair.

A good deal of forensic evidence was found at the scene which later identified the murder weapon as a .38 calibre Ruger revolver. It had been used to kill Larry Murchan, a Catholic newsagent near his shop at St James's Road, west Belfast, on 28 September 1991. It had also been used to murder Seamus Sullivan, a Catholic council worker, on the Springfield Road on 3 September 1991. Unfortunately, there was no further evidence to link any individual with the killing of Philomena Hanna. No one has ever been charged in connection with the incident.

Intelligence later established that the gunman was Stephen McKeag, a young member of the UFF, who was to kill many more times. McKeag, like the other active members of his gang, was arrested many times; but because of lack of evidence he had to be released without charge. The police and army carried out intensive surveillance on the group and made many arrests. Full-time surveillance was not possible in the confined environment of the Lower Shankill with its warren of side-streets. Here Adair reigned with impunity, enjoying the protection of the local community.

That same month, I was told by Special Branch that the IRA knew where I lived in Newtownards and was intending to target me. Normally, Special Branch is no more specific than that. I went to the head of CID in Belfast, George Caskey, and suggested that because I would now have to move home, I was entitled to know more. He arranged a meeting with high-ranking officers. They told me that a mole in the Census Office had discovered my address and that of two other officers and had passed on this information to the IRA. Their homes had already been attacked and I was the next target. I was advised to move and did so shortly afterwards. Anyone who has been in this situation will understand the stress involved. I left under a government scheme set up for people in my situation called SPED (Special Purchase of Evacuated Dwellings). The scheme paid me a conservative sum of money, then sold the property a few days later at a profit of several thousand pounds—a considerable sum in those days.

Bitter memories of the riots of 1969 leading to the burning of hundreds of houses and the displacement of thousands of people in the interface area between the Falls and the Shankill had not faded. Every summer tensions surfaced and often led to serious violence. In early July 1992, skirmishes occurred nightly in North Howard Street, one of the few streets in the area without a permanent security barrier. One of the reasons for this was the presence of an army barracks in the street which billeted soldiers. The primary role of soldiers on security duty at the base was the protection of the complex and the men in it. They took no interest in the rioting and saw it as the responsibility of the RUC. On 5 July, the police were called to the scene on a number of occasions when the clashes escalated. Land Rovers formed a barrier between the fighting factions, but left when the situation calmed down. Around 4 a.m. a Catholic youth, Kieran Abram, was walking his dog when he was attacked by a number of Protestant youths. They kicked and beat him with sticks. Soldiers on security duty realised what was happening and detained some of the assailants. They summoned medical help and contacted the police. Sadly, Kieran Abram died where he lay. I got a call shortly afterwards and hastened to the area. A short time later, a priest arrived and asked me if he could perform the Last Rites, an important ritual for Catholics at the time of death. I moved away as he knelt in prayer and blessed the body. Hopefully, it gave some comfort to the family.

Some hours later, I returned to Grosvenor Road where the five suspects apprehended by the army were being held in cells. They were legally entitled to a period of rest since they had been arrested in the early hours of the morning: interviews could not commence until 9 a.m. I assembled a team of detectives. During the interviews, all five made admissions and were subsequently charged with Kieran Abram's murder. At their trial some months later they were convicted of manslaughter, two of them were sentenced to nine years' imprisonment and a third to seven years. The other two, because of their age, received shorter terms.

The police and army were criticised by Nationalist and Unionist politicians and community groups for their handling of the disorder in the area. Security gates were erected in the week following the killing, after long-standing demands by local people.

August 1992 was a particularly busy month. I had several meetings with the Garda Síochána, who were investigating the killing of a young man, Raymond Healy, at Salthill, Galway, on 2 July. A number of men from west Belfast had been denied access to a nightclub because they were inebriated. A short time later, they threw a brick into the crowd queuing outside the club. Raymond Healy was hit on the head and died from the blow. We arrested various suspects. One of them was subsequently convicted of the killing and the others were prosecuted for affray.

In late August, I was summoned to a camp where a young Scots guardsman had been shot dead by a colleague. Inquiries and the results of a post-mortem indicated that it was accidental.

Late in the evening of 11 August, I got a telephone call informing me that a body had been found in an alleyway in Beechmount Gardens. It was that of a young man. He was wearing a white boiler suit; his eyes had been taped and his arms bound behind his back. It was a night of torrential rain, which made the forensic examination of the scene very difficult. The following day, we identified the body as that of Robin Hill, a 22-year-old from Ardmore Park in Coalisland. The post-mortem revealed that he had been shot in the back of the head. The pathologist observed that the body was remarkably clean and pale, suggesting that the victim had been immersed in water for some time prior to his violent death. The IRA alleged that he was an informant and had executed him. The family was devastated. They strongly denied the allegation. I spoke to Special Branch who declined to clarify the issue, in keeping with their policy of non-disclosure.

A forensic examination of the bullets recovered from the body showed that a .357 Magnum revolver had been used. The same gun had been used in the shooting of a UDR soldier, Brian Lawrence, in Duncrue Street, Belfast, in June 1991. It was later used in the killing of a good friend of mine, Constable James Douglas, murdered in the Monico Bar, Lombard Street, on 10 October 1992. He had worked with me at Donegall Pass; he and his wife were frequently in my company.

During the early part of the summer, intelligence reports from Special Branch and Garda sources in Dublin had indicated increasing tension between factions of the IPLO based in Dublin and the Lower Falls in Belfast. A former Belfast man had fled to Dublin after the murder of John McMaster in his hardware store in Church Lane. It was claimed that Mr McMaster was a member of the security forces; in fact, he was a lieutenant commander in the Royal Naval Reserve with no operational function in Northern Ireland.

The fugitive gunman teamed up with former INLA colleagues in Dublin and used his paramilitary muscle to establish a foothold in the lucrative drugs trade. They called themselves the IPLO Headquarters and laid claim to the weapons, money and policy-direction of that organisation. They supplied drugs to their Belfast counterparts at a competitive price. There was a dispute over missing money. Jimmy Brown, a prominent member of the IPLO and closely associated with the Dublin faction, came North to meet members of the Belfast group. He wanted to avoid a repetition of the 1987 feud which had claimed twelve lives.

It is known that he met a number of men in a car park at York Gate Shopping Centre in Belfast on 18 August. Forty-five minutes later, he was shot dead in Clonard Street in west Belfast. He had just left a house in the street and was travelling towards the Falls Road in his Ford Orion. A passenger in the car later described Brown pulling over to talk to a man, who fired six shots, hitting him in the head. A short time later, Brown died at the scene. His passenger fled and returned to Dublin.

The IPLO denied the killing—as did the IRA, who were increasingly frustrated by the criminal activities of the IPLO in their area. Members of the Belfast group were frightened of reprisals and took refuge in safe houses in the Rosetta and Carryduff areas of south Belfast.

The IPLO leadership in Dublin was anxious to avoid an escalation of violence and denied that the killing was part of a feud. The Belfast faction responded by denouncing the Dublin leadership as drug barons and said it no longer recognised Headquarters.

I went to the scene of the Brown shooting and realised that local people were fearful of further killings. Brown was a prominent republican. He was also a former chairman of the Irish Republican Socialist Party and had given the oration at the funeral of another prominent member, Martin O'Prey, shot dead by the UVF in August 1991. Many people condemned the Brown killing and made it clear that the drug-dealing activities of the IPLO were unacceptable.

The second victim of the feud was Hugh McKibben, shot dead on a bus outside the Lámh Dhearg GAA club in Hannahstown on the outskirts of west Belfast. He had supported Brown and acted as a minder at the confrontation at York Gate car park and had been part of the guard of honour at Brown's funeral.

This was a vicious killing, an execution carried out in front of children, women and football players. I arrived at the scene and saw a group of people standing around in shock. Many were silently praying. Mr McKibben's brother approached me and asked if he could pray over the body. I escorted him onto the bus and watched as he stroked his brother's arm and said a prayer.

The killing of the third victim was no less barbaric. Michael Macklin was shot dead in front of his wife and young son at his home in Whiterock Gardens in west Belfast. Attempts were made to kill other IPLO members. Several were shot and wounded; another was seriously injured after being hit in the head with a bolt fired from a crossbow.

Some of the Belfast faction responsible for these killings were to meet a similar fate at the hands of the IRA under the cover name, 'Direct Action Against Drugs'. Before the end of the year, the IRA had responded to public condemnation of the IPLO, forcing it to disband. On 31 October 1992, Sammy Ward, a prominent member of the group, was shot dead and as many as sixteen people were kneecapped. On 4 November the IPLO leadership announced that it had ceased to exist.

On 2 October, members of my squad who joined the RUC in December 1970 received our Long Service medal from the Chief Constable at the Training Centre in east Belfast. It was the first time I had seen most of them since then and we enjoyed the occasion. When we first joined, we were full of idealism and the hope that we could make a difference. The situation for policing had now become so difficult that even basic aims and objectives seemed a remote dream. Some members of the squad had been killed, others seriously injured; we remembered them during the ceremony.

Despite the huge effort of the police to prevent the disruption of Belfast city Christmas shopping, bombers managed to smuggle two devices into King Street on 9 December 1992. Inevitably this caused traffic chaos and dismay among the traders. As part of this operation, two houses were taken over by the IRA in west Belfast, and the cars belonging to their occupants were used to transport the bombs. Three men were arrested after being pursued by the police.

In their attempts to prevent further bombing incidents, the police mounted roadblocks at most of the roads into Belfast. This further aggravated the traffic situation and added to the misery of shoppers.

———

As part of the RUC strategy to address anti-social issues in west Belfast, operations mounted by the Stolen Car Squad were substantially increased. The previous year, they had made 107 detections and it was hoped that further patrolling would prevent young people from stealing cars and driving recklessly around estates. Local people had complained bitterly about these so-called 'joyriders' and we were anxious to tackle the problem.

Catholic housing estates in west Belfast had been the scene of conflict since the Troubles started. A legacy of this unrest and lawlessness was the emergence of a generation of young people with serious behavioural problems. Many parents, despite problems of poverty and unemployment, had done their best to instil a sense of discipline, but could not control their teenage offspring. Some in despair turned to alcohol and/or became dependent on prescription drugs. Others refused to believe that their children were part of the gangs terrorising the neighbourhood. Sadly, some took no interest in what their children got up to.

Thousands of cars had been stolen since 1970, many in the area itself, others from elsewhere, recklessly driven and subsequently dumped in west Belfast. Most of them were badly damaged or burnt. Obtaining car insurance became increasingly difficult and exorbitantly expensive.

Some of the offenders were as young as ten years of age and had learned their behaviour from older children. They took the cars for the excitement and seemed unconcerned by the risks involved. They taunted the police, doing hand-brake turns in the hope of teasing them into a high-speed chase.

The risk to the joyriders and people living in the area was enormous. Many young people had been killed or critically injured in crashes. In one incident, five youths travelling at 80 mph with the police in pursuit crashed into a tree. Three of the occupants were killed, the fourth suffered serious brain damage, and the fifth was paralysed from the waist down.

Several pedestrians were knocked down and killed, or left with long-term disabilities. There were instances of joyriders being shot by the police and army after crashing through roadblocks.

These were the realities which the police had to address when attempting to develop a strategy for dealing with joyriders in an urban environment. Where possible, the police tried to avoid high-speed pursuits in the interests of public safety. Joyriders realised this and became even more blatant in their behaviour.

Mena and Joseph Sheehy, my mother and father, outside 42 North Queen Street, Belfast.

I am in the front row, second from left, at Park Lodge School, Belfast, in 1958. Brother Holian is in the back row.

The funeral of Constable Robert 'Roy' Leslie in Moy, Co. Tyrone, September 1971.

A show of strength by the UDA on the Shankill Road in 1972.

The aftermath of the UVF gun and bomb attack on the Miami Showband in July 1975. Three members of the band and two UVF men were killed.

The burnt-out shell of the La Mon House Hotel outside Belfast. Twelve people died and dozens were injured in an IRA firebomb attack in February 1978. (*Pacemaker*)

The scene at Warrenpoint, Co. Down, after two IRA bombs killed eighteen soldiers in August 1979. (*Pacemaker*)

The funeral of Francis Hughes in May 1981. He was the second IRA hunger striker to die. (*PA Photos*)

The isolated bungalow outside Coalisland, Co. Tyrone, where Bernadette McAliskey and her husband Michael were shot by UDA gunmen in January 1981.

Jim Craig, the infamous UDA gangster and racketeer. (*Pacemaker*)

Donegall Pass RUC Police Station, Belfast, was extensively damaged by an IRA bomb in March 1992.

The funeral of Jimmy Brown, a prominent IPLO activist, killed in August 1992 during an internal feud. (*PA Photos*)

With Alex Maskey (front right) and Gerry Adams (back right) in a stand-off outside the Maskeys' house, after UFF gunmen had killed Alan Lundy, May 1993.

Hugh McKibben, shot dead during the IPLO feud in August 1992.

Paedophile priest Father Brendan Smyth was convicted of offences against children in both Northern Ireland and the Irish Republic.

Riot training in preparation for a Drumcree Orange March stand-off.

I received the RUC Long Service and Good Conduct Medal from the Chief Constable Sir Hugh Annesley (left) in 1992.

Me at the Ulster Folk and Transport Museum for the launch of the Drugs Awareness Exhibition. This became a permanent display in the museum.

Here I am delivering my closing speech at the US Drugs Enforcement Agency course in Washington DC, January 1990.

In 1990 I appeared on the *Gerry Kelly Show*, UTV, as head of the Drugs Squad, to explain the damaging effects of the drug ecstasy. (*Ulster Television*)

Me (left) with a medical team in Kosovo in 1998.

Me (right) with an RUC and British Army peace-keeping force in Kosovo, 1998.

Speaking with a local man in the market place in Pristina, Kosovo, 1999.

The police decided to target known and persistent offenders. Many of the older culprits, once apprehended, were given prison sentences ranging from six months to two years. In cases involving death or injury, longer sentences were imposed. For under-age offenders, the police endeavoured to involve the families and social workers, with limited success.

In contrast, the IRA's way of dealing with joyriders was kneecapping, punishment beatings, or expulsion from the area. Hundreds of young people ended up forcibly separated from their families, faced with the prospect of a lifetime in exile. Dozens continued to be kneecapped each year: some were shot in both knees and elbows, others received a 'Padre Pio' (i.e. shot through the hands and feet in a macabre replication of the saint's stigmata). This deterred some youths, but others flaunted their wounds as trophies of defiance and a challenge to the authority of the IRA in the area.

Efforts were also made to increase awareness of drug misuse among young people. The Drugs Squad worked closely with the voluntary organisations. I was invited as the ex-head of the squad into various local schools, including Corpus Christi and St Genevieve's, to give talks to members of staff. With the assistance of the squad, we also targeted large-scale traffickers who were catering to the demand for drugs in the area.

We also approached owners of pubs and nightclubs to highlight the dangers of drug-taking. I gave a talk to the Vintners' Association, who were very supportive. Unfortunately, like everywhere else in the world, drugs had taken hold and attempts to eradicate them had only limited success.

By the start of 1993, Johnny Adair and C Company had reached the zenith of their terror campaign against Catholics. Not only was Adair in control of the Lower Shankill, he was a major influence on UFF units throughout Northern Ireland. Attacks on Catholics had increased. His own unit targeted north and west Belfast. In March 1993, they shot dead Peter Gallagher, a father of six children as he arrived for work at Distillery Street. The following day, they shot dead a seventeen-year-old youth, Damien Walsh, at his place of work in the Dairy Farm Shopping Centre in Twinbrook.

One of their most audacious attacks was on the home of Alex Maskey, a prominent member of Sinn Féin, later to become Lord

Mayor of Belfast. Mr Maskey's Andersonstown home had been attacked before; on one occasion, he had been shot and seriously injured. The latest UFF attack, on 1 May 1993, took place in broad daylight and showed a reckless disregard for their own safety.

Alan Lundy, a fellow republican and good friend of Mr Maskey's, was building a porch at the house when UFF gunmen pulled up in a red Ford Orion and opened fire. Mr Lundy took cover in the house but was pursued by the gunmen, who then shot him several times. They searched the upstairs rooms but failed to find Mr Maskey, who had taken shelter in the bathroom.

A short time later, I arrived at the scene and spoke to Mr Maskey. He was understandably shocked and angered by what had taken place. He refused to allow police into the house to examine the body. A small group of onlookers, journalists and television crews assembled during the impasse. As head of a murder investigation team, I was legally entitled to enter the house, by force if necessary. I decided not to, because it would have heightened tension and furthered distress. I sent for Superintendent Timony, the sub-divisional commander in the area, and Detective Chief Superintendent George Caskey, the head of CID in Belfast.

Soon afterwards, Gerry Adams and his minder, Cleaky Clarke, arrived and spoke to Mr Maskey. When Mr Timony arrived, I explained the situation and he spoke to Mr Maskey and Gerry Adams. A few minutes later, he called me forward and introduced me. Gerry Adams responded to my name by saying, 'There's not much we can do about that!' Mr Maskey agreed that members of the investigation team, but not me, could enter his home. At that point, Mr Timony left and at once Mr Maskey returned to his original position. He refused entry. A couple of hours later, I informed him that we would enter by force if he did not permit a forensic investigation. He allowed two officers (excluding me) to enter and carefully observed them while they completed their work.

In June, the UFF threw a hand-grenade at the home of Gerry Adams, causing damage to the front of the premises. He was not there at the time, but his wife and son were. They were not injured.

In July, the UFF fired shots through the downstairs window of the home of Annie Armstrong, a Sinn Féin councillor in Twinbrook.

On 7 September 1993, three members of C Company drove up the

Falls Road in a hijacked car and parked at the top of the Donegall Road. Two of the men calmly walked across to a hairdressing salon and shot the proprietor, Sean Hughes, six times. They escaped in the vehicle, which was later recovered on the outskirts of north Belfast.

Two witnesses, a schoolgirl and a butcher in a nearby shop, gave good descriptions of the gunmen leaving and returning to the car. A number of arrests were made, including Stephen McKeag, one of the UFF's most active assassins. He always wore a baseball cap back to front and a thick gold necklace with a pistol-shaped pendant. He denied involvement. We placed him in an identification line-up. The two witnesses identified him as one of the gunmen. He was charged with the murder of Mr Hughes and was remanded in custody. In an attempt to influence the outcome of the trial, the UFF returned to the area some weeks later to shoot and seriously wound a member of staff in the butcher's shop.

In December 1994 McKeag was acquitted of the murder charge at Belfast Crown Court. The two witnesses courageously testified but the judge was not satisfied beyond a reasonable doubt with the identification evidence. In the circumstances, he had no option, because McKeag had been wearing a baseball cap, depriving would-be witnesses of a full facial view.

The Provisional IRA marked the close of 1993 with a mortar attack on Andersonstown police station. Fortunately, no one was seriously injured. In the early months of the new year, they used improvised Mark 15 and Mark 16 grenades filled with Semtex to attack army and police patrols. These were fired from hand-held launcher tubes and were powerful enough to immobilise armour-plated Land Rovers, causing many injuries, some of them serious.

During the course of the year, fifty-two incidents involving sixty devices were investigated by the police. Most of these were the work of a small IRA unit operating in the Woodburn area of west Belfast. The attacks were normally preceded by a house takeover; families were held captive until the operation was concluded. I helped investigate many of these incidents and knew the identity of every member of the unit. Most of them were arrested and interviewed on several occasions, but invariably had to be released without charge because of lack of evidence. Witnesses refused to make statements incriminating them and we could not connect them forensically to any particular incident.

It was disheartening to know that we were setting them free to cause further mayhem in a few days' time.

The UFF (Adair's C Company) continued their campaign in west Belfast. On 2 January 1994, they again fired shots at the home of Alex Maskey, but no one was injured. I later learned that they intended to repeat the attack the following day, but their car broke down. On 6 January, three UFF gunmen took over a house in Lenadoon with the intention of killing Una Gillespie, a Sinn Féin councillor. When she failed to turn up, they aborted the operation and instead shot and wounded a 24-year-old man. On 10 January, they travelled to the Rock Bar on the Falls Road and fired an RPG7 rocket at the front window. It bounced off the security grill and exploded on the road. They also fired shots at the bar. Up to sixty people were in the pub at the time and were fortunate to escape injury.

Sometimes an unorthodox approach to policing is necessary to get results. In January of that year, a police officer left a police issue Ruger revolver in his car in Belfast city centre. The car was stolen. We assumed that it had been taken by car thieves from west Belfast. Members of the Driving Away team were asked to make inquiries. They spoke to several known joyriders who 'owed them a favour'. A couple of hours later, a contact offered to locate the gun, provided no one at the address was arrested. I readily agreed. Guns stolen in similar circumstances had been given to paramilitaries and used to murder people. The arrangement held and the gun was recovered.

Later that month, Wilfred Monaghan, the Assistant Chief Constable in charge of Crime Branch, instructed me to investigate the killing of Robin Maxwell, who had been shot by police in an undercover operation at High Street garage in Donaghadee. Maxwell had been spotted acting suspiciously outside the garage on days leading up to the incident. It looked as if he was planning to rob the place. Uniformed officers from Newtownards were tasked to watch over the premises. One of them hid in a storeroom inside the building. Maxwell went into the garage near closing time and pointed a gun at the shop assistant. He then went behind the counter, threw the man to the floor, pushed a gun against his face and threatened him. The policeman came out of the storeroom and shouted a warning. In the excitement of the moment, Maxwell turned to face the policeman and inadvertently pointed the gun in his direction. In the belief that his life was in danger, the officer fired one shot and killed him. The shop assistant confirmed the account given by the officer. A forensic examination of Maxwell's gun showed that it was a replica pistol, incapable of being fired. Two solicitors from the Independent Police Complaints Panel supervised my investigation and judged it to be thorough and satisfactory. The police officer in question was exonerated both by the Director of Public Prosecutions and the coroner at the inquest which followed.

I was still working long hours, with early morning starts and late night finishes. In the last week of January, I worked eighty-three hours. As a detective superintendent, I did not qualify for overtime.

February started badly: on the second, Samuel Beers from Newtownards died in the Royal Victoria Hospital while being treated for an apparently non-life-threatening complaint. I asked my deputy, Detective Chief Inspector John Brannigan, to investigate the circumstances after the matter was referred to us by the coroner. An hour later, John telephoned to complain of a lack of cooperation from the hospital authorities. He told me that Mr Beers had died after a doctor mistakenly injected penicillin through an intravenous tube into his brain instead of his body. Mr Beers suffered convulsions and died soon afterwards. The hospital authorities told Detective Chief Inspector Brannigan that the doctor in question was now asleep, having worked a 120-hour week, and would be available for interview when the authorities deemed it appropriate. I telephoned the senior administrator and advised him that we would arrest the doctor and anyone else who obstructed our investigation. He assured me that the hospital would cooperate fully.

As part of the investigation, Detective Chief Inspector Brannigan decided to do a reconstruction of the fateful moment when the penicillin was wrongly administered. He asked the hospital authorities to provide the appropriate equipment. They were reluctant to do so because of the cost (£70). Eventually, they agreed and a reconstruction using a dummy and intravenous tubes took place.

The doctor was interviewed and later charged with manslaughter. She alleged that the most likely cause of the mistake was tiredness brought on by her long working hours. On the direction of the judge, she was acquitted. Neither we nor Mrs Beers wished to harm her career. But we both felt that it was in the public interest that the matter be highlighted to avoid a reoccurrence. It was a tragic case for all concerned. Mrs Beers had been widowed and left to bring up three young children.

That day had yet to run its course. I spent several hours at Castlereagh police office directing the interviews of three IRA suspects arrested in connection with recent rocket attacks in west Belfast. I also went to Beechmount, where a 'prig' (an improvised armour-piercing grenade) had been discovered during a house search. Later that afternoon, I helped investigate the abduction of a suspected sex offender at Colin Mill. In the evening, I went to Donaghadee and Newtownards to interview potential witnesses to the shooting of Robin Maxwell.

The following day, I went to the scene of a UVF shooting on the Springfield Road. The driver of a bus used to take relatives of republican prisoners to the Maze Prison had been shot and seriously wounded. A passing car was caught in the crossfire and a man and his wife were wounded. During a forensic examination of the area, four spent .762 cases fired from a rifle were found in the nearby Highfield Estate. An Austin Maestro car, hijacked earlier by two men and used in the attack, was recovered later in the day. Later that same day, the IRA shot a young man in the right thigh and left foot.

The violence continued: on 4 February explosives were discovered in Ross Street; on 6 February the IRA fired a Mark 16 grenade at a police and army patrol. A command wire was found in follow-up searches, along with a launcher tube, propellant assembly and a tail-fin from the device. While we were endeavouring to deal with these incidents, members of the UFF C Company slipped into the area and attached a hand-grenade to the front gate of Connolly House, the Sinn Féin headquarters in Andersonstown. The device was spotted by Alex Maskey as he was about to open the gate. It was safely defused by the army. A few days later, a rocket was fired through an upstairs window at Connolly House in the belief that a Sinn Féin meeting was taking place. It caused extensive damage, but no one was in the room at the time.

On 9 February C Company planted a bomb outside the Irish Language School at Nansen Street. On 18 February they returned to Connolly House and shot and wounded three men working on scaffolding outside the building.

The IRA was just as busy: on 20 February I went to the scene of a 'prig' attack on soldiers in the Woodburn area. Four had been injured.

Two houses had also been taken over as part of the ambush. On 21 February incendiary devices were planted in Dunnes Stores in the Park Centre. Later in the day, I went with other police to the Glenowen Inn, after a drinks delivery van had been hijacked.

On 22 February the son of a postmistress was abducted in Lisburn. I helped implement the Force Reaction Plan which sets out strict procedures for such cases. Police forces throughout the UK apply the same guidelines. The aim of the plan was to ensure a speedy and consistent response. Issues covered included command structures, surveillance, electronic aids, family liaison, trained negotiators and search teams. Three loyalists were arrested during the operation and subsequently charged.

In March, a frail 85-year-old woman called Mary Palmer, who lived alone, was attacked in west Belfast. She suffered broken ribs and severe bruising and was rushed to hospital. An examination confirmed that she had been raped and that the injuries had happened during the attack. The local community was stunned and could not believe that such a terrible thing could happen in their midst. Because of the nature of the crime, they were willing to respond to a police appeal for information and did their best to assist during house-to-house inquiries.

A prolonged and detailed forensic examination was made of Mary's clothing and the interior of her home. Everything was photographed and a mapper recorded the position of every object in every room. I knew that forensic work would play a crucial part if arrests were made. The location of Mary's house and the circumstances of the incident suggested that the attacker was probably someone that lived in the area. We made an exhaustive check on all sexual offenders within a one-mile radius of the house. Mary died in hospital: the inquiry was now a murder investigation.

Just before midnight on 5 April, I was contacted by the duty inspector and told that a man had walked into the local police station to confess to the rape and killing. I went to Grosvenor Road and spoke to a doctor who had examined the 33-year-old suspect, Martin Harper from west Belfast. The doctor said that while Harper was fit for interview, he had some concerns about his psychiatric state and vulnerability. I was concerned about the legal value of any admissions that Harper might make and spoke to his mother and uncle. The uncle agreed to be present during the interview as an 'appropriate adult', to ensure that the prisoner's welfare was adequately considered. Harper, through his solicitor, rejected the offer.

I and another detective questioned Harper about the circumstances of Mary's rape and death. He admitted the sexual part of the incident, but insisted that he had had no intention of injuring her. He agreed that he had used some force but suggested that severe bruising across her mouth had been caused unintentionally when he attempted to stop her calling out. He gave contradictory descriptions of the interior of the house and its furnishings. Without warning, he would deny his involvement in the incident.

The following morning, I asked my deputy, John Brannigan, and an experienced detective inspector, Alan Pentland, to question him on the same issues. Harper first admitted, then denied the rape. His descriptions of the layout of the house continued to be contradictory.

I stressed to forensic scientists the importance of comparing samples from the attack scene and samples from Harper. The following day, we got preliminary results from the DNA samples connecting Harper to the incident. This was sufficient to justify charging him. The DNA sample was sent for specialist examination to a laboratory in Birmingham; we were told it would take up to a week. Members of Harper's family were devastated by the whole experience and one of them kindly donated a sample of DNA to help with the comparative tests in Birmingham. A positive result followed. At his trial, Harper was convicted and sentenced to be detained in a secure psychiatric ward indefinitely.

On 9 March the IRA took over two houses in the Woodburn area and fired a Mark 16 rocket at soldiers. Over the next two days, the UFF bombed two houses. In one incident, a woman and her seven-month-old child were injured. In other incidents, the police recovered two explosive devices.

On 3 May, I went with other police to Whiterock Leisure Centre after a blue Ford Sierra was hijacked. The driver was held captive in a club on the Falls Road while his vehicle was used by INLA gunmen for the killing of Thomas Douglas on the Stranmillis Road in south Belfast. They alleged that Mr Douglas was a leading loyalist, but this was not so. I went to the scene and later to the Ormeau Road, where the hijacked car had been found abandoned.

The people of the Falls finally got the relief they deserved in May 1994 when Special Branch's E4A surveillance team and the Headquarters Mobile Support Unit reaction team followed C Company's top hit team to a house at Taughmonagh on the outskirts of west Belfast. They stormed the house and arrested four heavily armed UFF members: Richard Calderwood, Rob Bradshaw, Glen Esdale and Gary Smith, Adair's No. 2 and one of the UFF's most active gunmen. They had been planning to kill targets in west Belfast. It was seen as a very significant capture. A thorough examination was made of two houses and two cars.

The following evening, uniformed police arrested two UFF suspects after they threw a bomb at a Catholic house in Stockman's Lane. Later in court, all six were convicted of a series of offences, including attempted murder, conspiracy to murder, possession of firearms and explosives and membership of an illegal organisation. They were sentenced to long terms of imprisonment.

Over a two-week period in May, I was aware that Special Branch was working on a covert operation in my area of command. I gave them permission to use the services of one of my female detective constables. At breakfast time on 10 May, I was informed that a team of loyalists had been arrested during an attempt to hold the family of a postmistress hostage while they took her to a post office in north Belfast to hand over a sum of money. Three men (Stephen Quail, Colin Mitchell and Gary McMaster) were taken to Castlereagh police office for questioning. The following morning, I joined the detectives interviewing McMaster. He made admissions about a series of attacks in west Belfast during this and subsequent interviews, including the rocket and gun attack on the Rock Bar on 10 January 1994, and the booby-trap grenade and rocket attack in early February on Connolly House. Over the coming days, a number of other UFF suspects were arrested and taken to Castlereagh.

At one stage, I was contacted by the head of CID in Belfast and ordered to go to a meeting with Special Branch officers at Castlereagh. They told me that one of the men I was holding was an important informant, crucial to their work against the UFF. I informed them that there was evidence to connect this person to serious terrorist offences and that they would have to make a written submission when the time came to consider possible prosecution. They accepted this.

———

Late in the evening of 10 July 1994, an IRA unit took over a house at Donard Drive, Lisburn. They held an elderly couple captive overnight. The house was close to the home of Raymond Smallwoods (one of the gunmen convicted of the attempted assassination of Bernadette and Michael McAliskey) and gave a clear view of his front door. At around 9 a.m., as Smallwoods walked to his car, two IRA men armed with sawn-off shotguns confronted him and shot him several times. He died in an ambulance on the way to the nearby Lagan Valley Hospital.

I went to Donard Drive and took charge of the inquiry. David Ervine, the PUP leader, spoke to me outside the house. He knew Raymond Smallwoods well. David did his best to comfort the Smallwoods family.

A couple of hours later, the police were notified of a suspicious black Hyundai car, abandoned in the rear car park of a public house at Milltown Road, Derriaghy. The two sawn-off shotguns used in the attack were found in the vehicle. Despite an exhaustive forensic examination of the elderly couple's house, the Hyundai and the recovered weapons, nothing was found to identify the killers. Mr Smallwoods's family later stated that they recognised one of the gunmen as a leading IRA figure from west Belfast. After reviewing the circumstances of the shooting, I had doubts about the value of this identification and informed the DPP to that effect.

How will Raymond Smallwoods be remembered? As the cool-blooded, would-be assassin of the McAliskeys? Or the political analyst who in the 1990s attempted to lead militant loyalists towards peaceful co-existence with nationalists and republicans? The McAliskeys will remember him as a callous gunman; ministers like Dr Roy Magee and priests like Father Gerry Reynolds and Father Alec Reid will publicly acknowledge his contribution to the search for peace.

I will remember my involvement with him at Gough Barracks police office in the aftermath of the McAliskey shootings. He seemed a quiet, sullen man, very much in control of his emotions and showing no sign of genuine remorse. He and his two companions had spent days planning the attack. Smallwoods had driven them a considerable distance to attack their victims; they had forced their way into the cottage and had mercilessly fired a number of shots into Mr and Mrs McAliskey in front of their two young children.

Over the years, I mentioned Smallwoods to a number of high-ranking loyalists. They confirmed that he was an influential and respected political analyst on behalf of loyalist paramilitaries. However, they all agreed that he had a darker side. He had opposed talk of a loyalist ceasefire in 1992 when he knew that Presbyterian clergy were meeting with the Loyalist Inner Council. The same loyalists told me that he was a strong advocate of loyalist attacks on Sinn Féin and IRA activists as a way of extending loyalist terror to the Irish republican movement.

The shooting of the McAliskeys gave Smallwoods kudos within loyalism. When he was released from prison early in 1990, he was offered a position on the Loyalist Inner Council. He became a respected political analyst and spokesperson for the Ulster Democratic Party, the political wing of the UDA. He held meetings with Presbyterian clergymen who believed they could persuade loyalist paramilitaries to give up violence. More surprisingly, he responded to approaches from Father Reid and Father Reynolds, who were famously attempting to turn republicans from conflict. The clergymen were impressed by Smallwoods's contribution and believed that he would be an important influence in future peace discussions.

One of the most complex and sensitive investigations I ever undertook concerned the paedophile priest Brendan Smyth. John Gerard Smyth ('Brendan') was born in Nansen Street in west Belfast on 6 June 1927. In 1945, at the age of eighteen, he joined the Norbertine Order at Holy Trinity Abbey, Kilnacrott, Ballyjamesduff, Co. Cavan. He was an intelligent student and showed enough promise to be sent to Rome to study theology at the Gregorian University. In 1951 he returned to Ireland after graduating. He was seen as an energetic organiser of church activities around Kilnacrott and was popular with parents and children. Parents were delighted that many events involved the participation of children up to the age of twelve years. On his own initiative, he developed a system of punishments for children who turned up late for functions or talked during Mass. This normally meant beatings for the boys and improper touching and kissing of the girls. Although victims of this abuse, they did not report it to their parents. This is not uncommon in cases where children are mistreated by a paedophile.

Smyth made frequent trips to west Belfast, supposedly to meet old school friends. Through them he was introduced to other families in the area. Not surprisingly, many of the people he befriended had young children. Once he had gained their trust, they did not object to him visiting the children in their bedrooms or at school. On occasions, he took the children out for day trips in his car. He was respected as a playful and kindly priest who loved being around children. Parents were not concerned when, in their presence, he tickled the children or kissed them on the cheek. When alone with young boys and girls, he would sit them on his knee, kiss them on the lips and fondle their bodies through their underwear. Sometimes, he masturbated them, or encouraged them to do the same to him. Eventually some parents became suspicious and stopped him getting access to their children. A few were convinced that he was an abuser and reported their concerns to diocesan priests or clerics at the abbey.

The reports of alleged abuse appeared to have been taken seriously and assurances were given that Smyth would be sent for treatment. He does not appear to have been penalised in any other way. There is some suggestion that he received treatment in 1968 and 1973, but this is difficult to verify. One thing is clear: the Abbot of Kilnacrott moved Smyth from parish to parish and country to country in an attempt to prevent his abuse of children becoming a major scandal.

Smyth served in Wales in the late 1950s and was soon accused of child molestation. Senior clergy in the area dismissed him from his post and insisted that he be returned to Ireland. During the latter part of 1960, he worked in a parish in Providence, Rhode Island, USA. He was a popular and highly respected cleric among sections of the congregation. However, allegations of child abuse soon surfaced and in 1968 he was thrown out by the local bishop and returned to Ireland. In the late 1970s, Smyth was sent to North Dakota but was soon exposed as a paedophile and sent packing. Each time Smyth offended, the Abbot of Kilnacrott was informed. His response was always the same: move him somewhere else. No consideration was given by the Irish Church authorities to the effects of his molestation on children in various parts of Ireland, North and South.

While Smyth moved happily forward in his life, many victims struggled to cope with their violation and betrayal. It is probable that many have not revealed their terrible secrets to anyone. Others took many years to find the strength to confide in parents or friends.

Decades later, the lives of some victims are blighted by depression and addiction to drink and drugs, broken marriages, self-harm and attempted suicide.

The beginning of the end for Smyth as a paedophile—and for the Church authorities in Ireland who had failed to address his sexual deviance—may be dated from 23 February 1990, when a female victim of Smyth's unburdened her secret to a counsellor working for the Catholic Family Welfare Society in Belfast. The counsellor was in law obliged to inform the police and explained this to the victim. The girl then told her parents. They already had concerns about Smyth, because a family friend had recently confided to them that he and his brother had been abused by him in the 1950s and 1960s. Fearing the worst, they then spoke to their other children and were horrified to learn that he had also abused them.

The parents and abused children met with the RUC Care Unit officers. These are specially trained officers who work closely with social services and the medical profession in investigating instances of child sexual abuse. They have special facilities and techniques for interviewing young victims. Every stage of the investigation is discussed and agreed by the various specialists involved.

As a result of these allegations, arrangements were made to interview Smyth at Grosvenor Road police station on 8 March 1991. During a three-hour interview conducted in the presence of a solicitor, Smyth admitted the allegations made by five victims. He was charged with nine counts of indecency and released on police bail. He provided a contact telephone number and told the police that he would be staying at Holy Trinity Abbey, Kilnacrott. Through his solicitor, he indicated that he would continue to cooperate with the police investigation and make himself available when requested to do so.

A file of evidence was prepared by the police investigators and forwarded to the Director of Public Prosecutions. On 25 July, the file was returned to the RUC with a clear instruction to prosecute Smyth.

A preliminary inquiry hearing was arranged for 16 August 1991; it was postponed at the request of Smyth's solicitor. The purpose of an inquiry, held before a resident magistrate, is to ensure that the accused has been served with the necessary documents setting out the evidence against him. The magistrate then determines whether or not there is sufficient evidence to send the accused to trial.

Following Smyth's release, the police made many telephone calls to the abbey to make arrangements to have evidential papers served on him. Neither he nor the authorities in the abbey returned the calls. On 6 December 1991, Detective Constable Marks, the investigating officer at Grosvenor Road police station, made a telephone call to the abbey and recognised the person who answered as Smyth. He explained that papers containing evidence had to be served as soon as possible. He was taken aback when Smyth, seemingly unfazed by what he had been told, announced that he would not be travelling North until it suited him, and that would not be until the following year. Detective Constable Marks emphasised the seriousness of the situation and explained that Smyth's failure to make himself available would cause the RUC to seek his extradition. This appeared to have little effect on Smyth: he disdainfully repeated that he would be in Northern Ireland sometime in the following year.

Soon after I arrived at Grosvenor Road, in March 1992, Detective Constable Marks had a lengthy discussion with me about the case and explained Smyth's failure to cooperate. We agreed that he should apply for Smyth's extradition from the Republic of Ireland. At this time, the RUC had an extradition unit based at Headquarters which processed all extradition applications. The requests were then forwarded to the Attorney General's Office in London, which was responsible for making formal requests to foreign governments.

Detective Constable Marks had a close involvement with the victims and their families and spoke with them at regular intervals. They liked and respected him and placed a great deal of trust in his commitment to their campaign for justice. I made certain that they understood that the extradition process was complex and slow-moving. They were already frustrated by delays in the investigation. Their anguish turned to anger when they learned that Smyth was visiting west Belfast on a regular basis. They reported this to the police; but despite repeated attempts to locate him, Smyth was not detained. One of the families wrote to Abbot Kevin Smith and complained about Smyth's visits. In his reply, the Abbot pointed out that he was not in a position to stop Smyth leaving the abbey and suggested that Smyth was visiting a sex counsellor on two occasions each week.

The family was incensed by the Abbot's reply and attempted to make contact with the head of the Catholic Church in Ireland, Cardinal

Cahal Daly. They blamed the Church authorities for not tackling Smyth's abuse of children over many decades and saw their failure to force Smyth North as collusion and cover-up. In a strongly worded letter to Cardinal Daly, they made their views quite clear. The Cardinal, in his reply, said that he had spoken to the Abbot in the past about Smyth's behaviour and would do so again. In August 1992, the family again wrote to Cardinal Daly, including a further allegation of cover-up. A reply received by the family was deemed unsatisfactory and did not dispel their suspicions. It is known that the Cardinal did speak to Abbot Smith. It is likely that he emphasised the gravity of the situation for the Church and the potential damage that could result from allegations of collusion.

It was not until 23 April 1993 that the extradition warrant was available for execution. By 28 April, it was forwarded through RUC Headquarters to the Garda Síochána in Dublin. The following day, it was lodged at the Department of Justice and the Irish Attorney General's Office.

During the following months, Detective Constable Marks complained to me that the warrant had not been executed and expressed concern that the victims were dismayed by the lack of progress. On each occasion, I contacted the extradition unit at Headquarters and asked them to investigate further. In due course, I was informed that the Attorney General's Office in London had contacted the Irish Attorney General's Office on 20 September 1993, 14 October and 18 November, and was awaiting clarification on the issue.

In December 1993, Smyth unexpectedly agreed to meet the investigation team from the RUC. This was undoubtedly as a result of pressure from Cardinal Daly.[8] Smyth came to Belfast and preliminary inquiry papers containing details of nine offences were served on him. He was interviewed about other abuse allegations reported by victims in 1992 and charged with a further eight offences.

A trial date was set for April 1994. On the day of the hearing, to our and the victims' dismay, a barrister representing Smyth produced a fax message received that morning from a hospital in Gloucestershire alleging that Smyth had suffered heart problems and would not be fit to face trial for some time. The case was adjourned indefinitely.

On 10 June, he eventually appeared at Belfast Crown Court and pleaded guilty to seventeen counts of indecent assault on children. He was remanded in custody for one week to allow the trial judge an opportunity to examine medical and psychiatric reports and decide on an appropriate sentence.

I was shocked by Smyth's apparent indifference and lack of interest in the proceedings. He did not appear to notice the distress of his victims and their families. On his next court appearance, he was sentenced to four years in prison. Some victims felt that the sentence was too lenient, but were relieved to see him being led out of the court in handcuffs to begin his sentence in Magilligan prison.

The conviction of Smyth was covered extensively by the media North and South of the border. As a result, many more victims of abuse by Smyth and other clerics contacted the RUC and the Garda Síochána. By November 1994, special units North and South were investigating a multiplicity of new claims. I was appointed to the RUC team under the leadership of Detective Chief Superintendent Eric Anderson. He and I had many meetings with the Garda investigation team. We were fortunate in knowing many of these officers through working with them on murder and criminal investigations in the past. The inquiry teams were conscious of the political sensitivities surrounding both inquiries but were determined to give the interests of the victims a top priority.

I met the family of one of the principal complainants against Smyth, who was determined to make the Church authorities face up to their failings. They made formal allegations of a cover-up against Cardinal Daly and Abbot Smith, but nothing came of this.

Mr Anderson and I travelled to Magilligan prison to meet with a psychiatrist and prison staff who ran a much-heralded sex offenders' rehabilitation programme. We were anxious to understand the medical and psychiatric issues surrounding paedophilia—and in particular the underlying reasons these men were attracted to children.

As a result of further allegations following his conviction, I interviewed Smyth at Antrim Road police station on 7 December 1994. He seemed remarkably calm and unaffected by prison life. He said that he enjoyed prison food and found his sleeping quarters clean, warm and comfortable. He and other prisoners in his unit, mainly sex offenders, were segregated from the main body of inmates. I did not feel it was right to address him as 'Father'. He replied: 'If you do not wish to call me Father, you should call me Brendan.' He admitted the allegations I put to him, but his explanations indicated neither regret nor contrition. For instance, during questioning about indecent fondling of a seven-year-old girl, I put it to him, 'You must have known it was wrong to do that to a seven-year-old girl.' He replied: 'She did not tell me to stop; she did not say she did not want me to do it.'

Smyth seemed childlike and remarkably naïve. I asked him if he could recall any instances of abuse that had not been put to him. Suddenly he was calm and assertive and in a stern voice replied: 'I have answered all the questions you have put to me.' It was obvious that he was not going to volunteer information about past misdemeanours not known to the police.

As I left the police station after the interview, I was astonished to find several television crews outside. I was sure they had not been contacted by the police and assumed, rightly, they must have been arranged on behalf of the Catholic Church, probably in an attempt to demonstrate that the Church authorities were cooperating fully with the police investigations.

At an early stage in the inquiry, we had been told that Sir Hugh Annesley, the Chief Constable, had met with Cardinal Daly and his legal advisers and had agreed a process whereby suspect priests would be made available for interview and other procedures connected with our investigation. This was a sensible arrangement and undoubtedly speeded up the process. It also ensured that the recent political controversy surrounding Smyth's extradition would not be repeated. During the following months, several priests who had previously been based and transgressed in Northern Ireland travelled from the Republic to be interviewed by the RUC.

One of the most difficult problems encountered by the squad was identifying and locating alleged victims; we even sent two officers to Japan. In the new spirit of cooperation, the Church supplied us with files containing personal histories of children who, through no fault of their own, had been placed in Church-run institutions—young innocents who, because of family bereavement, marriage break-up, poverty, parental violence and alcohol abuse had been separated from their families and left dependent on priests, nuns and brothers for their physical and mental well-being. I, like other police officers who read these files, was disturbed and upset.

Many of the carers were untrained and unsuited to the task. While it is accepted that countless numbers of children benefited from the experience and prospered as a result, large numbers were beaten, bullied, abused and malnourished. As a result, many children's lives were destroyed by physical and sexual abuse. I was troubled and angry at the failure of Church authorities and the social services to prevent abusive practices in these institutions.

On 24 February 1995, I interviewed Smyth about further allegations of abuse. During the interview I told him that the Garda Síochána was also investigating his behaviour in the Republic and that several people had made serious allegations against him.

On 1 May 1995, Detective Chief Superintendent Anderson and myself met Detective Chief Superintendent Kevin Carty and Detective Superintendent Austin McNally, the heads of the Garda investigation team, at Dundalk Garda station to discuss their inquiry. They said they were anxious to interview Smyth as soon as possible. I contacted Smyth's solicitor, Denis Maloney. He agreed to make Smyth available for interview.

Because of the political sensitivities and huge media interest surrounding the case, Mr Carty sent two of his most experienced detectives to conduct the interview: the legendary Detective Sergeant Pat Lynagh and Detective Inspector Tadhg Foley. The atmosphere was tense as I introduced them to Smyth and Mr Maloney. I sat quietly in the interview room while the two Garda officers questioned Smyth at length. He was soon making admissions about the abuse of children in the Irish Republic.

This was the start of a process that would see him convicted in a Dublin court on seventy-four counts of indecency. He was sentenced to twelve years in prison in 1996. One year later, he died of heart problems in prison, broken and vilified. He was buried in the Holy Trinity Abbey grounds by the Norbertines after an early morning service. His grave was covered in concrete, possibly to prevent desecration. After a protest by one of his victims, the word 'Reverend' was removed from his headstone. On 24 March 2006, the *Irish Independent* reported that pilgrims were visiting the grave to lay floral tributes.

In the early 1960s, a member of my own family had been harmed by a paedophile priest, a visiting missionary from Africa. My parents reported this to our local priest, Father O'Rawe, a close family friend. A few days later, he reported back that the offending priest had been referred for medical treatment. My parents, being deeply religious Catholics, accepted this; during the family Rosary that evening, they prayed for the speedy recovery of the priest in question.

During the months I worked on the Smyth inquiry, I was shocked to learn of the widespread and horrific mistreatment of countless children. I understood for the first time how extensive and pernicious the cover-up by some senior Church figures had been. When I was young, I was taught to respect priests, to accept them as friends, comforters and spiritual healers. The Catholic Church I had admired now seemed deceitful and corrupt. Many of its most powerful figures lacked integrity and honour. I surmised that greed, ambition, patronage and dishonesty had played some part in the elevation of these people to high office.

I comforted myself that this particular issue, being sufficiently controversial, had rocked the powerful Church to its foundations and would lead to reform. There was evidence of the public shock and revulsion at the revelations made. Mass attendance in Ireland plummeted from 68% to 48% in the decade following the exposé of Smyth.

There were other casualties of the Brendan Smyth scandal. Abbot Kevin Smith was forced to resign in October 1994. On 17 November 1994, the Taoiseach, Albert Reynolds, resigned after Labour TDs withdrew their support for the coalition government. They were not satisfied by explanations given about the delays in executing the extradition warrant against Smyth. They also objected to the Irish Attorney General, Harry Whelehan, who was at the centre of the controversy, being promoted by Fianna Fáil ministers to the presidency of the High Court. Whelehan resigned from his new post four days after taking office.

The case also galvanised the debate about the relationship between Church and state. The civil authorities North and South are determined that the criminal law process will apply to clerical wrong-doers irrespective of procedures set out in Canon Law.[9]

The attitude of the Irish government was spelled out on 24 October 2002 by Michael McDowell, Minister for Justice, when he publicly declared: 'Under the laws of Ireland, Canon Law carries no more significance than the bye-laws of a golf club.'

Thankfully, the welfare and emotional needs of victims are now at last being acknowledged. Many have been compensated and offered psychiatric help. In February 2002, eighteen religious orders agreed to pay more than 128 million euros in compensation.

Chapter 10 ∿

I RETURN TO THE DRUGS SQUAD

Ashort time prior to my reappointment to the Drugs Squad in 1995, I was summoned to a meeting with Sir Hugh Annesley, the Chief Constable. He said that the issue of drugs was a matter of deep concern to the general public and that he intended to address it by increasing manpower and resources in the squad. He asked me to research the matter further and report back. Over the next two weeks, I spoke to members of the Drugs Squad, Headquarters' staff and Special Branch.

In April 1995, I duly reported back. On the basis of my report, he announced the following:

- the senior rank in the squad was to be increased to Detective Superintendent (from Detective Chief Inspector);
- twelve additional members of staff were to be appointed;
- drugs offices were to be opened at Armagh, Enniskillen, Ballymena and Londonderry to complement existing facilities;
- the Intelligence Unit was to be increased in size;
- a Financial Investigation Unit was to be created to examine the financial affairs of anyone indicted for a trafficking offence. The new unit could:
  - i. compel financial bodies (banks, etc.) to disclose details of financial transactions by a person suspected or charged with trafficking and prepare financial profiles on suspects for presentation at court;
  - ii. apply to courts for Restraint Orders to prevent suspects from disposing of assets;
  - iii. apply for Production Orders to ensure that all documents and details of the financial and property affairs of a suspect were produced in court;

iv. apply for a Confiscation Order to dispose of the assets of anyone convicted on indictment of a trafficking offence.

- secondments to the squad of uniformed officers were to be increased to enable them to develop specialist skills;
- Drug Liaison Officers, recruited from CID and Uniform Branch and totalling 150, were to be appointed to thirty-one police stations throughout Northern Ireland;
- education was to be a key element in the strategy.

Governmental departments, educational authorities and voluntary organisations had already invested heavily in the concept that information and education had an important role to play in persuading young people not to take illicit drugs. Selected members of the Drugs Squad delivered up to two hundred lectures each year to a variety of bodies, including parent/teacher associations, youth leaders and community groups. An assessment of each speaking engagement highlighted an amazing lack of knowledge and concern about the problem among older members of Northern Ireland society, particularly parents. Numbers attending the talks were often disappointing. On many occasions when I was invited to speak, fewer than ten people attended.

In July 1995, Henry Robinson from FAIT (Families Against Intimidation) invited me to address a gathering of townspeople in Downpatrick. I shared the platform with a representative of Lifeline, a highly respected and well-known drugs advisory group from Manchester. The meeting was widely advertised in the press; BBC TV sent a camera crew. Fourteen people attended—three from the Workers' Party and the rest from Sinn Féin. It was a waste of valuable time and, not surprisingly, developed into a points-scoring exercise between the two factions. Later that same month, at the request of the Lady Mayoress of Bangor, I organised a Drugs Education Day in a hall at Hamilton Road in the town. Several officers were on hand to talk to local people. We also set up display counters and made information packs available. At no time during the six-hour exhibition did members of the public outnumber police officers on duty.

Undeterred, we continued to talk to any group prepared to listen. We spoke to doctors, nurses, teachers, prison officers and voluntary counsellors. We also supported initiatives by educational authorities, district councils and voluntary organisations.

In early 1996, Omagh Lions prepared a drugs educational booklet for circulation to schools in the area. It was an impressive package and a praiseworthy initiative. They invited Patrick Kielty, the TV personality, to perform at the official launch. Towards the end of the show, I joined him on stage to discuss the merits of the booklet, congratulate the Lions and wish them success with their venture.

I have always supported an educational dimension to the issue of drug-taking. It is important that young people are given the necessary information. It is a complex issue and no one can be certain that the initiative will succeed. It is imperative that the information given is accurate and truthful. It must be clearly stated that not all drug-taking is harmful and unpleasant. Vast numbers of people take illicit drugs on a regular basis and enjoy the experience. Most schoolchildren over the age of fourteen years know someone who takes drugs. They see them living an apparently normal existence and hear stories of the wonderful time enjoyed while under the influence of drugs. Some people do suffer serious side-effects, both mental and physical, but they are in the minority. Most young people are inclined to believe that they will not suffer harm and are therefore not deterred by the prospect.

I believe that many young people will not be influenced by educationalists, parents or the police. This could have far-reaching consequences. At a regional conference on HIV/AIDS held at the Burrendale Hotel in Newcastle, Co. Down, I suggested that drug misuse in Northern Ireland would become a medical and sexual health problem, not merely an enforcement issue. In support of this assertion, I referred to a study in the USA regarding the relationship between drug-taking and sexual risk.[10] The study indicated that self-enjoyment while on drugs (ecstasy, cocaine, amphetamine) was paramount. The pursuit of pleasure took precedence over reason. Concerns about safe sex and sexual partners became irrelevant. This could result in earlier sexual experimentation and a reduced appreciation of the risks involved.

At every opportunity, I encouraged colleagues to engage in public debate on the health, welfare and social issues connected to drug misuse. We updated the RUC policy document on drugs and gave advice to the education department on guidelines issued to all the schools in Northern Ireland. We addressed a number of district councils and highlighted the dangers of drug-taking in places of entertainment under their control. We wrote articles for newspapers and magazines and gave interviews on television and radio. We engaged in bigger projects, such as the July 1995 recording of a documentary series for Teilifís Eireann called *Inside the RUC*. One episode featured the work of the Drugs Squad.

In April 1997, I travelled to Amsterdam with an Ulster Television crew to make a documentary on cannabis use. The programme considered whether cannabis should be legalised in Northern Ireland. I was filmed interviewing customers outside a café where cannabis was legally on sale. I also spoke to a journalist from a leading Dutch newspaper and a senior Dutch politician. Not surprisingly, young people I spoke to were in favour of further relaxation of the rules. The journalist outlined the debate currently taking place in Holland, where there was increasing concern about the liberal attitude to drug-taking and the harm it was doing to the country's reputation. Holland was a world centre for drug-smuggling and the distribution of cocaine, heroin and ecstasy; the problem was what role legislation could or should play in attempting to control it. The politician strongly favoured legislation to control the cafés. He was concerned that criminal gangs had taken over many of them, using them to sell more serious drugs which were illegal under Dutch law.

Nothing discussed in the programme changed my attitude to cannabis use. It is a dangerous and harmful substance. I get annoyed when 'informed' people refer to it as a 'soft' drug. The reality is that it is far more powerful than it was thirty years ago. Small amounts can affect the memory and concentration; heavy, prolonged use can cause serious illnesses, such as bronchitis and cancer of the lungs and throat. It can also cause psychological dependency and psychosis. I am strongly opposed to legalising/decriminalising or re-classifying the drug.

I represented the RUC as a keynote speaker at a number of major conferences: the Association of Chief Police Officers Drugs Annual Conference at various locations in England; the Scottish National Drugs Conference;[11] an American Customs Conference held in Dublin; an RUC Symposium on Drugs and a Drugs Awareness Conference in Donegal.[12]

On 1 May 1996, I accompanied the Deputy Chief Constable

Operations, Ronnie Flanagan, to the House of Commons to give evidence to the Northern Ireland Affairs Committee on the local drugs situation. We were questioned on a range of issues, including the extent of the problem, the RUC response, the allocation of resources to the Drugs Squad, and the involvement of paramilitary organisations in drug-trafficking. On 30 October 1996, Mr Flanagan (by now Chief Constable) and I gave further evidence to the committee. We were accompanied by Mrs Christine Jendoubi from the Department of Education and Rob Phipps, Health Promotion Agency Northern Ireland Office. The discussion focused on educational and community initiatives.

In November 1997, I made a submission to the Northern Ireland Forum for Political Dialogue[13] on the subject of men's health in Northern Ireland. I was also a member of the Drugs Advisory Committee, which met at Stormont several times each year.

The submissions to these political bodies ensured that the RUC's strategy was an integral part of a uniform, inter-agency approach to the drugs situation in Northern Ireland. It was important that we should not be seen merely as an enforcement agency, in some way detached from the work of educational, welfare and voluntary bodies. A great deal of our time was spent ensuring that this did not happen.

————

These initiatives represented a laudable and determined response by the RUC to the developing drugs problem. I quickly realised, however, that the Chief Constable's public initiative was hampered by other priorities. The threat of paramilitary violence remained. Although there was talk of a possible ceasefire by republicans, the initiative pioneered by Gerry Adams was facing opposition from within. It was not certain that he would carry the day. Dissidents were threatening to leave the Provisional and Sinn Féin movements and continue the struggle on their own. In the previous twelve months, the IRA, INLA, UVF and UFF had been involved in killings, shootings and bombings.

When the IRA declared a complete cessation of military operations in August 1995, followed a month later by the announcement of a truce by the combined loyalist military command, the police were not in a position to dismantle the structures set up to combat violence. These had taken years to develop into the present, sophisticated state and, if removed, would take too long to rebuild, should it become necessary at some future date. Through Special Branch and the security services, the Chief Constable knew what the policy-makers within these paramilitary groups intended. He knew that they had no intention of disarming, discontinuing the targeting of security force personnel or disbanding. Within their ranks there remained skilled bomb-makers and known killers. Some of these issues would be resolved years later, but in the intervening years, the killing continued.

As part of our new initiative, I was anxious to harness the skills of Special Branch, their surveillance unit and its technical sophistication. They readily offered their services, but made it clear that the degree of commitment was dependent on the security situation. We made use of their specialist surveillance team (E4A) and their uniformed back-up (HMSU) on many occasions. They did magnificent work and assisted in the arrests of many suspects and the recovery of substantial quantities of drugs.

The problems of availability and the length of time they could work with us, however, impacted on our effectiveness. Their commanders were always pleased to hear from us, but invariably asked: 'How long do you need them for?' Operations lasting two or three hours were fine; anything longer tended to cause difficulties. Special Branch operatives were particularly effective in jobs of short duration focused on traffickers exchanging drugs and moving to another location. Their involvement guaranteed success.

———

The history of intelligence gathering in the RUC oscillates between noted successes, glaring failures and damaging public scandals. No one outside the small, elite band of policy-makers will ever know all the secrets because it is likely that the full story will never be told.

As head of the Drugs Squad, I was required to comply with existing procedures for handling informants and recording intelligence. I did my best to do so, but it was a secret world to which I was not accustomed, and one I did not enjoy nor fully trust.

By now, I had twenty-three years' experience in CID. I had been seconded to the department in 1972 as a young and inexperienced constable; but over the years, I had been promoted four times to a senior position of Detective Superintendent. It was a job where attention to detail, thoroughness, intuition, skill and experience were paramount. Everything done in an inquiry was committed to print and eventually submitted for scrutiny to a higher authority. It was then filed or processed for prosecution. For relatively minor offences, a file was forwarded to a Process Office manned by uniformed officers. They presented the evidence to a Magistrate's Court. Papers on more serious matters were sent to the Office of the Director of Public Prosecutions. He decided whether there was sufficient evidence to prosecute.

The interests of suspects were protected at every stage of an investigation. Arrests had to be justified: houses could only be searched under warrant; interviews were conducted in the presence of a solicitor; medical and forensic evidence was handled by suitably qualified professionals; during judicial proceedings, an accused person was represented by a solicitor and barrister; court proceedings were open to the family of the accused and the general public; the court proceedings could be reported by the media with the minimum of constraint. Everything done by the investigating officer was scrutinised at various stages of this process. The successful outcome of any case was dependent on the officer proving that his actions were legally sound and that the rights of the suspect had been safeguarded.

Sensitive information relating to the investigation was submitted to the Director of Public Prosecutions in a separate file. This might refer to the involvement of an informant, details on intelligence, or previous convictions. The Director of Public Prosecutions decided how much of this data could be disclosed to the court and to defence counsel.

Special Branch had the same rank structure; many officers had served the same period of time as me and were promoted in a similar fashion. The chain of command in CID led through an operational Chief Superintendent to an Assistant Chief Constable and ultimately to the Chief Constable. Special Branch's line of command led in the same way to the Chief Constable, but became less clear at this point. The influence of the security services (MI5 and MI6) was much in evidence.

Over the years, Special Branch had taken the lead in the RUC's efforts to defeat terrorism and was seen as crucial to national security. The resumption of the IRA bombing campaign in England after the deaths of the IRA hunger strikers made this inevitable. In July 1982, eight soldiers were killed in an explosion in Hyde Park; in December 1983 a bomb exploded at Harrods, killing five people; in October 1984 a bomb demolished part of the Grand Hotel in Brighton where the Prime Minister, Margaret Thatcher, and her Cabinet had gathered for the Conservative Party conference. Five people died. In a chilling statement after failing to kill Mrs Thatcher, the IRA made its intentions very clear: 'Today we were unlucky, but remember we have only to be lucky once. You [Mrs Thatcher] will have to be lucky always.'

Special Branch was given the responsibility of intelligence gathering in Northern Ireland. The number of officers attached to the department had been increasing steadily since the start of the Troubles. They were provided with a huge budget by the Chief Constable and, I suspect, central government to train officers in surveillance, handling informants and the collation and analysis of intelligence. Substantial sums of money were paid to agents who provided high-grade information leading to the recovery of firearms and explosives, the arrest of suspects and the prevention of further attacks. The department worked closely with the security services and army intelligence and made use of undercover units from the RUC and the army, including the SAS.

MI5, whose principal remit was national security, assumed the lead role in counteracting the IRA bombing campaign on the mainland. It forged a close working relationship with the RUC and Garda Special Branches and relied on them to provide intelligence on impending attacks.

CID had its own Criminal Intelligence Unit (CIU) based at Headquarters. Details on all informants and their police handlers were registered there. The Drugs Squad and the Anti-Racketeering Squad also collated information of significance to themselves. Each divisional headquarters' station ran a small collation office where uniformed officers could access intelligence of local interest. All intelligence from these sources was forwarded to CIU.

Special Branch had access to everything held at CIU, including details on informants. This was not a two-way process, however: no one had clearance to access Special Branch intelligence. Any information released by them was carefully monitored and strictly controlled. Based on the premise that knowledge is power, this process gave them overall dominance. Some of the most senior officers in other departments were former members of Special Branch, including Blair Wallace (the Deputy Chief Constable), Ronnie Flanagan (at that time, an Assistant Chief Constable), and Raymond White (the Assistant Chief Constable in charge of CID).

Special Branch was the undoubted expert in intelligence gathering in Northern Ireland. It had in place procedures which maximised its effectiveness and gave it numerous successes against republican and loyalist paramilitaries. I have knowledge of some of its work, which saved lives and interrupted bombing missions. Its efforts helped bring about the end of hostilities and contributed to the IRA ceasefire of 1994.

It manned a twenty-four-hour telephone which ensured that informants and police handlers were always in contact. Details of all informants and handlers were stored in a central register at a Source Handling Unit. Any contact with an informant was sanctioned by senior officers in the unit. Everything discussed was recorded on tape or in writing. Handlers were debriefed after every meeting to ensure that the intelligence submitted was accurate. No omission or distortion of facts was permitted. Other informants were secretly quizzed about this intelligence in an attempt to verify its accuracy and quality. Senior officers regularly analysed the quality of the work and information provided by each informant. Intelligence from electronic surveillance ('bugging devices', telephone intercepts), the security services and Army Intelligence was also analysed.

Special Branch also established a specialist group (TCG) which controlled all undercover and surveillance work. In particular, they directed the operations of E4A (the elite Special Branch surveillance unit). It also worked closely with army undercover teams and the SAS.

Central control of surveillance was necessary to limit the danger of undercover officers being mistaken as terrorists by uniformed officers. In the early 1970s, before the centralisation and control of surveillance was established, several clashes between army and police resulted in deaths. TCG placed areas 'out of bounds' when it was operating in a particular location. All other police officers and army were ordered to stay out of the area until the 'All clear' was given.

These sophisticated systems helped achieve remarkable success against paramilitaries, but they had the unfortunate effect of restricting the operational effectiveness of other departments, including the Drugs Squad: e.g. our ability to conduct surveillance operations. All surveillance had to be sanctioned, including details of the location, duration and targets. Operations could be terminated at short notice and without explanation, no matter how important or advanced.

All house searches and arrest operations proposed by the Drugs Squad had to be approved in advance. If permission was denied, no explanation was given. This caused a good deal of frustration: Drugs Squad officers anxious to arrest a suspect or search premises assumed that a refusal meant that a particular subject or premises was of some interest to Special Branch. It was never clear to me how much Special Branch knew about the drugs trade or how many of their informants were involved in trafficking. They may have had good reasons for these constraints on our work, but it made us question the value of our role.

My brief, on appointment to the Drugs Squad, was to give the squad a higher profile. Every Chief Constable since then, in his Annual Report, has recognised the importance of the drugs issue and declared that the police are doing everything they can to tackle the problem. I could not therefore help wondering why the RUC's strategy for tackling paramilitary violence was being allowed to impact so badly on our work. It was obvious to me that all paramilitary groups in Northern Ireland were deeply involved in drug trafficking and that the lucrative returns from this were helping in no small way to finance their military activities. So there ought not to have been any clash of priorities: we were all working towards the same end, viz., to put the paramilitaries out of business and thus protect the community.

I had encountered similar problems as a member of the Anti-Racketeering Squad. It had been set up in response to complaints from the business community that they were being held to ransom by the paramilitaries. Although we made significant inroads against the gangsters and gave businessmen some hope, I was never satisfied with our level of success. We were never able to prosecute individuals who were of value to Special Branch. A possible compromise could have been achieved by setting up a joint committee of senior CID and Special Branch officers to ensure that conflicts of interest were kept to a minimum. In 1996, I asked the head of CID in Belfast, Detective Chief Superintendent Martindale, to consider setting up a joint subcommittee with the Drugs Squad to ensure that all informants registered at the Criminal Intelligence Unit reported on all types of criminality, including drug trafficking. He declined my offer.

——

Most members of the Drugs Squad were decent and hard-working, although only a few were capable of delivering on the really big jobs that made a difference. A couple of exceptionally talented members endowed with imagination as well as enthusiasm managed to penetrate the secret world of the traffickers. They secured the intelligence that made possible surveillance operations, arrests and seizures. They were the individuals I enjoyed working with. I encouraged them and did my best to provide the resources they needed.

I soon realised that the investigative skills that were so important to CID were of limited value here. They could still be applied when interviewing suspects, handling exhibits and recovering forensic evidence; but intelligence gathering and the recruitment and handling of informants were more important. This was because information from Uniform Branch, CID and Special Branch tended to be vague, fragmented and seldom specific enough to achieve results. They had their own concerns: Special Branch concentrated almost exclusively on paramilitary violence; CID on crime, and Uniform on public order situations and traffic.

The Drugs Squad had a limited range of tactics: surveillance, searches and the arrest of suspects. Surveillance involved a huge drain on manpower and financial resources. It also required access to a large fleet of vehicles which could be changed regularly. Everything was dependent on intelligence: the better the intelligence, the greater the prospects of success. Like Special Branch, the Drugs Squad graded information according to its content: A1 to F6 (i.e. from high quality to imprecise and/or speculative).

The rules governing CID's handling of informants was set out in the Walker Report of February 1981. A memo was issued to all officers of Detective Inspector rank and above in the RUC. The purpose was to ensure an effective interchange between CID and Special Branch, guaranteeing the fullest possible consultation and cooperation. It made recommendations on informants who were in a position to report on subversive (paramilitary) and non-subversive (ordinary) criminality.

From this date onwards, Special Branch took the lead role in handling informants belonging to paramilitary organisations. On rare occasions, informants insisted on maintaining contact with their CID handler. In such instances, joint handling was authorised; but Special Branch had primacy.

In 1995, under revised rules, CID officers ceased to handle informants involved with paramilitary groups. This development gave Special Branch unprecedented control of the process. It now determined what intelligence could and should be made available to CID and Uniform Branch. In time, all planned arrests, searches and surveillance operations by these groups had to be cleared by Special Branch. They had the power of veto.

CID was now obliged to intensify its intelligence gathering from criminal (i.e., non-paramilitary) informants. Although procedures were already in place, they were periodically reviewed and updated. Despite existing legal restraints and attempts by RUC management to specify and limit the parameters within which informants and their police handlers were permitted to operate, serious issues remained which could not be eliminated without abolishing the use of informants.

Drug traffickers and dealers led a secret and dangerous existence. They parted with large sums of money in exchange for illicit drugs, which they then sold on, hopefully at a profit. The suppliers had similar ambitions and had no interest in the well-being of dealers or users. Some were unpredictable and very dangerous. Inexperienced dealers were often robbed, beaten, or had poor quality drugs dumped on them. They also faced the danger of detection by police and customs. Seizure of drugs meant a substantial loss of money. Eventually they distributed the drugs to smaller dealers, who used a host of 'runners' to sell them on their behalf. The criminal code of loyalty and accountability was rigidly applied: the theft or loss of drugs belonging to someone else resulted in punishment beatings of considerable savagery which sometimes led to death. Potential profits were huge, and as long as things went according to plan, everyone in the chain of supply could expect to benefit.

Few dealers gave information to the police because they genuinely disapproved of drug-taking or had a conscience. None of them did it for money. The budget available to the Drugs Squad was miniscule compared to the sums of money dealers could hope to make in one night of trafficking. Most of them did it out of self-interest: some had been arrested in possession of drugs and sought to make a deal in the hope of avoiding prosecution; others had been ripped off by rivals and wanted revenge; a few had fallen foul of suppliers and wanted protection. Most of them were deeply involved in the drugs trade and had no intention of giving up.

I convinced my bosses that the existing level of rewards paid to informants was too low and they agreed to increase the budget; but it was still lower than the amounts accessed by Special Branch.

I quickly learned that large payments did not guarantee success. The primary aim of a police handler was to use intelligence given by an informant to make seizures and arrests. The informant's intention was to meet his handler's need without risking his own safety by passing on information that could be traced back to him by his criminal associates. This often resulted in withholding or distorting information. The situation was further complicated by traffickers working as double-agents: i.e. pretending to work as police informants while helping criminal and paramilitary associates to avoid detection. Sometimes they passed on information on rivals to divert attention from themselves and their associates.

Dishonesty and ingenuity on the part of informants meant that the police had, at best, an incomplete picture of illicit drug use in Northern Ireland. Raymond White, a former Assistant Chief Constable who was head of CID at this time, told *The Sunday Times*: 'Just because someone was registered as an informant or agent, it did not mean we had complete control of him. People with relevant intelligence might hold back information to suit their own agendas or protect friends.'[14]

The integrity of intelligence gathering was also dependent on the honesty and professionalism of police handlers. Information obtained from a source which produced results reflected favourably on them; an unproductive informant or faulty information reflected badly.

Nuala O'Loan, in her report on the Special Branch informant Mark Haddock,[15] alleged that he 'had been involved in a number of murders with the knowledge or suspicion of his police handlers: adequate records of meetings with him had not been kept.' She also stated that 'Records were minimised, exaggerated, fabricated and must also have been destroyed.'

Attempts to control the accuracy and reliability of information provided by informants and handlers were not sufficient to prevent public scandals that undermined public confidence in the police. In 1977, a case involving Anthony O'Doherty, another Special Branch informant, and his police handler highlighted the difficulties and dilemmas faced by senior officers. The police handler, a detective sergeant in Special Branch, had been charged with the murder of a fellow police officer, Sergeant Joe Campbell in Cushendall—and twenty-six other charges, including armed robbery and the illegal possession of firearms and explosives. O'Doherty alleged that Special Branch officers had visited him while he was in prison and he agreed to work with them. He was told 'to get in on the Provies' scene'. Over a period of time, he passed on information concerning the Provisional IRA. His handler gave him guns, recovered during searches, for his own protection. O'Doherty also alleged that his handler committed armed robberies and conspired with him to murder Sergeant Campbell. The detective sergeant was convicted but later acquitted on appeal.

By assigning two experienced officers to work with the Serious Crime Squad Surveillance Unit at Castlereagh, I managed to increase the surveillance capability available to the Drugs Squad. The new arrangement also gave the squad access to additional telephone intercept facilities not being fully utilised by CID. The availability of the CID surveillance team enabled us to make greater use of high-grade intelligence. Members of the unit were highly trained and had in their ranks undercover officers who had been recipients of bravery rewards from the Queen at ceremonies in Buckingham Palace.

———

By late 1995, Brendan Fegan, a young trafficker from Newry, had become one of our main targets. He had a reputation for enjoying fast cars and reckless driving. Intelligence indicated that he was supplying drugs to many areas in South Down, west and north Belfast, and Bangor. He had narrowly escaped capture on two occasions, thanks to his driving skills.

On 23 October 1995, I got a telephone call from an unexpected source. I knew the male caller was a sleekit, unsavoury character with a recent involvement in thieving as well as a brothel. Not surprisingly, he insisted on a financial arrangement before telling me what he knew. His story was of great interest to me: one of the biggest trafficking gangs, based at Carryduff in south Belfast, was planning to bring a consignment of drugs into Northern Ireland from Belgium that weekend. He gave me the name of the driver. Members of the squad and DLU (Drugs Liaison Unit) officers in central Belfast also confirmed that a consignment of drugs was expected. We placed surveillance on the suspect driver and his home. I spoke to HM Customs in Scotland and Northern Ireland and got permission for the import operation to run. On 26 October the suspect driver was seen boarding a ferry for Scotland. Special Branch agreed to place their E4A surveillance team on stand-by over the weekend.

Late on 28 October (Saturday), I got a phone call from the informant to say that a handover of drugs had taken place south of London and that the consignment was on its way north. At 5.30 a.m. on 29 October, I was told by the police portal unit in Stranraer that the car was on a ferry heading to Larne. E4A was immediately scrambled and set up a surveillance operation. The suspect vehicle was followed through Belfast city centre and up the Saintfield Road to Carryduff. Undercover officers observed it being parked outside a house in one of the estates. The driver took a bag from the car and entered the house.

Officers in the control room waited to see what would happen next. They had a number of issues to ponder: Were the drugs still in the car? Had they been carried into the house? Who exactly was in the house?

Just then, a surveillance team spotted the leader of the gang (Liam 'Fat Boy' Mooney) driving up the Saintfield Road. It was agreed that if he entered the house, an order would be given to storm it. Disappointingly, he turned off and went elsewhere. About the same time, the driver left the house and drove off. Minutes later, a man carried the bag from the house and placed it in a car. He was followed to the car park of the nearby Royal Ascot public house and restaurant. He left the car and entered the premises.

Nothing happened for some hours. In the late afternoon, a different man left the pub and drove the car out of the car park. He turned left onto the Hillsborough Road. Surveillance officers radioed their base and arranged for a roadblock. The suspect vehicle smashed through it, causing severe damage to a police vehicle. A car chase ensued, reaching speeds of 80 mph along narrow, winding roads heading towards the M1 motorway. The target entered the motorway against the flow of traffic and proceeded along the hard shoulder at over 100 mph, with the police in pursuit. By now a police spotter plane and high-speed police traffic vehicles driven by specially trained drivers had joined in. The target left the motorway at the Blacks Road intersection, still driving against the oncoming traffic. Suddenly he stopped, leapt into another car (presumably arranged during the chase) and made his getaway. A search of the abandoned vehicle uncovered £.5 million of cannabis and ecstasy. Over the coming days, we learned that the driver was Brendan 'Speedy' Fegan.

Three weeks later, we had another encounter with him: we learned that he was using the grounds of an isolated monastery outside Banbridge to hide a stash of drugs. We made a cursory search of the location, but found nothing. We knew that a Belfast dealer intended to do business with him over the coming days and we put undercover officers into position as part of a surveillance operation. They spotted Fegan driving onto the carriageway that runs between Lisburn and Newry and followed him, at times reaching speeds of 100 mph (his normal speed). We contacted Traffic Branch on the M1 motorway. They were soon on Fegan's trail; speeds were now in excess of 120 mph. They forced him to stop at a roadblock on the Stockman's Lane exit. He was arrested and his car seized. A subsequent search failed to turn up any drugs, but £5,000 was found behind the panel of the driver's door. He had not much to say during interviews and was released. The following day, we searched part of the grassy verge along a section of the motorway in case he had thrown drugs out of the window during the chase, but nothing was found.

I submitted a report to Headquarters detailing all the information we had on Fegan. The Deputy Chief Constable agreed that the Special Branch surveillance team (E4A) would carry out surveillance on him, but stressed that this would be intermittent and subject to other priorities. Over a fourteen-month period, we received high-grade information on him and some of his associates, but it failed to give us an opportunity to arrest Fegan. That would have needed intensive work over an indefinite period.

The periodic but invaluable work of Special Branch's surveillance team showed that he tended to do most of his business along the border, in the car park of the Skylon Hotel in the Republic and in the Sheepsbridge Inn outside Newry. He met his customers by arrangement and negotiated a price. Once they handed the money over, they were directed to a collection point on nearby roads. For security and political reasons, we were not allowed to work in these areas; but on three occasions, good intelligence enabled us to intercept dealers returning from the rendezvous. On 30 April 1996, we arrested two men in possession of £100,000 worth of cannabis. It was the detained men who suffered a financial loss, not Fegan. We were not getting any closer to him.

I made a further determined attempt to catch him in the act of moving drugs. On 19 January 1996, David Ervine and Billy Smith of the PUP (Progressive Unionist Party) invited me to a meeting at Tennent Street police station. They told me that the Shankill area had been 'flooded' with drugs. This confirmed what I already knew. Members of the squad had been working on the problem for many months and were certain that the main supplier was Brendan Fegan. Intelligence indicated that he was dealing with one particular family. I explained to David that the best way to deal with him was to catch him on a supply run into the Shankill. I asked David to discuss the issue with community activists and members of the UVF in the hope that they, as concerned members of the community, would provide the information needed to catch him. Three weeks later, David telephoned to say that the plan had backfired: the UVF had 'arrested' and interrogated a number of suspect dealers and had issued threats against them. I did not tell David that my own bosses were less than pleased. Some of the people 'arrested' were important sources for Special Branch.

By July 1997, we had compiled a comprehensive dossier on Fegan's activities along the border. Intelligence indicated that he was delivering cannabis, ecstasy and cocaine on behalf of the infamous Gilligan Gang, who had murdered the journalist Veronica Guerin on 26 June 1996. I decided to share this intelligence with the Garda Síochána and met Detective Chief Superintendent Kevin Carty plus members of the Dublin Drugs Squad in a hotel outside Dundalk. I brought senior members of the CID surveillance team along. It was agreed that the Garda would lead the investigation into Fegan and that the RUC would assist in any way necessary.

I have been told that the Garda National Drugs Unit eventually followed Fegan to one of Gilligan's warehouses in north Dublin. A search of the premises uncovered 25 kilos of cannabis—a bitter disappointment to the Gardaí, who were expecting a much larger haul. Fegan was detained; he agreed to work as an informant. Over the next two years, he gave information which enabled the Gardaí to recover huge amounts of drugs. In one operation at Balbriggan, Gardaí made a multi-million punt seizure: 250,000 E-tabs, cannabis worth 1,570,000 punts and a substantial quantity of cocaine. He also provided information resulting in the seizure of 1 million punts worth of cannabis in September 1998.

During this period, Fegan's behaviour was becoming more excessive and erratic. He was under threat from rivals and the IRA. In 1998, he was shot and wounded in an attack in Belfast widely blamed on the IRA. He started to carry a gun for his own protection and could not resist flashing it in order to impress. He used it to threaten bouncers at various nightclubs in Monaghan and to intimidate rivals. In May 1999, two men wearing false beards and moustaches calmly walked into the Hermitage Bar in Newry, where he was drinking with friends. He had just lost £25,000 after his trotting pony was beaten by a rival. He was shot a number of times and died at the scene.

Returning to the Carryduff operation and the gang leader, 'Fat Boy' Mooney, we kept a careful eye on him and his associates. In December 1996, we received information that he was planning a drugs run to the Continent to cater for Christmas revellers in Belfast. A late-night raid on his home in Carryduff surprised him and three associates as they counted £64,000 into a shoe-box. No one was arrested, but the money was seized. Traces of illegal drugs were found on various notes; no one laid claim to the money.

In October 1997, a source reported that 'Fat Boy' and his gang were planning to pick up a consignment of drugs in Dublin destined for the North. I immediately contacted the Garda National Drugs Unit and sent one of my officers to work with them. They carried out surveillance on Mooney and his associates over a number of days. During the evening of 24 October, they stopped two cars in Lucan on the outskirts of Dublin and recovered £250,000 worth of cannabis. Three men from Northern Ireland (including 'Fat Boy') were arrested and charged with drug offences. Mooney was released on bail and promptly absconded to Holland.

In late 1995, two members of the squad asked me if they could register Saul Devine as an informant. He had been released from jail a number of weeks earlier on charges of handling stolen goods. Intelligence indicated that he had previous involvement in drug dealing and was trying to re-establish himself. They were hopeful of using him against a man from Northern Ireland who had established a supply base in Manchester. I had already discussed this man's activities with Greater Manchester police. They had confirmed that he was part of an international gang responsible for importing huge quantities of cannabis, ecstasy and cocaine into the UK. We had been investigating his links with traffickers operating in Northern Ireland.

Thousands of lorries enter Northern Ireland from England and the Irish Republic each year. It was not possible to intercept drugs, alcohol and cigarettes hidden in lorries without specific intelligence. Drugs were often hidden among the cargo, which could be furniture, electrical goods and canned foodstuffs, or in concealed compartments. It was a difficult decision to break the seal on a consignment of perishable goods without being confident that drugs would be found. It was known that this Manchester dealer used lorries to transport his drugs into Northern Ireland.

In November, Devine reported to his handlers that a consignment of cannabis, ecstasy and cocaine was destined for Crumlin, Co. Antrim. The drugs would then be delivered to Devine, who had an apartment in the Russell Court complex in the Donegall Road area of Belfast, by a leading figure in the INLA. Because of the sensitive nature of the information and safety concerns for the informant, I decided that the operation would have to run beyond the delivery of the drugs in Crumlin. I engaged Special Branch's E4A Surveillance Unit. It carried out surveillance on the suspects and the premises in Crumlin. I met the informant with the handlers in Hillsborough and made it clear to him that this consignment of drugs would be intercepted. After a great deal of persuasion, he agreed to cooperate.

E4A followed the consignment from Crumlin, through Moira and up the M1 motorway towards Belfast. Members of the HMSU (Headquarters Mobile Support Unit) decided that an interception on the motorway was too dangerous in darkness. We mounted a roadblock instead on the Donegall Road a short distance from the Broadway roundabout. The surveillance team reported that everything was going according to plan and that the car carrying the drugs was approximately half a mile short of the roadblock. The car suddenly pulled into the hard shoulder alongside Milltown Cemetery. This section of the road was unlit and the surveillance vehicles had no option but to drive past. One of the team spotted the driver carrying a bag and hitching a lift. A white van stopped and picked him up within seconds. It passed through the roadblock before the uniformed officers could be alerted. They were ordered to break off and head immediately to the Russell Court complex.

There, they gave chase to a man who dropped a bag while escaping. It was found to contain a large quantity of ecstasy and some cannabis with a street value of £180,000.

Anyone who knows the area of the M1 motorway at Milltown Cemetery would not dream of stopping there to pick up a stranger on a dark winter's night. There is no doubt in my mind that the driver of the car moving the drugs was tipped off that a roadblock was awaiting him half a mile further up the road and that the timely arrival of the white van was no coincidence. There was no reason for anyone to tell Devine that the roadblock was in place. So who informed the INLA driver of the car? I am left to consider the possibility that it was a member of the Force who had some interest in the INLA man or Devine.

The INLA man was an infamous character. In December 1995, the INLA tried to kill him at a house on the Falls Road, when they peppered the front room with shotgun fire. It is believed that he shot a man dead outside the Glengannon Hotel in Dungannon a week after being ejected from the premises for selling drugs.

On 8 December 1995, Devine was shot dead close to his flat. Despite claims of responsibility by DAAD, a prominent figure in the INLA was arrested and questioned about the murder. He too was later shot dead.

In 1996, three seemingly unrelated incidents caused an on-going inquiry into fraud and money-laundering involving an Ulster businessman, Colin Lees, and his associates to develop into an international drugs investigation of a complexity and magnitude never before experienced by the RUC.

(a) On 4 May 1996, I boarded a ferry to Scotland en route to a conference at Blairquhan Castle in Ayrshire. I was to join delegates from a variety of professions: local government, finance, education and business to discuss political issues of national importance. Everyone invited had taken part in a similar conference at Windsor Great Park in June 1985, which I had attended with Sir John Hermon and Ronnie Flanagan.

During the crossing, I was disturbed by the incessant ringing of a mobile phone. Each time, the call lasted no more than five or six seconds and the response was always the same: 'We are on the ferry. We are on our way.' After the sixth call, I decided to take a closer look. I watched as a stout man with ginger hair took another seventeen calls in as many minutes. His response never varied. There were five other men with him who appeared to be keeping an eye on the other passengers. I later followed the group to the car deck, where they dispersed. I noted the registration number of the stout man's car and telephoned the Drugs Squad, who identified him.

(b) On 30 October 1996, three Garda officers went to a beach at Bambas Crown on the Malin Head peninsula in County Donegal following a report that a boat had run aground. They encountered five men with Northern Irish accents: Noel Morrison, Ian Symington, Samuel Adams, Noel Johnston and James Miller. They were immediately suspicious. The area had a strong republican history. A few days earlier, in the same area, the Gardaí had broken up an IRA training camp.

Back in 1988, Gardaí manning a roadblock had stopped a van near Five Finger Island on the same peninsula. The driver was a local man with known republican connections. They found traces of sand in the back. A cursory search was made of the nearby beach. In a shallow hole, they uncovered two plastic tanks filled with automatic weapons, ammunition and Semtex explosive. It was later established that these were part of a shipment from Colonel Gaddafi in Libya.

Morrison told the senior Garda officer, Detective Sergeant Carroll, that he was the owner of the maroon boat and a Land Rover parked nearby. He described how the boat's engine had cut out the previous evening, causing it to drift onto the rocks. Detective Sergeant Carroll was an experienced seaman and knew this part of the Donegal coastline well. He decided that the damage to the rudder indicated that the engine was still running when the boat ran aground. The Gardaí also found sleeping-bags, transmitters, gas cylinders and food nearby. They decided to arrest the men under Section 30 of the Offences Against the State Act, 1939, on suspicion of being members of the IRA. The men were questioned at Burnfoot Garda station. Checks were made with Special Branch in Northern Ireland who, in turn, contacted the Drugs Squad. We confirmed that Noel Johnston was a drug dealer and a target.

It soon became clear that none of the men were involved with the IRA; instead, they were loyalists with criminal connections. Nothing useful was uncovered during questioning. Despite inconsistencies in their versions of events, there was no evidence that they had committed a criminal offence and were released two days later.

In a further search of the Land Rover, which had been retained by the Gardaí, Detective Sergeant Carroll found a road map of Ireland. He noticed two x's marked on the Donegal coast and was convinced that the men had intended to rendezvous at sea.

(c) On 1 November 1996, the day after the men were released, a six-berth motor cruiser, the *Plongeur Wisky*, moored in Kilrush Harbour in County Clare with engine trouble. A search of the boat by customs officers uncovered 1.7 tons of cannabis—in Irish terms, a huge haul with a street value of £17 million. When Detective Sergeant Carroll heard of the find, he realised that the men he had spoken to at Malin Head had been waiting to offload this cargo.

The following day, I went to meet the Drugs Squad in Dublin. They were certain of the link between the *Plongeur Wisky* and the activities of the men at Malin Head. They gave me all the information available and asked me to make further inquiries.

On 4 November, we discussed this at the RUC Drugs Squad weekly policy meeting. A detective constable told the group that one of the men arrested at Malin Head was a casual informant for a uniformed officer based in Larne. Later that afternoon, I travelled with other squad members to interview the officer in question. He confirmed that this man occasionally gave him information leading to the recovery of stolen, high-quality vehicles. The man did not ask for anything in return, nor was he paid any money. The officer dismissed my suggestion that this individual might be involved in criminal activity, including drug dealing. I was unhappy with the outcome of the meeting and decided that the relationship could not be allowed to continue. I spoke to a senior uniformed officer in Larne and Detective

Chief Inspector Cook, a senior CID officer in Ballymena. It was agreed that the constable should terminate his involvement with the informant. As far as I was concerned, the man was now of interest to the Drugs Squad.

On 4 and 5 November, I discussed this man with the CID surveillance team (C1.2) at Castlereagh and asked them to look at the possibility of mounting a surveillance operation.

On 6 November, I discussed the matter further with Detective Chief Superintendent Eric Anderson, the head of CID in North Region. He gave me permission to meet the suspect. I travelled to Larne with a fellow squad member in an unmarked police car fitted with a hidden recorder. The man was apprehensive and very suspicious. He refused to sit in the car and insisted on talking outside the vehicle. I immediately recognised him as the stout, ginger-haired man who had taken the telephone calls on the boat in May. He was unnerved when I quoted his own words back at him: 'We are on the ferry. We are on our way…'

I told him that the Gardaí had worked out the link between Malin Head and the *Plongeur Wisky* and would wish to speak to him in the near future. After a great deal of persuasion, he conceded that there was a connection. He said that the cannabis was to be distributed in Northern Ireland and Britain. He then revealed that the main financer of the operation was Colin Lees; that Lees had organised a further eighteen shipments of cannabis, ecstasy and cocaine into the UK; that Paddy Farrell from Newry and large-scale dealers in Dublin had pooled their finances to pay for shipments; that the money was delivered to a man called 'Rocky' in Liverpool, who arranged deliveries of millions of E-tabs from Holland and Belgium and huge loads of cannabis and cocaine from Spain. The bigger the order, the cheaper the price. The drugs were brought through ports in containers, vans and buses. Some of the vehicles had been fitted with hidden compartments. These alterations were made at a garage near Toomebridge. He also said that Paddy Farrell laundered his money at the *bureau de change* on the border on the Newry to Dundalk road. The drugs were offloaded at a huge warehouse in an industrial complex outside Manchester before being distributed to various parts of the UK, including Northern Ireland, and the Irish Republic.

As he spoke to me, I recalled an incident when HM Customs at Dover had become suspicious of an empty bus leaving for France. The driver (who was from Northern Ireland) said that he was collecting schoolchildren in France who were on an educational trip. The Customs officers were suspicious and flagged up their colleagues on the French side. On the return journey, French Customs checked the bus and reported back to British Customs: they had checked the passenger manifest and found no trace of a school party. On its return to Dover, the driver and co-driver were detained and the bus thoroughly searched. A false compartment in the floor of the bus was found to contain 13 kilos of cocaine, 400 kilos of cannabis and 100,000 E-tabs.[16]

On 14 November, Detective Chief Superintendent Anderson authorised me to hand the tape and notes made of the Larne meeting to a senior member of staff at the Director of Public Prosecutions' Office in the Royal Courts of Justice. I was advised that the poor quality of the recording (the conversation had taken place outside the car) and the circumstances in which it was made (I merely wished to evaluate the man's relevance to my inquiries and did not formally caution him) limited its evidential value.

After further discussions with Mr Anderson and Assistant Chief Constable Raymond White (head of CID), I was instructed to prepare an intelligence brief on the information he had provided and circulate it to appropriate departments. I invited representatives from HM Customs (Northern Ireland and England), senior CID, RUC, Manchester police and members of the National Criminal Intelligence Unit to a meeting at the Drugs Squad. Copies were also given to the Fraud Squad and the Financial Investigation Unit under the command of Detective Chief Superintendent Jimmy Molloy. The intelligence on Lees was given the code name 'Operation Kilbreck' and that on Paddy Farrell 'Operation Palmette' by Operations Branch at Headquarters from a list compiled by the National Criminal Intelligence Section.

With drug smuggling an added dimension to Mr Molloy's investigations, I seconded some of my most able officers to his inquiry, including Detective Constable Marks (the young officer who had pursued Brendan Smyth on behalf of his victims and their families) plus a member of the Drugs Squad Financial Investigation Unit.

Since 1992, Fraud Squads in the RUC and Scotland had been investigating Colin Lees after an examination of his accounts by Price Waterhouse uncovered irregularities and debts totalling £15 million when his companies went into receivership.

For seven months prior to the *Plongeur Wisky* incident in County

Clare, the Financial Investigations Unit had also been examining the financial affairs of Lees and his business associates. They were convinced that a myriad of national and international bank accounts, limited companies and other financial transactions were being used to launder money.

By 1997, several police forces in the UK and the Gardaí were involved. Over half a million documents were seized and examined. Members of the RUC investigation team travelled to New York to examine financial links with two Mafia crime families, Bonanno and Genovesi, who had been indicted on charges related to fraudulent stock dealings in the USA and Canada. A senior prosecutor from the US Department of Justice visited Belfast as part of the investigation.

Premises in Blackpool were searched, also the home of Lees' former book-keeper and the Loughside Inn on the Shore Road, Belfast. Police uncovered incriminating paperwork implicating Lees in the purchase of the *Plongeur Wisky* and established his connection with the five men at Malin Head. His fingerprints were also found on a number of faxes connected to the investigation. An examination of mobile phones confirmed that he had been in contact with the crew of the *Plongeur Wisky* on its fateful journey from Gibraltar to Ireland.

On 11 October 1997, Lees was charged in connection with the *Plongeur Wisky* saga. This was the first time the RUC had used the 1971 Misuse of Drugs Act (Section 20) to prosecute an individual for offences outside the jurisdiction of Northern Ireland.

Lees was remanded in custody while a series of prosecutions were arranged. On 23 November 2000, he was sentenced to twelve years' imprisonment on drug-trafficking charges. He received lesser sentences for his money-laundering and tax evasion, to run concurrently.

Samuel Adams was sentenced to four years' imprisonment; Ian Symington received a two-year suspended sentence, James Miller a suspended three-year sentence. Noel Johnston was not arraigned for offences connected with the Malin Head incident. The Drugs Squad had caught him in possession of £250,000 worth of cannabis, for which he was serving a three-year sentence. Noel Morrison went into hiding and is still being sought. The trial judge, Mr Justice Gillen, praised the vigilance of the Irish Customs and the painstaking work of the Gardaí and the RUC.

The conviction of Colin Lees represented a huge fall from grace.

His father, William, was a self-made man who had built his concrete production works and sawmill into a profitable business worth £38 million. My good friend, Robert Hastings (a prominent solicitor in the area for many years) described William Lees as a 'hard-working, honest and highly respected businessman'. He said that he would be turning in his grave at how his son Colin had squandered the family business and brought shame on the family.

In 2003, Lees was released from prison. He immediately resumed contact with his drug-trafficking associates. In September 2005, aged fifty-three, he was sentenced to twenty-five years' imprisonment for his part in a smuggling operation to supply huge amounts of illicit drugs throughout the UK. During a surveillance operation at Fieldhouse Industrial Estate in Rochdale, north of Manchester, police observed a consignment of drugs being delivered. It consisted of 470,000 ecstasy tablets and 437 lbs of amphetamine powder and paste, with a street value of £30 million. His accomplice, Peter Giannasi, received seventeen years' imprisonment.

The investigation into Paddy Farrell identified him as a major money-launderer for drug dealers, criminals and the IRA. It also uncovered a multi-million-pound laundering operation involving the *bureau de change* and other businesses in South Armagh.

In the early months of 1997, a well-known drug dealer, Michael Cahillane, domiciled in southern Spain, was planning to import large quantities of cannabis into Northern Ireland. He had absconded from his native Bangor in 1990 after being released on bail on fraud charges. He was looking for a lorry driver who made regular deliveries to and from the Continent, including Spain, believing that HM Customs would take less interest in a driver who regularly passed through English ports.

We located an experienced undercover officer in the Serious Crime Squad who held a heavy goods vehicle licence. He had already done undercover work in Northern Ireland and England. Arrangements were made for him to meet a member of the gang. Over the course of four meetings and several phone calls, he gained their trust. It was imperative that the gang believed that he was a long-distance driver and a frequent traveller to the Continent. With some help from contacts in the Northern Ireland haulage business, we arranged for the officer to make a delivery of goods from a firm in Carrickfergus to southern Spain. On his return, he made further contact with members of the gang in Bangor and arranged to drive a consignment of cannabis from southern Spain into Northern Ireland.

Political and legal differences between European Union countries meant that existing protocols had to be rigorously adhered to. Spain was one of the major distribution countries for cannabis in Western Europe. Huge quantities of the drug were being shipped into the country from north Africa—in particular, Morocco. The demands on the manpower and resources of the Policía Nacional (Spanish Police) were enormous, so we had to present a convincing and worthwhile case to them. We introduced our undercover officer and sent Drugs Squad and HM Customs officers to liaise with them. HM Customs successfully negotiated the uninterrupted passage of the consignment through Spain and France.

This took a number of weeks to arrange. Unexpectedly—and before we had agreed a plan of action with our European counterparts—the gang announced that the consignment was imminent. We needed to play for time and considered ways of stalling them. The wife of one of my colleagues worked in the casualty department of a local hospital. She kindly agreed to fit a plaster of Paris to the arm of the undercover officer. He then met with the gang and convinced them that he was unfit to drive for three weeks. He made a suitably miraculous recovery once our plans were finalised in March.

Arriving in southern Spain, he parked at the pre-arranged spot. During the night, the lorry was taken away and the drugs loaded on board. The journey back to the UK was uneventful. During the ferry crossing from Stranraer, officers from the RUC Technical Support Unit fitted a tracking device to the consignment. We were then able to follow it to a house in Bangor.

In a search of the premises, £250,000 worth of cannabis was recovered. We were bitterly disappointed that it was not a lot more. Cahillane did not hold our undercover officer responsible. In October 1997, he sent a further consignment of cannabis with a street value of £340,000. Three men were arrested in the two operations and sentenced to three, four and a half and five years in prison. Cahillane's fingerprints were found on the packaging and wrapping. It was not until 2006 that the new Police Service of Northern Ireland (PSNI) managed to extradite him from Spain. He was charged with the March and October 1997 incidents and sentenced to four and a half years in prison.

In June 1997, we made our biggest ever seizure of cannabis. Intelligence from an informant indicated that Robert McNeill, a driver with one of the biggest haulage firms in Northern Ireland, was planning to bring a consignment of drugs into County Antrim from England. The drugs were to be concealed in wine boxes which he kept in his cab. Surveillance in England confirmed that five white boxes were being carried by McNeill in his lorry.

The operation took much longer than expected. On three occasions, McNeill drove towards Liverpool port to board a ferry for Belfast. Each time, as he neared the port, his managers in Northern Ireland, unaware of our interest, re-directed him to other destinations in England. We decided to approach senior management in the firm. I located a senior CID officer in Armagh who knew the managing director well and asked him to make the approach.

The following day, the lorry arrived in Belfast. A surveillance team followed the lorry to Duncrue Place in the docks area, where McNeill met up with his brother-in-law, James Steele, and another accomplice, Gregory Montgomery. All three men were arrested; 200 kilos of cannabis with a potential street value of £2 million were recovered. The men claimed that they were involved in a drink-smuggling, not a drug-smuggling, operation. They were subsequently convicted of possessing drugs with intent to supply. McNeill was sentenced to five years' imprisonment; Steele and Montgomery were each jailed for four years.

In some dangerous and difficult situations, we used undercover officers posing as customers to buy drugs from dealers. The tactic, known as 'controlled buys', was sparingly employed because of legal restraints and operational difficulties. It required written authorisation from an Assistant Chief Constable and was closely supervised. When successfully executed, it provided strong evidence and was accepted by courts when the police could prove that they had not acted as *agents provocateurs* (i.e. did not incite or encourage the dealers to sell drugs to them). We avoided this by carrying out surveillance work to prove that dealing was taking place. The tactic was used to great effect at clubs in Lurgan, Banbridge and Portrush. Undercover officers watched dealing taking place and identified the drugs on offer. They then joined the queue of customers. The money paid to the dealers was marked and its serial number recorded. The dealers were arrested in the car park at the end of the night. This avoided dangerous confrontations between police and revellers inside the building.

This strategy was used to arrest a number of taxi drivers making home deliveries of drugs after taking orders by telephone. It was most useful in tackling the problem of 'dealing houses' on estates in Lurgan, Craigavon, Belfast, Antrim and Ballymena. Dealers bricked up windows in unoccupied council houses, leaving a small gap ('serving hatch') to take money and pass drugs through. Doors were heavily fortified with steel panels and bars with the intention of stopping rival gangs, paramilitaries and the police gaining entry.

Obviously, the police had the equipment to force their way into any property, but the delay in breaking through these defences gave the dealers time to dispose of the drugs in the fire or down the toilet. To counteract this, we blocked drains and carried fire extinguishers when storming these places.

During April and May 1996, residents of Clifton Park Avenue in north Belfast complained that dealers were operating from vacant, heavily fortified houses in the area. We carried out surveillance and arrested customers as they left, to establish what drugs were on sale. Several houses were forcibly entered and a number of suspects arrested. Unfortunately, Belfast had no shortage of empty properties.

By the end of 1997, the Drugs Squad had recovered £6.5 million worth of drugs—a rise of £3 million on the previous year. Some £1 million worth of ecstasy was seized, compared to none in 1990. In one operation alone in Newry, 90,000 LSD tablets were recovered with a street value of £360,000—the biggest single seizure of LSD ever made in Northern Ireland, amounting in value to the combined total of LSD recovered over the previous ten years. I put the following on record: 'It is time the community took stock of the drug problem here. I would like to see it being regarded as the next enemy after terrorism ...'[17]

———

In December 1996, the Drugs Squad and Traffic Branch became the first departments of their kind in the UK to be awarded the Charter Mark for outstanding service to the public. The awards, announced at a ceremony in London, were warmly welcomed by the Chief Constable and received a great deal of media attention. Ronnie Flanagan publicly stated: 'Charter Marks are awarded in recognition of not just a good quality service but an outstanding one and the RUC's Drugs Squad and Traffic police are to be congratulated on their dedication and commitment in winning this recognition. I know that not only were they comprehensively assessed on their work and performance but the assessors also took on board the views of the public...'

In 1997, I was surprised and delighted to be awarded an MBE in the Queen's Birthday Honours List. On 8 December, I flew to London for the ceremony, accompanied by two members of the Drugs Squad. This was a break with tradition: it is normal practice to invite family members. Instead, I chose two officers as representatives of the Drugs Squad in recognition of the team's hard work and commitment.

Prior to the presentation, we stayed at the Union Jack Club, where we enjoyed a traditional afternoon tea of cucumber sandwiches and tray-bakes. In the evening, we went to Terry Neill's wine bar. Terry was a former captain of the Northern Ireland football team; he had also played for Arsenal for many years. He made us very welcome and was a wonderful host. He introduced us to a number of his friends and produced champagne to celebrate my award. Later that evening, he invited his close friend, the superintendent of the nearby police station, to join the party: he turned out to be an old friend from a ten-week CID course I had attended at Hendon Police College in 1976. The following morning, I went with my two colleagues to Buckingham Palace for the investiture by the Queen. It was a moment I will remember and treasure.

Chapter 11 ∾

I MOVE TO THE PRESS OFFICE

On 17 November 1997, I learned from Personnel Branch that I was being moved the following week to the Force Information Department—one of the two wings of the Press Office (F1 and F1.1), as its new head. The BBC reported my 'promotion' in a news bulletin. I had some concerns, because it meant forfeiting my detective status, which I had held since 1972. But I was under the impression that the move had been arranged by the Chief Constable, Ronnie Flanagan. He had mentioned a transfer to the Press Office some months before, after a charity rugby match involving past members of Ireland and Ulster and stalwarts of the RUC rugby club, including himself. The match had been organised by Trevor Lyttle, a member of the RUC, on behalf of cancer charities. Trevor was well-known in rugby circles; he was also a much-loved and respected colleague. Sadly he too was suffering from cancer and died not long afterwards.

I had the highest regard for Mr Flanagan and liked him a lot. I told him I would be happy to move if I could be of any help to him. I began work in the Press Office on 24 November. My new post lacked the intensity and unpredictability of life as an investigative detective. I knew something of the Press Office's function and how it operated. I had done work with it during my time in the Anti-Racketeering Squad, the Drugs Squad at Donegall Pass and as a CID officer in west Belfast. The department stored information on a range of topics, including historical data on paramilitary violence, road accidents and public statements by senior officers, including the Chief Constable. Regional newspapers were studied each morning and any references to the RUC were included in a circular sent to senior officers before 8 a.m. Requests from the media for interviews with serving police officers of any rank, from Chief Constable to Constable, were processed by us. A press officer was present during authorised interviews. UK television channels and radio stations were monitored twenty-four hours a day and recordings were made of issues of interest to the RUC. Briefing papers were sent to the Chief Constable when necessary.

The department had a deserved reputation for accuracy and reliability. Friction sometimes arose when we refused to disclose information or make officers available for interview. These matters were referred to the Chief Constable for guidance.

From the day I started on the job, no one in the Press Office offered me the slightest guidance on what my position involved. Fortunately my good friend, Jim McDowell, the Northern editor of the *Sunday World*, offered some timely advice: I should never confuse my role as a press officer with that of a journalist. The primary purpose of a journalist was to gather news, mine to represent and project the interests of the RUC. I should expect journalists to respect what I told them in confidence; they should not cause me any embarrassment or harm, but on occasions I should expect the organisation to be criticised. I should be helpful and have a drink with them if necessary, but should always remember that my job and theirs were different. It was wise advice and I did my best to follow it. Sadly some journalists did not reciprocate.

Ronnie Flanagan was Chief Constable during the three years I spent in the Press Office. He was a gifted, articulate and impressive communicator. He had an extraordinary memory and was able to retain and recall, when necessary, vast amounts of information. I saw a great deal of him during the three-year period. I sometimes represented the department at the weekly senior officers' policy meeting, which he chaired. I often accompanied him for television interviews and at ceremonial events. He seldom asked me for advice and, like Margaret Thatcher, was not a good listener when it was offered. He was polite and affable and I enjoyed working with him.

Two incidents highlight some of his qualities. During the spring of 1996, when I was head of the Drugs Squad, I did some work with the educational officer of the Presbyterian Church who was preparing a drugs information package for circulation to Church members. On 26 June 1996, Mr Flanagan and myself were invited to the Presbyterian headquarters at Church House, Fisherwick Place, Belfast, for the official launch of the 70-page booklet, *Get Real*, which highlighted the dangers of illicit drug use. On his arrival, Ronnie Flanagan was taken for coffee by the moderator and senior clerics. Minutes before he was due to speak, he gave me thirty seconds to explain the layout and content of the publication—then proceeded to address his distinguished audience for twenty minutes with authoritative references to it.

In December 1997, I accompanied him to Antrim Road police station for a visit by Prime Minister Tony Blair. Mr Flanagan handled the situation with consummate ease. Afterwards, he invited me to join senior police and army officers for a drink in the divisional commander's office. During the next hour, he reminisced about his life and experiences in the police. An hour with Peter Ustinov could not have been more entertaining.

There were moments like that in the job. I will never forget the time John Prescott, the Deputy Prime Minister, visited Northern Ireland. It happened that he, Detective Chief Superintendent Eric Anderson (another manly figure) and myself ended up squashed into a tiny loo in a country police station. All three of us were aiming at the single urinal when Mr Prescott spotted a piece of chewing gum in the receptacle. Quite spontaneously, he burst into a chorus of the Lonnie Donegan hit song, 'Does your chewing gum lose its flavour on the bedpost overnight?' and we joined in with gusto. Boy bands? We invented the concept years before Take That appeared on the scene.

But these were moments of light relief against the background of a tenuous peace process punctuated by many horrendous acts of violence and murder by loyalist and republican paramilitaries, of which by far the greatest was the Omagh bombing.

At 3.10 p.m. on 15 August 1998, an explosion devastated Omagh town centre. Twenty-nine lives were lost, including eighteen-month-old and twenty-month-old girls and unborn twins. More than 250 people were injured, some critically. Many others suffered deep shock and trauma. The bomb caused the biggest loss of life in any incident during the Troubles.

Immediately after the bombing, an emergency plan was set in motion at the Information Department at RUC headquarters. An information helpline number was circulated in the media and extra staff were brought in to man the telephones. We initiated a system for collating and cross-referencing details concerning victims and missing persons. Although communication cables under the main street of Omagh had been destroyed in the blast, we managed to establish and maintain contact with the police in the town, including those manning the temporary mortuaries at Lisanelly army camp in Omagh, local hospitals, the ambulance service and staff at Omagh Leisure Centre where relatives awaiting news had gathered.

It soon emerged that a group of Spanish holidaymakers had been caught in the blast: schoolboy Fernando Blasco and his teacher, Rocio Ramos, on a bus trip from Buncrana in Donegal, had been killed. With some difficulty, I made contact with the Spanish Consul and kept him informed of developments.

The blast was news throughout the world. During the night, I gave interviews to radio stations from Japan, Germany and the USA. At first light, I went to Omagh. Television crews, journalists and professional cameramen were descending on the town from many different parts of the world. I met up with other members of the Press Office who had been there since the previous day. We did our best to facilitate the media corps, but our priority had to be the identification of the dead and injured and the location of missing persons. I spent much of Sunday at the leisure centre, where social workers, medical staff, clerics and volunteer workers from St John's Ambulance and the Red Cross did their best to offer practical assistance and comfort.

Dozens of relatives were still waiting for news. Hundreds of people had been reported missing a short time after the blast, but by 9 a.m. on Sunday, the number had been lowered to fifty-five. Relatives handed photographs of loved ones to the police and gave detailed descriptions of distinguishing marks, jewellery and clothing to help with the process of identification. Casualty lists were posted on the walls and periodically updated. On two occasions, I assembled the press to update them on casualties. Local taxi drivers brought people to and from the leisure centre free of charge. Many times during the day, police cars took relatives to the mortuary or nearby hospitals.

I worked discreetly with police officers at the centre. My job was to provide accurate information on casualties, a clinical but necessary undertaking which obliged me to keep my personal emotions in check. The human dignity and love of so many in that centre was evident and tangible.

Mary McAleese, the Irish President, arrived and spoke at length to relatives and volunteers. Gerry Adams and Sinn Féin officials were standing by hoping for a photo opportunity with the President. Her officials were aware of this and ensured that it did not happen.

Over the following days, we worked closely with the press corps. We took agreed numbers to areas outside the police cordon so that they could record the scenes of devastation, and arranged interviews with uniformed police officers who had helped the injured in the immediate aftermath of the bombing. We also arranged interviews with senior members of the investigation team.

Many dignitaries visited the town in the following weeks, including Prince Charles, President Bill Clinton and Prime Minister Tony Blair. The American Secret Service took charge of security during the presidential visit. Their media relations people imposed strict conditions on coverage of the visit. They were professional and exceedingly thorough. Just before Mr Clinton was due to meet townspeople and members of the emergency services, I was asked to arrange for him to meet senior members of the RUC and Garda investigation teams. For me it was important to show the world that the two police services were committed to working together. A Secret Service agent told me that it was too late to include anything else in the President's schedule: that he had eleven seconds of free time if he was to remain on schedule. Some time later, I approached him again. He directed me to an impressive, distinguished-looking lady who had just flown in from Moscow. She was sympathetic to my request and told the agent to arrange it. Within minutes, the President was shaking hands and addressing the four senior officers by name.

Gerry Fitt, a former parliamentary representative for west Belfast and then a member of the House of Lords, also visited Omagh. I found him wandering the Main Street in tears. I knew Gerry well and took him down to the police cordon. I explained the sequence of events on the fateful day and introduced him to members of the investigation team.

The town was still in shock and in deep mourning during the seemingly endless procession of funerals. The media responded to family and police requests to maintain a discreet distance.

I have watched with deep sadness the continuing tragedy of Omagh. The recent decision of Mr Justice Weir[18] to dismiss all charges against one of the alleged bomb-makers was a bitter disappointment to the relatives. Mr Weir is a man of great integrity and an expert in law and rightly identified serious weaknesses in the prosecution case which prevented him from coming to any other conclusion. In his judgement, he severely criticised processes used in the gathering and storage of evidence. The biggest flaw in the prosecution evidence was its reliance on Low Copy Number DNA testing. Once the judge questioned the validity of the technique, the case was doomed to failure.

It is over ten years since the bombing. The anguish and sense of loss felt by the relatives can only be imagined. The failure of the prosecution has left them with a sense of betrayal and disbelief. Ten years of campaigning, hoping, expecting and demanding that someone should be brought to justice has not resulted in any satisfactory outcome. The Chief Constable of the PSNI made a very pertinent comment on the predicament of the police when he said that intelligence was not the same as evidence. He also confessed that it was highly unlikely that anyone would be convicted for the Omagh bombing unless those who know who did it were prepared to stand up in court and identify them.[19]

One of the controversial issues raised in the Ombudsman's Report on Omagh[20] concerned the informant, Kevin Fulton. I had had some personal dealings with Fulton. In June 1996, while still head of the Drugs Squad, I had met him at the request of one of my detective sergeants who was hoping to recruit him as an informant. Fulton did not appear to know much about drug dealers. He told us that he had previously been involved with the IRA around the early 1990s, but had had no dealings with them since. He offered information about two major frauds, one involving members of the Italian Mafia in London. He also told us that he had been a Special Branch informant between 1992 and 1994, but that they had dropped him after he had given them inaccurate intelligence. I told the detective sergeant that he could register Fulton, but in view of the fact that Fulton did not appear to know much about drugs, he should involve members of the CID Serious Crime Squad. Special Branch later confirmed that it had terminated its involvement with Fulton because he was considered 'an intelligence nuisance' by them.

In the following weeks, the detective sergeant convinced me that Fulton had crucial information about two frauds involving St

Brendan's Cream (a firm in the drinks trade) and the theft of computer parts in London. I gave him permission to work with the RUC Serious Crime Squad and detectives in London. By July 1997, the inquiries were progressing. The detective sergeant submitted a file on the investigations which led to Fulton being granted 'participating informant' status by the Assistant Chief Constable in charge of Crime. The authorisation permitted Fulton to participate in the two frauds, but not as an instigator. The aim was to bring about the arrest of the principals. A number of people were arrested and successfully prosecuted. The financial sums involved had totalled a minimum of £27 million. I had no further involvement with Fulton.

I am aware that Fulton contacted a senior member of the Omagh investigation team, offering information on a possible location for the manufacture of the Omagh bomb. Two officers travelled to Carrickmacross in the Irish Republic in search of the isolated farm buildings described by him. They passed the information on to the Garda. After researching the matter further, both the RUC and Garda investigators concluded that Fulton was wrong about the location, therefore his allegation was of no relevance to the Omagh bomb investigation.

I am also aware that Fulton made financial agreements with a TV company and at least one newspaper. Two English newspapers negotiated with him for his story. *The Mail on Sunday* offered £30,000 but withdrew when the RUC refused to lend credibility to it. *The People*, however, was happy to run with the story without consulting us and paid Fulton substantially more. He alleged that he had told his police handler on 12 August 1998 (three days before the Omagh bombing) that the Real IRA 'was about to move something North over the next few days'.

This information would be considered low grade and of limited value (F6 category) by any intelligence service in the world. In the context of the Troubles in Northern Ireland, non-specific intelligence of this type was received by the RUC hundreds of times each month.

One of the Special Branch officers who considered the information provided by Fulton about the Omagh bomb was a friend of mine and had previously worked with me. He was a highly experienced and competent officer. I do not know of anyone better placed to assess intelligence. On the basis of his conclusions, the head of Special Branch in August 2001 described Fulton as an 'intelligence nuisance'; and in September 2001, the Chief Constable referred to him as a 'Walter Mitty type'. I am inclined to agree with this assessment.

My next big responsibility was a visit to Kosovo by Ronnie Flanagan and Adam Ingram, the Security Minister, in December 1998. The purpose of the visit was to meet a contingent of RUC officers (including Ronnie Flanagan's son) who were part of the UN peace-keeping mission. We were accompanied by Jilly Beattie, a well-known journalist from the *Daily Mirror*, and a film crew from Ulster Television. The war had just ended, but ethnic and religious differences between the Albanian and Serbian communities were much in evidence. Whole towns were divided by barbed wire and UN soldiers; individual families were trapped in blocks of flats in the wrong side of town and needed soldiers permanently positioned outside their doors to stop them being killed. The atmosphere was one of fear, suspicion and hatred. It was not hard to see similarities with the Northern Ireland situation.

We visited an ancient church complex where a small group of elderly nuns was guarded by French peace-keeping tanks. We spent a couple of hours with them; they were kind, generous and deeply religious. They made a huge impression on me.

During our four days in Kosovo, a university professor and his daughter were murdered in broad daylight in a busy street simply because they were Serb nationals; the bodies of two men were found shot dead outside a derelict building. Ominous-looking characters dressed in black leather jackets drove around in top of the range Mercedes cars, their wealth derived from drug- and people-trafficking, both of which the RUC officers were investigating. During our brief visit, five children disappeared off the streets.

I travelled with the Ulster TV film crew on visits to a school and a university. We were impressed by the resolve of the two staffs to keep going. During the war, members of staff and some students 'disappeared', presumed murdered. I arranged interviews with Sir Ronnie Flanagan and other members of the RUC contingent. We filmed them on patrol and also the large quantities of arms seized by them.

The following year, I returned to Kosovo with Sir Ronnie to attend a UN medal presentation ceremony involving RUC officers. It was a proud day for the individuals concerned and for the RUC.

In early April 2000, I worked with Headquarters staff and the Northern Ireland Office preparing for the Queen's presentation of the George Cross to the RUC. We spent several days at Hillsborough Castle, where the presentation was to take place, working with media and journalists.

On the day itself (12 April) I took up position alongside the Chief Constable, Sir Ronnie Flanagan, to organise media interviews. The Queen paid tribute to the courage and commitment of the RUC: 'This award is an exceptional recognition of the outstanding contribution made by the RUC to peace in Northern Ireland ... a singular acknowledgement of the gallantry and courage shown and, in all too many cases, the ultimate sacrifice paid by the members of the Constabulary during the past thirty years of terrorism and civil unrest.'

The award was the highest decoration for Commonwealth civilians—the civilian equivalent of the Victoria Cross. It was the second time in history that it had been awarded, the other occasion being to the people of Malta who had endured an unrelenting German bombing campaign in 1942.

The award was accepted on behalf of the RUC by Constable Paul Slaine, who had lost both legs in an IRA rocket attack in Newry in 1992. A colleague, Constable Colleen McMurray, died in the blast.

Sir Ronnie Flanagan responded to the award: 'This most gracious honour ... is not only recognition of outstanding past achievement, but also the most tremendous incentive to us all, now and in the years to come, to draw on our experiences to work in partnership with all our people for the future benefit of us all ...'

This was my final big job as press officer. I had enjoyed my time working with the media; but within the organisation my reputation and status had come under unexpected scrutiny.

| FALL FROM GRACE

During my first weeks in the Press Office I had attempted without success to get access to Sir Ronnie Flanagan through his police secretary, Superintendent Keatley, to find out what was expected of me. A number of things were happening which caused me concern: I had not been invited to any Christmas functions at Headquarters, nor to the Drugs Squad Christmas party. A very close civilian friend who had attended a police function in mid-December told me that a superintendent in Special Branch had hinted that 'Sheehy was finished' and that he should have nothing further to do with me.

The same superintendent would later fall foul of his masters during the IRA spying scandal at Stormont in 2005 which 'outed' Denis Donaldson as an informant.[21] In the ensuing controversy, the officer resigned.

In Christmas week, several uniformed officers told me that Detective Chief Superintendent Martindale from Special Branch was heading a team of experienced detectives investigating the Drugs Squad. It was suggested that the Deputy Chief Constable, Blair Wallace, had initiated this investigation into the arrest of two alleged drug dealers, Mr A and Mr B,[22] on 14 February 1997.

On 5 January 1998, I spoke to Mr Wallace in the senior officers' mess at Headquarters. He told me that the matter was being examined at the request of the Director of Public Prosecutions and that, as far as he was concerned, I was not personally under investigation. Later that same day, I was told that members of the investigating team had seized notebooks, special property registers and the controlled drugs register from the Drugs Squad office at Ballymena. No explanation was given. The arrest of Mr A and Mr B was not connected to the Ballymena office, so the raid suggested an extension of the investigation.

I wrote to Detective Chief Superintendent Anderson, deputy head of CID, and sought clarification: 'I think I am entitled to know whether I am being investigated on criminal or disciplinary matters in view of the fact that numerous people know about an investigation and the investigation team refuses to specify the nature of their inquiries. As a result, rumours abound and my reputation is being damaged.' I delivered this by hand. Mr Anderson confirmed that an inquiry was on-going. According to the RUC disciplinary code, every member has a right to know, as soon as possible, that they are under investigation.

I had known Mr Martindale since my time in Londonderry (1974). He had a reputation for thoroughness and efficiency. He made it clear to me that his investigation would be 'rigorous' and 'wide-ranging' and would involve an examination of the various practices of the Drugs Squad. While I was taken aback by his declaration, I had no reason to be concerned about anything he might find.

Over the next two and a half years, it seemed that everyone in the Drugs Squad was under investigation without knowing exactly why, expected to function as normal in a Kafkaesque atmosphere of suspicion, concern and fear.

I discussed the matter with the secretary of the Superintendents' Association. I believed that an insurance policy, originally taken out on the recommendation of the Association, would cover legal expenses should I feel the need to seek legal advice. A few days later, however, I was informed that the terms of the policy only covered the cost of legal representation in the event of my being charged or prosecuted. Eventually I felt the need to seek legal advice—it was to cost me £5,050.

I hired the services of Ted Jones, a solicitor from a highly respected legal firm in Belfast. He advised and encouraged me during the long-drawn-out investigation. On three occasions, I was interviewed under caution in the cell block complex at Antrim RUC station. Mr Martindale, accompanied by another officer, interviewed me on each occasion. He was polite, but very formal and businesslike. Although I was invited to these interviews, it was clear that I would have been arrested had I not attended. Other members of the squad had a similar experience.

It was also clear from the line of questioning that while the arrest of Mr A and Mr B formed a major part of the investigation, it was looking at allegations made by them that members of the squad, myself included, were involved in drug trafficking and other criminal acts.

We began by discussing the circumstances of the two arrests. I told them that on the morning of 13 February 1997, I had been working in the Intelligence Office at the Drugs Squad at Antrim Road police station. A detective sergeant entered the room and told me that Mr A was intending to move drugs from his home in County Down to Belfast; that a surveillance operation had already been put in place, but that no uniformed officer was available to make the arrest. I telephoned the duty inspector at Downpatrick RUC station and informed him of our predicament. He agreed to take Mobile Support Unit officers away from a house search and make them available to the surveillance team. A couple of hours later, I was informed that two men (Messrs A and B) were in custody at Newtownards police station and that £40,000 of drugs had been recovered. They were charged with drug offences the following day.

On 18 February 1997, Mr A telephoned me and asked me to meet him. I arranged a rendezvous at Holywood RUC station. He asked me how long it would take for his trial to come to court. He reminded me that he had done work for CID, Special Branch and myself in the past. I assured him that this would be brought to the judge's attention.

I had been involved with Mr A on two important investigations in the past. I worked with him for the first time during the build-up to and during the IPLO feud in west Belfast in 1992. He had been involved with the Belfast faction in drug-trafficking operations. Three people had been killed during the dispute and a number seriously injured. He was concerned about his own safety. I discussed this with a detective superintendent in Special Branch and arranged ways in which he could contact Mr A. I believe that Mr A then worked with Special Branch over a period of time.

On 13 September 1994, Mr A telephoned me out of the blue and said that he needed to see me urgently. He gave me details of a scam involving the manufacture of counterfeit tapes and CDs in Castlebellingham in County Louth in the Irish Republic, including the location of the recording machines and the persons involved. At this time, I was in charge of the CID in west Belfast and was too busy to handle the matter personally. I discussed it with members of the Anti-Racketeering Squad and introduced them to him.

Over the coming weeks, two officers from the Anti-Racketeering Squad and myself met several times with Mr A and developed the intelligence further. On 12 October, I arranged for the informant and the two officers to meet with Garda detectives in Banbridge. Later in the month, the Garda Síochána seized 2.5 million tapes and recording and printing equipment during a search in Castlebellingham. A number of people were arrested. I later received a letter from the European Phonographic Industry via Assistant Chief Constable Raymond White congratulating me on the outcome of the operation.

Mr A had been a full-time criminal from an early age. He was undependable, dishonest and amoral. During the investigation, I was under the impression that he had made allegations against a few police officers in the Drugs Squad, CID and Special Branch. I later learned that he had alleged impropriety on the part of several dozen people, including prison officers and medical staff. He also alleged that I had allowed other informants to deal drugs in Northern Ireland. On 6 January 1998, after I had left the Drugs Squad, he was arrested in Belfast in possession of drugs.

My main priority while head of the Drugs Squad was to prevent illicit drugs finding their way onto the street. For that reason, there is no way I would have tolerated anyone (such as Mr A) dealing in drugs, informant or otherwise. Two instances will illustrate this. In February 1996, a CID officer recruited Christopher 'Cricky' O'Kane as an informant. O'Kane had former associations with the IRA and was a well-known drug dealer and criminal in the northwest. I discussed the matter with my brother, Paul, a community beat sergeant in Londonderry. He confirmed that it was common knowledge that O'Kane was a big-time dealer. During a study of intelligence reports, I noticed that O'Kane had provided information that had led to the seizure of small amounts of drugs (£10,000–£15,000). Each time a small seizure was made, it coincided with information from police sources and informants indicating that O'Kane had taken receipt of large amounts of ecstasy, cannabis and 'speed' (amphetamine) from an English supplier.

Later in the month, I told O'Kane's handler that I was concerned by this. He arranged a meeting with O'Kane and told him that I was aware of his dealing and that it would have to stop. I was not happy with O'Kane's response; I told him that he would be arrested the next time he stepped out of line.

My concerns with O'Kane's dealing continued. On 11 April 1996, I discussed the matter with Detective Chief Superintendent Anderson, the then head of North Region CID. He agreed that O'Kane should be struck off the informants register. I had two further meetings with senior CID officers in the area, at Strand Road, Londonderry, and Strabane on 22 and 26 April to ensure that no further contact was maintained with O'Kane. A number of arrests and seizures were made in the area; although some of O'Kane's associates were detained, we never managed to prosecute O'Kane himself.

We continued to monitor the activities of dealers in the northwest and, when possible, take action against them. In April 1997, after a surveillance operation, we arrested a man from Harlesden in London in possession of £25,000 worth of cannabis. We knew that he was one of O'Kane's principal suppliers. In October, we carried out a number of searches in the Waterside area of Londonderry and recovered £80,000 worth of cannabis and ecstasy in two locations. In November, we seized £50,000 worth of cannabis. While these were not huge amounts, it was enough to unnerve the dealers and cause them a substantial loss.

O'Kane's lifestyle of holidays in Tenerife and expensive sports cars brought him to the attention of the IRA. In 1995, the IRA raided a house in Londonderry with the intention of killing him; but he was not there. The INLA was also anxious to hold him to account for his theft of an Armalite rifle from one of their hides. It was later used to rob £15,000 from a post office. In an attempt to pacify these groups, he smuggled cigarettes and diesel on their behalf. In December 1999, he and four henchmen were jailed for a baseball attack on a group of teenagers. On his release, he continued to torment the residents of Curryneirin Estate in the Waterside. He fitted his home with security cameras and an intruder alarm system, but it failed to protect him: he was later murdered by DAAD (the IRA's Direct Action Against Drugs), as part of a purge of dealers.

In early March 1997, a detective sergeant in the Drugs Intelligence Unit brought to my attention that a drugs liaison officer working in Belfast had registered Brendan Campbell as an informant. Campbell was one of the best known and most active drug dealers in Northern Ireland. The officer was young and enthusiastic, but I knew that this relationship would be of no value. Campbell had no other discernible source of income and enjoyed a high-profile, decadent lifestyle. He wore expensive jewellery and clothes bought from exclusive boutiques and drove top of the range cars. He loved the company of women and openly flaunted his wealth.

On 5 March 1997, I discussed the matter with a chief inspector in CID and a detective inspector in the Criminal Intelligence Unit. I explained to them that Campbell was deeply involved in importing large amounts of drugs into Northern Ireland. His main source of supply was a dealer from Northern Ireland living in Greater Manchester. He was a close associate of major dealers in Belfast, including Mickey Mooney, Ed McCoy, Tony Kane, Paul Daly and Saul Devine. These men had a number of things in common: they detested the IRA and refused to come to a financial arrangement with them in order to be allowed to deal drugs in republican areas. They frequently had violent confrontations with IRA members in Belfast city centre bars and invariably emerged victorious. A couple of months before his death, Campbell threw a hand-grenade at Connolly House, the Sinn Féin headquarters in Andersonstown. No one was injured in the blast but it sealed his fate. All of his associates mentioned above were killed by the IRA's DAAD (Direct Action Against Drugs).

Soon after Mr Martindale's inquiry started, I learned that an anonymous letter had been submitted to senior officers in CID. It contained allegations about the handling of a number of operations during my period in charge of the Drugs Squad. The source of this letter has never been officially established. Fingerprint and hand-writing examination failed to identify the sender. The content suggested that it had originated within the Drugs Squad. I know the identity of the originator of the letter, a man of little honour or loyalty, and that he composed it with the connivance of a more senior officer in CID.

One of the most serious allegations involved the recovery of drugs in a town north of Belfast. I cannot be more specific lest I identify an informant. On a Saturday night, close to midnight, I received a phone call at home from one of my detective inspectors. Earlier in the week, we had agreed on a surveillance operation to recover drugs imported from Scotland. It was an important job and we were hopeful of catching a drug-trafficking team which had been operating in this provincial town. We had engaged E4A (the Special Branch surveillance team) and HMSU (Headquarters Mobile Support Unit) to do surveillance and make arrests. The inspector informed me that the two teams had to pull out of the operation at midnight because of other commitments. A short time later, he phoned back to say that the local Mobile Support Unit he was hoping to use instead was not available.

The situation was critical: we had a car containing a large amount of drugs in the possession of an informant waiting to be collected by a trafficking gang. I made it clear that the drugs were to be recovered and, at the same time, that all necessary steps should be taken to protect the informant. I authorised them to take whatever course of action they deemed necessary. It was later alleged that I should have cleared this with an Assistant Chief Constable. I saw no point in getting an ACC out of bed to sanction a course of action that was unavoidable. That's what robots do. As far as I was concerned, it was an unavoidable but correct decision.

With the permission of the informant, members of the Drugs Squad removed the car from the town and made it appear as if it had been stolen. They broke a small side window and threw in a couple of beer cans. The drugs were safely recovered.

Other serious complaints focused on the handling of informants and payments made to them by the Drugs Squad. In a previous chapter, I have referred to potential difficulties involved in the handling of informants. It is not possible for officers to give guarantees that their informants will not commit criminal acts without their knowledge, nor can they be certain that intelligence given to them by informants contains details of everything they intend to do.

Where there is an intention on the part of an informant to commit a criminal act, the matter has to be referred to the Assistant Chief Constable Crime Branch under a process known as the 'participating informant' scheme. The application must give details of the part the informant is expected to play and the likely outcome. The Drugs Squad sought such authorisations in every instance, to my knowledge. On rare occasions, hastily arranged operations sometimes meant that this authorisation was requested by telephone. The rules clearly state that it should be in writing. In such cases, this was submitted as soon as possible.

One such instance was investigated by the Martindale inquiry team. It involved the movement of cannabis into Northern Ireland from the Republic. HM Customs in Belfast provided the intelligence.

Their source was a disgruntled member of a criminal gang who gave information that a fellow gang member who happened to be a Drugs Squad informant was preparing to bring in the drugs later that day. A joint surveillance team of HM Customs and Drugs Squad was speedily dispatched to Newry. Permission for the operation was sought by telephone under the 'participating informant' scheme. Later in the evening, with the help of uniformed officers, we stopped the informant's car travelling through Newry. The informant explained that his involvement in the incident had been due to circumstances beyond his control; and £100,000 worth of cannabis was recovered. Customs seized the drugs and the informant's car. They later disposed of it at a public auction. Although the informant was not prosecuted, he was warned about his future conduct. He also suffered a substantial financial loss.

This one incident highlighted some of the difficulties caused by informants. Unfortunately, Drugs Squad officers were very much dependent on the intelligence they provided. A full-time surveillance team dedicated to the Drugs Squad and greater access to technical aids such as telephone intercepts would have enabled us to monitor their activities more closely.

I highlighted this very issue in a discussion with the Director of Public Prosecutions and Assistant Chief Constable White in a meeting at the Royal Courts of Justice in March 1997. The Director had convened the meeting to voice his concerns about three drugs cases due to come to trial. In each incident, suspects were arrested and charged after receiving drugs from informants operating under the 'participating informant' scheme. The Director made it clear that the use of the scheme was the responsibility of the Chief Constable. He emphasised that lawyers acting as defence counsel for the accused could apply to have the informant named and produced in court. I explained to him that our dependence on informants would have to continue until we received assistance from a full-time surveillance team and other resources.

Drugs Squad informants were paid through a central fund controlled by Assistant Chief Constable White at Crime Branch. Requests for payment were forwarded in writing by me or my deputy. In instances where an application exceeded £1,000, my deputy or myself was required to meet with a detective chief superintendent at

Crime Branch (during my time, Detective Chief Superintendent Caskey, later replaced by Detective Chief Superintendent Anderson). A week or more after an application was submitted, a cheque for the required amount was forwarded to the Drugs Squad. The cheque was cashed by a nominated member of the Intelligence Unit and was later given to the handler against receipt. The handler in turn paid the informant, also against receipt, although there were instances when this did not happen. It was alleged that I interfered with this process without proper authority and was therefore guilty of the misappropriation of funds. At no time did I handle money myself. I adopted the informant payment scheme used by my predecessors and made no alterations to it. The major weakness in the process was the delay between an application and the receipt of payment at the Drugs Squad.

Occasionally, a handler asked for an urgent payment to assist an informant with a domestic or personal problem, such as the payment of rent or car tax and insurance. In such instances, I authorised payment from the fund. This sometimes meant that other informants were not immediately paid money owed to them. The deficit was paid as soon as possible. On one occasion, a detective constable told me that the life of his informant was in danger and that he needed to leave the country immediately. He asked for a payment of £2,000 to help him with the move and to assist his family. I contacted the Chief Superintendent Crime Branch and was told that the money would not be available for several days. I gave the detective constable £2,000 from my personal finances and recovered the money some days later.

An entry in the notebook of a handler which indicated that an informant was owed some £1,400 was not brought to my attention before I left the squad. Had he done so, I am sure the matter could have been satisfactorily resolved.

There was no question of the misappropriation of funds. None of us had received official training in book-keeping. No one in the squad or at Headquarters hinted at a problem or suggested changes to the system.

It was therefore somewhat hypocritical that my superiors should charge me with financial inadequacies when they themselves were so strongly criticised for their financial failures by the Ombudsman in her Report of 2007:[23] 'The Police Ombudsman is most concerned that there could have existed a system for the payment of informants which was so lacking in proper accountability mechanisms' (30.8) and 'The Police Ombudsman regards the financial arrangements for the payment of informants as a significant failure by RUC/PSNI management to provide a proper system of control of payments and, to arrange for a proper audit of payments made' (30.10).

Another serious allegation levelled against me was that I permitted illicit drugs to be imported from Liverpool for distribution in Northern Ireland. The officer who made the allegation was not involved in any specific operation connected to Liverpool. One of my responsibilities as head of the Drugs Squad was to address any drugs issue that affected Northern Ireland. This required a good deal of lateral thinking. I had identified Liverpool as being a major concern as a supply route for drugs. One of the men arrested at Malin Head in the *Plongeur Wisky* incident had given details of the involvement of Irish traffickers, North and South of the border, with major international dealers based in Liverpool. Their operation resulted in huge amounts of cannabis, ecstasy and cocaine being distributed throughout the UK, including Northern Ireland. Two Liverpool dealers had been arrested after a surveillance operation in Belfast. Each was sentenced to seven years' imprisonment for bringing drugs into Northern Ireland.

I had raised the issue with the Northern Ireland Affairs Committee at the House of Commons on 30 October 1996. In answer to a question from Mr Couchman, a member of the committee, I replied: 'We have identified the main trafficking gangs; some of them are resident in England and some in the Republic, and we are working very, very closely with the authorities. We have been to Liverpool, Manchester, London and Scotland in recent weeks and the Liverpool police are coming to Belfast next week.'

I introduced the head of the Liverpool Drugs Squad to two informants I intended to send to Liverpool in the hope of increasing our intelligence on Northern Ireland dealers operating in the city. They exchanged telephone numbers with the Liverpool Drugs Squad. It was nonsense to suggest that anything improper existed in this arrangement. At no time was anyone authorised to work outside this formal arrangement or import drugs into Northern Ireland.

The same officer alleged that I had given him permission to remove a package of drugs in transit through the post office. I was on leave at the time and had no knowledge of this incident.

There was a number of less serious allegations against me personally and other members of the Drugs Squad. I was interviewed on three occasions under caution by Mr Martindale and for twelve hours by officers from Complaints and Discipline. It was right and proper that they should thoroughly investigate all allegations against me. I cooperated fully with the investigation, which lasted approximately two and a half years. A file was submitted to the Director of Public Prosecutions, Complaints and Discipline and the Office of the Ombudsman. No criminal or disciplinary proceedings were instigated against me.

My last day in the RUC was 21 January 2001. I went for lunch with a couple of colleagues from the Press Office and two dear friends, Eric Anderson and Philip Boyd. We were joined by Jim and Lindy McDowell, Hugh Jordan, Dennis Murray and Michael Beattie, among others. During the lunch, Eric received a telephone call from Sir Ronnie Flanagan telling him that the Ombudsman had authorised my departure from the job with the words, 'Mr Sheehy can go'. Eric asked Sir Ronnie if he wished to inform me personally. He did not.

I was the holder of an MBE, a Police Service Medal, a Police Good Conduct Medal and twenty-seven commendations but, as the old Irish proverb goes: If you want to see how much you will be missed, stick your arm into a bucket of water, pull it out, and the hole that remains is the extent to which you will be missed. It is the law of life.

I have no recriminations or bitterness about much that happened in my career. But I was hurt and dismayed by the investigation that overshadowed my final years. It is my considered opinion that the real point at issue was my comments at the Scottish National Drugs Conference in 1995. A whole new political situation was developing in Northern Ireland and yesterday's enemies were now at the peace table. To remind the world of their on-going criminal activities, including deep involvement in drug dealing, was not deemed appropriate or helpful. Political expediency carried the day.

I fully support the concept of policing and wish the PSNI every success. Just after I retired, I gave an interview to Donna Carton of the *Sunday Mirror,* in which I urged Catholics to join the new policing service of Northern Ireland. For it is only in this way that the community as a whole can move forward.

APPENDIX 1

DRUGS AND TERRORISM: MAKING THE LINK
Detective Superintendent Kevin Sheehy
Royal Ulster Constabulary
(Scottish National Drugs Conference, 1997)

I suppose some of you might be wondering what an Ulsterman discussing Northern Ireland terrorists is doing at a Scottish Drugs Conference. Hopefully by the end of this short presentation I will have highlighted my concern that terrorist organisations in Northern Ireland are deeply involved in drug dealing, not only throughout the whole of Ireland, but within the whole of Britain and in countries in Western Europe. Their involvement is increasing all the time and my forecast and my deep concern is that in the very near future Irish terrorists will be a major factor in the drugs scene in Britain.

Anyone who knows anything about terrorists knows that their main function in life is to cause as much harm and damage as possible to the populace and to the economy of any society. Northern Ireland terrorists are no different.

We can see in parts of Europe how violent the drugs situation has become. The break-up of the Soviet Bloc countries has caused great hardship. Soldiers came back from Afghanistan totally disillusioned. Life to them is cheap. Two hundred pounds will buy a hit in parts of Western Europe. Anyone involved in international investigations in drug trafficking is very aware of that. I have to tell you that in Northern Ireland we have terrorists in abundance with the same make-up, completely devoid of moral concerns for anything. They don't value life whatsoever. Anyone who stands in their way, be it a brother or sister, is in danger of being eliminated.

What I would like to do for the first part of the presentation is to remind you of the organisations we are talking about. There is a misconception that because a ceasefire exists in Northern Ireland we no longer have to concern ourselves with terrorist organisations. This is not so. We have two terrorist camps, one which we will call republican. This involves IRA groupings. The other camp we will euphemistically call loyalist terrorists, who are committed to the retention of the Union. It comes as no surprise to me that in each camp we have one faction which failed to sign up to the ceasefire. On the republican side we have the Continuity IRA, which continues to plant bombs. They have been responsible for a number of serious bombing incidents in the last couple of months. On the loyalist side we have the Loyalist Volunteer Force who continue to kill Catholics simply because they are of a different religious persuasion.

The disturbing news for the rest of Britain is that these killers move freely about these islands. Many are domiciled on the mainland. Some of them are working with drug dealers in Liverpool, Newcastle, London, Manchester and Blackpool. Many are involved in importing large amounts of drugs into Britain from the Continent. Most, however, operate within Northern Ireland. It is difficult to believe that a small country with a population of approximately one and a half million people could harbour a substantial number of terrorist organisations.

There are a number of terrorist organisations with which you are no doubt already familiar. The Provisional IRA—we all know what they have done. The Irish National Liberation Army, who killed Airey Neave outside the Houses of Parliament, using a booby-trap bomb, some years ago; the organisation on the republican side that is currently causing the most concern—the Continuity IRA. Many of the IRA militants who are opposed to the current peace process have moved to this organisation. The strength of this organisation is increasing. They have expert bombers and committed killers in their ranks. The main objective of these republican terrorist groups is to break the constitutional links between Northern Ireland and Britain and secure a United Ireland. These groups will do anything in their power to complicate Britain's existence. My concern is that they will do everything they can to prevent the British people securing a solution to the drugs problem. They will try to undermine any initiative aimed at finding a solution. They will involve themselves in extremes of violence to complicate the situation; they will give assistance to leading drug traffickers. They are, in their own right, sophisticated internal organisations; they will use their contacts to assist international drug traffickers to get their merchandise into Britain.

On the loyalist side we have as many 'intellectuals' involved in a variety of organisations. They have no concerns about killing people and destroying property. They are deeply involved in drug trafficking in the British context. The main objective of the loyalist organisations is the preservation of the constitutional link between Northern Ireland and Great Britain. The biggest group is the Ulster Defence Association. Their military wing is the Ulster Freedom Fighters, who have killed many Catholics over the past number of years. Publicly, at least, they have tried to distance themselves from drug trafficking, but interviews of many arrested UFF men have revealed a deep involvement with drugs. It was often the case that after a killing, UFF volunteers would be rewarded with new clothes, drugs such as ecstasy, or trips to Rangers matches. Such was their kudos that they could walk into public houses in areas where they had dominance and secure the attention of admiring women.

Then we come to the Ulster Volunteer Force. This organisation has also been responsible for many atrocities. It is deeply involved in drug trafficking in Northern Ireland. Its members use contacts in the criminal world in Scotland and England to assist in the supply of drugs into Britain. Until recently it was content to supply cannabis and ecstasy. Intelligence reports indicate that it now has access to powder drugs, particularly amphetamine and cocaine. I feel that in the foreseeable future this particular group will concentrate on the supply of cocaine.

The Loyalist Volunteer Force has not signed up to the ceasefire and is responsible for killing a number of people. It is the most militant loyalist organisation in Northern Ireland at the moment and has the capacity to cause mayhem. Its members are deeply involved in trafficking. Like the other loyalist organisations it has criminal contacts in Scotland and England.

Terrorism is rampant and alive in Northern Ireland. The people in all these organisations, both republican and loyalist, are debased, violent, vulgar and immoral. Over the past twenty-five years they have inflicted pain and destroyed Northern Ireland society: 3,235 people killed, 39,664 injured as a result of terrorist activity; 10,000 explosions and 14,180 persons charged with terrorist offences. To some of you these statistics may not convey very much, but if you put them within the context of a population of 1.5 million people, they represent a great deal of pain and suffering. Few families in Northern Ireland have not been affected by terrorism in some way.

The statistics relating to the number of persons charged is, in my view, particularly relevant to the conference: 14,180 persons charged with terrorist offences. These people serve long terms of imprisonment, they get out of jail, they have no future, many don't want employment, or haven't the discipline to take jobs. Unemployment is running at a high level in Northern Ireland in any case. Ex-prisoners do not want to go back to jail so they don't want to take risks in doing armed robberies. Instead, a large percentage of these ex-prisoners are turning to drug trafficking because they believe it to be safer. They have already in place international and criminal contacts. In one operation, with the minimum amount of risk, they can amass ten fortunes.

These organisations need money to finance the purchase of guns, explosives and other equipment. Guns are extremely expensive to buy. Some members are away training and others live away from home for operational units: for example, IRA 'sleepers' working in England. Every prisoner's family, in theory, is entitled to a weekly payment. The organisations are finding it increasingly difficult to make these payments. Drugs are becoming increasingly important as a source of income to enable these payments to be made. All these organisations have offices with full-time staff. They have fax machines, photocopiers and telephones. Every time they fight an election they spend huge sums of money. They have sophisticated propaganda machines working for them—this involves the production of doctrinal booklets, election leaflets and the production of newspapers.

Most of the organisations have political parties. The Provisional IRA has Sinn Féin—Gerry Adams and Co. The Ulster Volunteer Force has the Progressive Unionist Party, and the Ulster Freedom Fighters have the Ulster Democratic Party.

All of these parties are involved in the current peace process and have met the President of the United States and Mr Tony Blair, the Prime Minister. Gerry Adams travels frequently to the United States.

Loyalist politicians meet many prominent public and political figures. Many people believe that the involvement of these groupings is essential to the preservation of peace and democracy in Northern Ireland. Many ordinary people remain cynical or are depressed and deeply frightened about the future prospects for peace.

All terrorist organisations throughout the world have traditional sources of finance. Terrorist organisations in Northern Ireland are no different. A major source of income is pubs and clubs. They have pubs and clubs galore. They are properly registered, they pay VAT. Breweries, as a business venture, give them hundreds of thousands of pounds to upgrade their premises. Again, as a legitimate business venture, they obtain loans from banks and other financial institutions. They run rackets involving counterfeit money, tapes, clothing and perfume. They are involved in building site frauds involving tax-exemption documents, which enable them to avoid paying income tax; or in providing security on building sites. They run taxi firms and organise insurance and diesel for the vehicles. Many of the drivers are ex-terrorist prisoners. They are involved in extortion, blackmail, robberies and every conceivable form of fraud.

The long-term aim of these organisations is to generate large amounts of cash which they want to reinvest in legitimate enterprises, or legally buy over existing businesses. In this way they hope to become self-sufficient, However, I don't think they will be able to achieve this aim. This is one of the reasons why I believe that drugs will become a major issue with terrorist organisations.

Over the years the RUC has been very effective in curbing many of the criminal activities of these organisations. In 1982 the Anti-Racketeering Squad was established by the Force to identify and eliminate sources of paramilitary finance. The government made available financial and legal advisers to help the squad. Many rackets have been closed down by the introduction of legislation or strict operating codes. Legislation has been introduced which has enabled the RUC and various governmental departments to get access to illegal monies. At long last we can confiscate profits from any criminal organisation—courts are very sympathetic to our need and are doing everything they can to assist us.

At this conference in 1990, I first mooted my concerns about the link between terrorists and drugs. At that time I would have estimated the percentage income to terrorist organisations from drug trafficking as being in single figures, possibly 5 to 10 per cent. Now I would estimate the figure as being closer to 50 to 60 per cent. All organisations, republican and loyalist, recognise that high sums of money can be generated by drug trafficking. Their long-term strategy will not allow government, police, Church or the educational system to interfere.

It was estimated in 1990 Northern Ireland didn't have a serious drugs problem. Cannabis was the most popular drug. There was not a serious problem with heroin or cocaine. Today cannabis, LSD, ecstasy, amphetamines, heroin and cocaine are available. Drugs are now a multi-million-pound industry. Terrorist organisations are turning to trafficking as an increasingly important source of finance. In time Northern Ireland, with its small population, will reach saturation point.

The whole of Ireland, which has a population of six and a half million people, in theory could one day be saturated. As Kevin Carty said yesterday, Ireland is being used as a transit point by international traffickers. It is becoming the Achilles heel of Britain and the Achilles heel of Western Europe. Our forecast is that the amounts of drugs moving through Ireland will substantially increase over the next number of years.

The Customs in Northern Ireland and Britain know all too well how deeply involved Irish lorry drivers are in the drugs trade. There is a concentration of these drivers in Armagh, which is on the border between Northern Ireland and the Republic. These people work openly with the IRA; they work under the protection of the IRA, and they make huge financial donations to the IRA.

We had a shooting about two months ago when a man with an estimated fortune of anything up to a hundred million pounds was killed. It is believed that he and people like him make high donations to the IRA on a yearly basis. Some would say it runs into millions of pounds. Little or nothing is known about these drivers in this particular area, but these people pass through Britain on a weekly basis, to go to Western Europe and to Eastern Europe and they come back through Britain the same week. The difficulty for Customs and ourselves working in these areas is connected to the terrorist situations. Without the presence of maybe fourteen or sixteen uniformed police officers and soldiers it would not be safe.

As I said earlier, trafficking by terrorists is not confined to Northern

Ireland or to the Republic. There are established terrorist links with many cities on the mainland. One man who allegedly killed thirty Catholics in Belfast is apparently in custody in Spain charged with possessing twenty-six million pounds worth of drugs, which were destined for Britain. Another terrorist who is currently living in London is responsible for at least ten murders. One of the murders was of two men in their fifties who were abducted on their way to work. They had to pass through a Protestant area. They were stopped, taken away and tortured. Their bodies were found in a burnt-out car.

Terrorists and criminals are working together to import millions of pounds worth of drugs into Britain. One group has been involved in at least thirty major importations. A typical load would be up to 800 kilos of cannabis and 200,000 ecstasy. Up to 90 per cent of the load remains in England and 10 per cent comes to Northern Ireland to satisfy our need. Manchester has the same problem. Top criminals work with terrorists to supply terrorist organisations in Northern Ireland. When we talk about terrorists we are talking about killers.

In conclusion, I wish to record my deep concern about the increasing involvement of Irish terrorists in drug trafficking. In my view it will become a major and a regular source of income. I believe it will have far-reaching and violent consequences for the drugs trade in Britain. The IRA will not go away until they achieve a United Ireland. Because the IRA will not go away, loyalist terrorists will not go away. They match each other, stride for stride, in their savagery. They need finance to buy weapons. They need finance to train their people. They need finance to keep their people happy. They need finance to pay the families of people who go to jail, to make them believe that their husband or father, who has been sentenced to fourteen or sixteen years, is doing something necessary and worthwhile.

APPENDIX 2

**NORTHERN IRELAND FORUM FOR POLITICAL DIALOGUE
STANDING COMMITTEE C
Thursday 20 November 1997**

**MINUTES OF EVIDENCE
Supt Sheehy (RUC Drugs Squad) and Dr Patterson (Shaftesbury
Square Hospital) on DRUGS ABUSE**

The Chairman: Good afternoon, Supt Sheehy. Welcome to this meeting
of Standing Committee C, which deals with health issues. At the
moment we are looking at the drug problem and also at the suicide rate
among young males. I am going to have to leave, but I wanted to be
here when you arrived. I have a planning meeting in the City Hall.

May I, first of all, congratulate you and your team on the enormous
amount of success that you have had in recent months and on the
tremendous job you have done in your field. We understand from press
reports that you are moving on. I believe that that will be a very sad
loss. We all appreciate the difficult task that you have. While Northern
Ireland may not be like the Dublins and Birminghams of this world, we
want to ensure that we do not get anywhere near them. It is you and
your tremendous staff whom we have to thank for ensuring that, while
things are bad, they are not just as bad as they might be. I want to thank
you on behalf of the committee for the tremendous job that you have
done and to wish you success in whatever you do next.

The norm is that you make a presentation and that members then
have the opportunity to cross-examine you for the purpose of
information. As I said, I have to leave, but I wanted to be here to thank
you personally. My deputy, Mrs Joan Parkes, will be taking over. Thank
you very much for coming.

Supt Sheehy: I will give a brief account of the current situation. During the past five years, there has been a serious deterioration in the drugs situation in Northern Ireland. If I were to make a comparison with other areas of the United Kingdom and the Republic of Ireland, on a scale of one to five I would say that Liverpool, Edinburgh and Dublin are at scale four, and Northern Ireland is at scale three. Over the last three years we have been moving rapidly through scale three and are now approaching scale four. I am making that assessment on the basis that there are far more drugs available in Northern Ireland than ever before—every town, every village has drugs—and there are more people taking drugs than ever before. Within those general statements there are a number of issues that must cause us deep concern.

The first issue is that the people taking drugs are much younger than ever before; it is quite common for people of twelve and thirteen to be involved in taking drugs. The second issue is that, because there are so many different types of drugs available, we can categorise the most popular drugs in Northern Ireland as culture drugs—drugs associated with entertainment. Three drugs in particular—LSD, ecstasy and amphetamine—are the drugs of choice with these younger people. I would say that a big proportion of people under the age of twenty-five taking drugs are taking one or more of those three drugs.

The deep concern I have about these three particular drugs is that they all attempt to serve the same purpose. They are all attempting to do things to the central nervous system and to the body. They are all attempting to give people a state of mind that is conducive to their enjoying themselves. Instead of taking one drug, it has now become increasingly common for young people to take more and more of these different types of drugs—they are mixing them. It is quite common for kids to buy ecstasy and amphetamine on the same night and to take both drugs. The worrying thing is that the kids have absolutely no idea what effect any of these drugs will have on them, but when they mix them it becomes increasingly dangerous because, again, they have absolutely no idea of what the effect of the mixture will be. When the drugs take effect, it becomes increasingly difficult for young people to take sensible precautions and take care of themselves.

We have had a couple of deaths in Northern Ireland associated with the taking of ecstasy. The people were killed not because of the effects of ecstasy; they were killed because, under the influence of this drug, they were not able to take care of themselves. One little girl actually drowned herself. She drank up to twelve pints of water over a short period of time, and, because she had taken the drug ecstasy and had been dancing in a very confined space, her body heated up, the organs started to malfunction, the lungs and kidneys were not able to process the water and she actually drowned herself. That is becoming of more concern to us.

One further concern I have is that very few people in Northern Ireland have any idea of how dangerous drugs are. We hear public statements by people who should know better suggesting that certain drugs should be decriminalised or legalised. I know this to be the case because we have an increasing number of instances of people having their drinks interfered with when they are in pubs and clubs. They go to the toilet, someone puts drugs into the alcohol or into the Coke and when they come back and consume the Coke or the alcohol, they have no idea that it has been contaminated by LSD or ecstasy. There are an increasing number of instances where people become very frightened under the influence of these drugs. They have no idea what is happening to them, and, really, that is something that public bodies are going to have to recognise and do something about. There needs to be publicity about the dangers associated with people interfering with drinks in public houses and so on.

The situation, I think, will continue to deteriorate in Northern Ireland. I was at a conference in England recently, and the whole of America, Europe and Britain is now being targeted by these designer drugs. There are more and more of them coming onto the market, and Britain has a serious problem with these drugs. They are all drugs aimed at an age group and they are all associated with entertainment. To get the message through to young people that they should go out and enjoy themselves and not take these drugs is becoming increasingly difficult. In the future these designer drugs will become a major issue.

Of further concern to me is the increase in powder drugs in Northern Ireland—amphetamine, cocaine and heroin. We are making more and more seizures of heroin and cocaine. Amphetamine is probably the drug that is causing me most concern. We have seized 19 kilos of it this year. Amphetamine comes in powdered form. The purity level tends to range from 0% to 100%. When people bring one kilo of amphetamine base into this country, they tend to add other ingredients to it to make five kilos, so by the time it has been injected, swallowed and ingested, it is probably 10% pure. That means that our young people are taking 10% amphetamine, but they are also taking 90% adulterated products into their bodies, and, again, they have no idea what they are taking.

Drug dealers have no interest in the welfare of their customers. As long as amphetamine, which is a stimulant drug aimed at affecting the central nervous system, has some effect on the central nervous system, the dealers are quite content to mix ingredients that will ensure that reaction. In the future I see an increase in these powdered drugs. The higher the purity level the more dangerous the drug, but it is equally as dangerous the lower it is because it means that the drug has been adulterated by other products.

Heroin, in particular, is taking a hold. We have a developing problem in Ballymena and Belfast. The problem for us is that every major city in Britain has a serious heroin problem. I was in Scotland recently talking to police and they were telling me that Stranraer has a very serious heroin problem. There are 2 kilos of heroin being consumed every month in Stranraer among a population of 17,000 people. That is quite frightening. When you think that Stranraer is only twenty-one miles from Northern Ireland, we have really no defence against this. With heroin will come injecting. We do not have an injecting culture here at the moment, but that will increase. It will lead to needle-sharing and to an increase in hepatitis and perhaps AIDS. Injecting is a very dangerous process. We have intelligence to suggest that, even now, people in Belfast and Ballymena are crushing prescription drugs, mixing them with water and injecting them into their veins. From a medical point of view, that is exceedingly dangerous.

The situation will continue to deteriorate. The police have put on record that they alone cannot deal with this problem. Enforcement is very important but it is only one part of the strategy. There is a recognition in the police that we have to be very much part of the educational development. There has been a huge financial contribution from the government to education about drugs. I have concerns that even education may not be the answer. No one anywhere in the world has come up with dialogue that young people have listened to, have been influenced by or that has solved the drugs problem. We have to keep trying, but the news for the Forum is not good: we have a deteriorating situation in Northern Ireland.

The Vice-Chairperson (Mrs Parkes): Thank you very much. We do appreciate your coming. Your presentation was very enlightening and it paints a very depressing picture. I am the mother of a young daughter and her school has had the drugs officer come to talk to the girls.

Dr Patterson from Shaftesbury Square Hospital is also here.

I will now open it up for members to ask questions. May I just emphasise that they should keep their questions brief.

Mr King: That was a very enlightening presentation and, unfortunately, it is the message that has been recurrently presented to the Forum. You talked about the scaling of cities and regions. I come from a legal background and have spent a lot of time working and living in Manchester. I have some experience of the scale the problem can get to. How do you categorise a city or region as scale three or four? Is it the type of drugs, the predominance of use of drugs or the age group of the users? If you could give us a definition of a scale-three and a scale-four area, I would be much obliged.

Supt Sheehy: There are a number of scaling measurements. The first one is the number of people believed to be involved in taking drugs. Also, the number of registered addicts, the number of arrests, seizures and the number and types of drugs available are all involved in that assessment. Part of the problem is that you cannot isolate one city and say that Manchester or Liverpool has this particular problem. We all know that drugs do not recognise geographical, political or religious boundaries. We do a lot of work in Manchester and Liverpool, in particular, which are major problems for Northern Ireland. We have a sound working knowledge of the situation in these cities. Part of our problem is that many major drug dealers from Northern Ireland leave here and go to live in Manchester. We are also doing work in Bolton, Blackpool and Liverpool. These people reside permanently in these cities and do all their dealing from there. What we can say is that things that happen in Liverpool and Manchester, in particular, have a direct bearing on what happens in Northern Ireland. There is increasing evidence that the people in these two cities in particular are involved in a major international operation which imports into Britain. This involves millions of pounds every month and a part of the load, say 10%, comes into Northern Ireland. The remaining 90% stays in

Manchester or Liverpool. Using that knowledge and looking at statistics from these cities, I think we can say with a degree of confidence that Northern Ireland is probably at scale three if we want to measure it.

Mr Robinson: In your presentation you painted a very bleak picture for the future, and that is probably quite justified. But what do you see as the answer? You mentioned that it may not be education—is there an answer? Is it going to get worse or can legislation help? How do you think the situation can be controlled?

Supt Sheehy: I have to be very honest and say that I do not think there is an answer. But that does not mean that there is not a moral obligation on us to keep trying.

Enforcement is important because for every ounce of drugs and every tablet that is seized by us and taken off the street, we can say with certainty that those items have not caused harm to our young people. Seizures this year are at record levels—430 kilos of cannabis, compared to 160 last year; 135,000 units of LSD, compared to 8,000 last year; and 20 kilos of amphetamine compared to 6 kilos last year. These statistics might not in themselves be very meaningful, but they are an indication that there are more and different types of drugs available, and the arrests indicate that more people are taking drugs. So it is a very bleak picture, and I am not certain that there is an answer to it.

We have to work with education, and the investment by the government in this area is very much welcomed by the RUC. They have produced a magnificent document, and I have no doubt that it will influence many young people against involvement in drug taking. However, I am not so certain that anyone has an answer to give to those young people who are determined to take drugs, and that is the problem.

Mr Robinson: You mentioned that enforcement is important. Quite recently there have been accusations made—and I am sure you are well aware of them—that the hands of the RUC Drugs Squad have been tied in some way. How do you respond to such accusations?

Supt Sheehy: First, that is not the case. People must appreciate that there are departments within the RUC that have to deal with the terrorist situation, and they have rules and methods of working. My problem is that if I want to make arrests, conduct house searches or carry out surveillance, I must, because of the terrorist situation, get clearance from these departments, in particular Special Branch. It is easy for people to suggest that they are interfering, but because of the dangers involved in surveillance and undercover work, someone has to take the lead and structure it in such a way that everyone knows what everyone else is doing. There are different priorities within the RUC, and terrorism is the top priority. Most of the specialist units are geared towards dealing with it. The Drugs Squad is probably the second priority. But as far as I am concerned, we have all the manpower, equipment and access to specialisms that we require.

Mr Robinson: Perhaps I misunderstand you, but are you suggesting that there are occasions when you cannot do your job because of certain circumstances?

Supt Sheehy: There are occasions when terrorism is the priority, and if I am doing work in a specific area and work in relation to terrorist activity is required there, I have to move out for safety and efficiency reasons. That is a fact of life. But overall, I do not see that my hands are tied or that efficiency is dramatically affected. It means that for a limited period of time I cannot work in an area, so I move out. And as soon as the terrorist issue is resolved, I move back in. There might be some delay, but it does not affect efficiency.

Ms Rice: Thank you for coming—what you had to say was very interesting and very frightening. I take the point that you were making about coke and heroin coming in—it would be a natural progression for people taking E-tabs and LSD to move onto the harder drugs.

I do not know how you feel about education. Are we not doing enough at primary-school level? I never knew what a drug or an E-tab was until the Drugs Squad came to a community group one night and gave us a talk on it. I do not think that many people know what drugs look like or would know if their children were taking drugs. Do you feel that the government or even local government should be doing more to warn younger children of the dangers of drug abuse because currently we are looking at fifteen-, twenty-four- or thirty-year-olds who are actually taking the drugs. Perhaps children could be educated before they got to that age and were encouraged to take drugs at school. Perhaps parents could be better educated to enable them to educate their children about the dangers.

Supt Sheehy: The government's investment in the education package is very substantial. We were consulted when the document was being prepared, and I think it is a magnificent document; it is as good as anything anywhere in the world. The government, rather than just producing and issuing the document, is, through the Health Promotion Agency, doing research into how effective the package is. It is also investing in three television advertisements about the dangers of taking LSD, amphetamine and ecstasy. I have seen the videos, and they are magnificent. Government investment is very extensive—it covers every school in Northern Ireland. It is excellent, and it has our total support.

You have touched on the major issue as far as information is concerned—that of getting access to parents. We get invited to hundreds of lectures every year and most of them, unfortunately, are really a night out for women. These little groups have a guest speaker once a month—it will be drugs one night and something else another night, but for most of the people attending, it is a social night out. They find it interesting, but I do not believe that many of them leave the room feeling that they have been educated. And I do not feel that they are going to do anything with the knowledge that they have obtained, because most parents believe that it is not happening to their families. There is still a degree of snobbishness among many parents. Better off, middle-class people do not think that this can happen to their families. So they are not interested in coming to these talks.

And it is well nigh impossible to get access to those in working-class areas with their attendant problems and where mothers have so many other problems to deal with. The Rotary clubs and other groups produce little booklets and documents for parents, but it has to be the most simple message for those parents. However, getting access to them is the major problem as far as education is concerned. We can speak to the kids at the schools, but we cannot reach the people we most need to because when the children leave school they are subject to many other influences. If the parents do not have the knowledge, they cannot get involved in discussions with their children about drugs. And they cannot recognise the signs of drug abuse either.

Ms Rice: Perhaps local government might be able to help with this because it is more involved with local communities.

Supt Sheehy: Yes, there is some merit in working with the local community. If they can set a group up, they should be given funding. To try to do it on a regional basis or to try to cover the whole of Belfast will not work. You want councils to take an interest in these very localised issues and to assist, if possible, any group working on the street at the lowest level.

Ms Beattie: You say that a greater quantity of drugs is being seized. Do you know if those involved and those who are being arrested are the message boys or the drug dealers?

Supt Sheehy: We are in a very privileged position in Northern Ireland because of our very sophisticated intelligence gathering system, which has evolved and developed because of terrorism. The Drugs Squad is quite certain that it knows all the major dealers who are operating in Northern Ireland or operating outside Northern Ireland and pushing drugs into the province.

At the start, I identified six major gangs. We have dealt successfully with four of those gangs, and we are involved with the fifth gang, so we are making significant progress, but there is a lot of work still to be done. The problem with drugs is that as soon as a job finishes, even if it is successful, it immediately becomes history because as soon as you arrest a suspect, someone else will take his place. It is a never-ending fight and today I can say 'Yes, we are doing well,' but if you were to ask me in three months' time, I might have a different answer to give you because new gangs will be operating. It may take six months to penetrate these new gangs, so for those six months these people are extremely dangerous to society. It is never-ending. We have made satisfactory progress this year, but I still have deep concerns that anyone with whom we have dealt will have been replaced within two or three months.

We are doing more and more of our work outside the province. We are doing major work with the Garda Síochána and we are working with Customs and Excise and a number of other police forces. Much of our work is done outside Northern Ireland. The priority for us is to stop the product coming in and to take it off the streets of Northern Ireland once it is in. It is a big bonus to arrest dealers, and we are currently arresting a significant number of dealers.

Mr Foster: You referred to the education process. You must be amazed, as I am, that in this more enlightened age and in spite of the known dangers of drug taking, the younger generation continues with it.

You referred to someone from the west of the province who had drowned. About six weeks after that I interviewed a young man who was being held in a police cell on a drugs charge. We talked about the young girl who drowned herself by over-indulging in water and he said quite casually, 'Oh well, she really gulped it into her; she should have drunk it slowly.' This is how casually some young people take it. How do you feel about that?

Secondly, is drug taking a social issue or has it increased in Northern Ireland because of terrorism? I remember attending a drugs conference in 1986 in the Hague. I spoke to a Belgian policeman and he said that Western Europe would be flooded with drugs from the East, that terrorists would get hold of them and that it would be disastrous. Is it terrorist-related in Northern Ireland or is it a social issue?

Supt Sheehy: Let me look at your first point. Part of the problem of drugs is that they are incredibly pleasurable to take. If kids are under the influence of LSD, ecstasy or amphetamine and if it is a good-quality product, they will really enjoy themselves. There is no point in our going with an educational message and saying that anyone who takes ecstasy will die because that is not the case. It is also not the case that anyone who takes ecstasy will have physical or psychological problems as a result of taking it. So for every child who either dies or suffers an adverse reaction, there are thousands who do not appear to suffer anything at all. Part of the problem is that drug taking is a very secretive activity and if in a group of ten children going to somewhere in the province to take ecstasy, one child gets home at night and cannot sleep, suffers serious pains and suffers from dehydration, he is not going to tell his friends. Young people tend to keep it secret until a problem has developed that cannot be disguised, and only then will they confide in their friends or their parents.

In response to the second part of your question, yes, all terrorist organisations in Northern Ireland are deeply involved in drug trafficking, and increasingly so. A greater percentage of their income is through drug trafficking, and part of the reason for this is that the Anti-Racketeering Squad of the RUC, which was set up in 1982, has identified all the rackets that they were previously involved in—building site frauds, extortion, counterfeit clothing and tapes and so on. And working with the Northern Ireland Office we have introduced new legislation that has effectively prevented terrorist organisations from continuing with those practices. So, there are fewer and fewer opportunities to make big money, and all terrorist organisations have prisoners and prisoners' families to take care of. They have a structure, they have active-service units, and they have a propaganda machine—these all require finance.

Then we have the other problem of 17,000 people having gone to prison during the last twenty-eight years because of their association with serious public disorder or terrorism. When those people get out—a large percentage of them having maybe done ten, twelve or fourteen years in jail—they find it very difficult to get work, and this is exactly the same as has happened in Eastern Europe. When all the soldiers there got back from Afghanistan, they had not been paid for years, and they had also been corrupted because of their introduction to heroin—so they are the people running most of the major drug-trafficking rackets in Europe. If you want someone eliminated, you pay them £100 and they will kill anyone, even a prime minister or a president—that is the price of life to those people.

So, we have a situation where these terrorists are being released, and it would be very naïve to assume that they are all reformed characters. Some of them are unemployable and some of them just cannot get employment. But they need money, and then there is also all the glamour which is associated with being a successful drug trafficker—a new car, phones, jewellery and expensive clothes. And once they get access to that, or once some of their friends have got access to that, it is very difficult to persuade them to give it up.

So, in my view, we are going to have serious problems with more and more people connected to terrorist organisations getting involved in drug trafficking and introducing the type of violence that we see in Eastern Europe. I also think it is conceivable that in the future, with all the guns that are about, we will have executions associated with drug trafficking, and committed with increasing violence as well.

Mr Gardiner: As a member of Craigavon Borough Council, I would be interested in hearing how active drug taking is in that area, and, moving from Craigavon to the city of Armagh, can you see any link between those two council areas?

Supt Sheehy: We have quite a serious problem in Craigavon which extends to Lurgan, Portadown and Armagh. The most popular drug down there appears to be cannabis, although there obviously is some ecstasy about also. But the prevalence of cocaine, heroin, LSD and amphetamine does not seem to have taken hold down there. Part of our problem is that there are sprawling housing estates down there, and so when a dealer sets up house he tends to have other people living close by who act as lookouts and, of course, they all have mobile phones now.

Moving from Craigavon to Antrim for one moment, there are a couple of housing estates there which are causing a major problem—as soon as a policeman gets within one mile of certain estates in Antrim, or Craigavon for that matter, the word is out that the police are in the area, and the dealing tends to stop.

But three female residents from Craigavon approached me recently, and I went to meet them. We talked about two specific dealers, and as a result of what they told us we gave these dealers the highest priority and arrested one of them—he is now in custody. But there are still a couple of big dealers there who are either from Craigavon, or who have moved from Craigavon but still have criminal associations there. I see the problem continuing down there—it seems to be cannabis at the moment, so it could get more serious. But it is obviously causing great concern to people living on a housing estate from where drugs are being dealt—they are concerned for their children.

Mr Gardiner: Are these houses mainly based in the Lurgan area, or are they in the Brownlow area in Craigavon, or Portadown?

Supt Sheehy: We have big paramilitary involvement in drug trafficking around Portadown, we have criminal dealers in Lurgan, and in Brownlow we have small-time cannabis dealers working from different houses. So I think the situation will get worse before it gets better.

Mr Gardiner: Can councillors from those areas assist you in any way?

Supt Sheehy: Yes. I had a meeting with the Northern Ireland Office the other day about the regulation of licensed premises and about the regulation of drugs, and we are in the process of drawing up a document that will be discussed with all the councils in Northern Ireland—that document will be more effective than anything that has gone before it. But councils really do need to examine all the places of entertainment in their area. If, after consultation with the police, the police express concerns about a specific premises because of drugs activity, they have to be brave enough to take effective action on any front—be it on safety, fire prevention, overcrowding, lack of proper facilities or late opening. So, rather than the police taking the lead in that, our recommendation to the Northern Ireland Office is that councils should become increasingly involved—they can attack these clubs and pubs from the fire prevention and health and safety angles, whereas we act in a law enforcement capacity. But while the police are going to work more closely with councils, the councils really need to take the lead in letting publicans or club owners know that wholesale abuse of drugs on their premises will not be tolerated, and they need to be doing that more than they have been.

Mr Gardiner: I appreciate that. As a councillor it certainly has my full support, and I will welcome that report when it comes out. I can assure you that Mr Cander, our public health inspector, will fear no evil—he is very efficient, and he will certainly go a long way in supporting and carrying out whatever is laid down.

Dr Patterson, are there any illegal drugs which you think would be better legalised? I am thinking about drugs such as cocaine which could be of medical benefit to people suffering pain in hospital.

Dr Patterson: The question about legalising certain drugs for medical reasons is, perhaps, a red herring. Some drugs which are illegal on the drugs market are used normally in medicine—for example, heroin is a very valid medical drug: it is well proven; it is effective; it does ease suffering; and it has been properly tried and tested in medical circles.

In my view, any drug which is useful for medical purposes should be legalised for that purpose, but that is quite different from the issue of legalising drugs for leisure use. The question about legalising cannabis arises frequently, and there is a suggestion that it may be of value in treating certain medical conditions.

Mr Gardiner: Is that the one that can be of benefit to people suffering from MS?

Dr Patterson: Yes, that is right. But the drug has not yet been properly tried and tested in that setting. If it were found to be effective in the medical treatment of that condition, my view is that it should be allowed as a medical treatment, but only after the normal, stringent tests which are carried out on any pharmaceutical drug have been completed—and certainly not as some back door method of legalising it for leisure purposes.

Mr Gardiner: Where does cocaine come on your list?

Dr Patterson: I find it very difficult to envisage a medical use for cocaine. Now, cocaine in different forms is used as a local anaesthetic— it was originally used as a skin anaesthetic, and in very altered forms it is still commonly used for that purpose—but the drug which is used bears no relation to the cocaine which is on the streets, other than in its chemical composition. I would find it very difficult to envisage any use for the cocaine that is on the streets.

Mr Gardiner: How does it affect the body when it is taken into the system as a skin anaesthetic?

Dr Patterson: Drugs which are applied topically, that is, to the affected part, tend to have very little effect inside the body, and for that reason many drugs are now developed so that they can be used topically—for example, many painkillers are sprayed onto the skin, and some asthma drugs are delivered by mouth and breathed in so that the drug does not get into the bloodstream and acts only at the small, local area where its effect is desired. Any drug which is related to cocaine and used for topical anaesthetic would not enter the bloodstream and would not have an effect on the body.

Ms Marshall: Supt Sheehy's presentation was the gloomiest that we have heard. Obviously, people are involved with drugs to make money. Have you enough powers to enable you to get hold of money from the drug dealers' bank accounts and to stop it being laundered?

Supt Sheehy: Yes. The importance of money to organisations was recognised, and in 1982 the Anti-Racketeering Squad was set up by the RUC with the aim of going after the organisations' finances. Since then the legislation has been refined, and we now have in place the strongest financial legislation in the world with which to recover their money— it has been very, very effective. Last Christmas we raided a house and four drug dealers were counting out £64,000. They fled from the house, but were detained. When interviewed, none of them accepted responsibility for the money, and using the legislation we were able to recover the money and put it back into the public purse. So the legislation, as far as finance is concerned, is excellent. The courts are also responding in a very positive way—they have had meetings with us, and they also appreciate the importance of money to drug traffickers.

Ms Marshall: Are you allowed to liaise with the Social Security Agency when people are ostensibly living on benefits, yet have a high standard of living?

Supt Sheehy: Yes. We have a very quiet, but very effective working relationship with a number of departments, and we get great assistance from them. There is a compulsion, under this legislation, on anyone who can give us assistance to do so, and that includes solicitors, financial institutions, and, indeed, any institution which has a financial connection to the suspect, whether it be statutory or private. We are finding that all these groupings now realise that the legislation is there, and there is a greater willingness on their parts to work with us. So, the financial legislation is very strong at present. It might need to be refined again some time in the future, but for the time being it is proving very effective.

Mr Calvert: I congratulate you on your presentation and on the vital work that you are doing in relation to drug seizures. It is very risky work and in view of that, you and your team should be commended.

Can we be assured that those dealing in drugs will be pursued and brought to justice, no matter what side they come from?

Are searches being carried out at places of entertainment where you know that drugs are being peddled? I am a member of Lisburn Borough Council—we have had the privilege of having you there—and I will certainly try to ensure that our council does all it can to clamp down on the peddling of drugs in our area.

Supt Sheehy: Religion plays no part in drug trafficking; there are people from all religions and all persuasions working together to traffic drugs. Market forces are the main factor; drug traffickers want to get the product as cheaply as possible and in order to do that, they join forces and bulk buy. They want to get the product out as quickly and as safely as possible to as many customers as possible, and they are not interested in religion at all.

The Drugs Squad's attitude to where we work is that we work everywhere and anywhere. I could not give you any breakdown of the religion of the people we have arrested because we do not see that as relevant.

Sorry, I cannot remember your second question.

Mr Calvert: Although you have brought religion into it, my emphasis was not on religion but on paramilitary groups—the UDA and the IRA could be infiltrated by those sorts of people. Are searches being carried out at places of entertainment? We all know that there are certain places where drugs are being peddled—I know of such places in the Banbridge area. Are searches being carried out effectively to try to catch these drug pushers, especially those who are targeting young people in discos?

Supt Sheehy: There are a number of safety issues associated with the police raiding places of entertainment. It is very dangerous to go to premises at, say, 10 p.m. where there are 3,000 or so people, some of whom have taken drugs, and where drug traffickers are working, because they will start a stampede—they will light a fire. So we have to bear in mind the whole issue of young people being killed in any sort of chaotic or excitable situation. I am glad you mentioned Banbridge because next week, you will see very effective action being taken in relation to premises in that town. I hasten to add that the owners worked very closely with us; we have been doing undercover work in these premises for the last three weeks. That is the best way of doing the work, and there are other, very well-known places in Northern Ireland where we are also doing that. We have a list of premises that cause us deep concern and we prioritise them. Undercover work is very time-consuming; it is also very dangerous. If you put someone in somewhere, you need to have the capacity to extract him very quickly so it is not just a case of putting five or six people in; you need fifty people who can go into a place very quickly to get them out. We have a total commitment to do one place. But you will see very good results in Banbridge next week.

The councils can help us with these premises. If we have a deep concern and we bring that concern to a council, there is nothing to stop it seeking to take effective action by making sure that the premises do not get occasional licences for particular nights and by imposing restrictions about closing time. This is quite common for places in Belfast. If you buy the *Belfast Telegraph* on a Thursday night you will see all these clubs mentioned—some of them go on to six o'clock in the morning. They stop serving drink at one o'clock, so what does the club owner get out of keeping his premises open until 6 a.m. if no money is crossing the counter after 1 a.m.? That is a five-hour period when, on the face of it, the owner of these premises is actually providing a service to customers and he is not getting any financial reward. There are all those issues.

We cannot afford to close all premises down because kids are entitled to go to raves; they are entitled to listen to any type of music they want. There is a very fine line between being prejudiced against that type of music and premises that run raves and taking effective action. Places can get a bad reputation because they are running raves, but that does not necessarily mean that there is wholesale drug abuse in those premises.

As regards the premises in Banbridge, we feel the need to do this. The owner brought the problem to our attention; we have worked closely with him for the last month, and he is to be congratulated on his cooperation. My concern is that when the arrests are made and the story hits the papers, his premises will, in some way, suffer because of what appears to be adverse publicity. So, we have to be fair to pub-owners and club-owners as well. If they work with us, we will be understanding; but if they do not, we will be looking to the councils to assist us in closing them down.

Mr Calvert: Lisburn Council is concerned about the buses which travel from Lisburn to the likes of Banbridge and then back to Lisburn in the early hours of the morning. Are these buses ever stopped and searched en route to see if the dealers are on them?

Supt Sheehy: Yes, but drug dealers are very cautious and clever people. Occasionally, we mount major operations to stop these buses but the problem is that if we stop them once, the dealers will take other action. They will, for instance, take orders for drugs on the bus and take the money, and then someone will be sitting in a car somewhere about Banbridge and the customers will get off the bus and get their drugs that way. We have had many situations where we have recovered drugs but, unfortunately, you only do that once with a particular dealer, or with a particular group of dealers—they learn so quickly. And then you have the problem of people who have two ecstasy and who, when the police mount the bus, swallow them, which is incredibly dangerous, of course—kids have no appreciation whatsoever of the dangers of these drugs, and they are quite happy to do that. They will swallow LSD and ecstasy at once, or swallow a quarter ounce of cannabis to stop us getting access to it. There is a major security problem associated with stopping these buses: you only do it effectively once. Sometimes we put undercover people on the buses and do it that way; the buses do get some consideration from us, but they are not a high-priority area because you could put man-hours and resources into this activity and often the results are negligible.

The Vice-Chairperson: We have been looking at the general area of men's health and, more specifically now, how that connects with drugs.

I would like to ask both of you about the male:female ratio. Are there more males than females with a drug problem?

Dr Patterson: At the health end, of the people presenting to my service—people who inject drugs—it is almost equal between the sexes. There are a very few less women, but the number is almost equal. At the other end of the drug range—people who are taking the likes of cannabis and ecstasy—there are more men than women. So, there is a slight male predomination—more so with the less dangerous drugs—but when you look at the more dangerous drugs, the sexes are equal.

Supt Sheehy: That would be very difficult to work out from an enforcement point of view—all you could do is base it on arrests—but I think that girls are a bit more cautious. There are hundreds and hundreds of people manufacturing drugs. Take ecstasy for instance. Over 200 different types of ecstasy have come into Northern Ireland and over 2,000 different types of drugs have been used in the production of these types of ecstasy. In spite of that, males, for a variety of reasons, are prepared to swallow these, but females are a bit more cautious. However, the common denominator tends to be a certain type of music. These drugs are geared towards an age group with specific tastes in music and socialising, and I do not think there is a big difference between males and females.

Mr Foster: What sort of music? Is it heavy rock, or something?

Supt Sheehy: Yes, it is this rave music. Where I live, there is a big forest behind my house. One morning, at five o'clock, I heard this rave music blaring out; you can hear it for miles—it is like Indian drum music. There is a continuous beat and the other notes are incidental; there is no melody or anything to it, just fancy sounds and rhythms. It is like a tribal rhythm thing, but the problem and the danger with that type of music is that some of the records last for twenty-five minutes, and as one is finishing, another is starting. When I went to dances, there were fast dances and slow dances, and you had a choice, but the kids now tend not to take a break at any stage, so they could be gyrating to this very dramatic and very haunting music for six hours.

Mr Foster: An assault on the ear-drums.

Supt Sheehy: It is an assault on the ear-drums. From the point of view of safety, I am sure that the noise level in these places is causing untold damage. We went into one place and the noise was like five jet engines at full throttle—it was horrifying. In fact, we were disorientated because of the noise level, the cramped conditions and the heat. But the kids love all that. Ecstasy is known as the love drug, not because it makes people want to have sex, but because it does something to their minds that does not incline them towards violence. They lose their inhibitions and their shyness and they can communicate more easily and more freely—there is very little violence associated with raves now; you seldom see people stabbed or badly assaulted.

Ms Rice: You made an interesting point about noise pollution and public health. Unfortunately, we are not in line with the United Kingdom legislation on this. If noise levels are causing a problem, this is a prosecutionable offence under our local government legislation. Could you close some of these premises down on that basis?

Supt Sheehy: Dr Patterson might be in a better position to answer from a medical point of view, but the noise level in some of these places is undoubtedly extreme, and it has to be damaging to hearing, and so on. Councils are entitled to impose restrictions and if a club is misbehaving, we should attack it on any front, be it the noise level, safety, overcrowding, abuse of opening hours, abuse of drinking legislation, drugs found on the premises or the bad behaviour of people leaving. Rather than the police taking the lead and going off to these clubs, it would be more effective if they worked with the councils and encouraged them to attack on any front whatsoever. And what we want to do then is encourage magistrates almost to read between the lines and give a very positive response by imposing heavy penalties. However, imposing financial penalties is a waste of time; what you really want to do is affect their business by closing them down.

We worked very hard to deal with the drugs problem in a major premises outside Armagh. The owner, in desperation, decided he would change the type of music, but that did not work, and he is now being forced to sell the premises. But there was serious misbehaviour there, so really I have very little sympathy in that case.

As regards noise pollution, yes, we could attack on that front.

The Vice-Chairperson: Thank you both very much. This has been a very educational afternoon. I think that all of us appreciate the gravity of the situation we are facing and will face in the years to come. It was good of both of you to give up your time. We wish you well for the future.

REFERENCES

1. Jonathan Bardon, *A History of Ulster* (Belfast: Blackstaff Press, 1992), p. 417.
2. John Campbell, *Corner Kingdom* (Belfast: Lagan Press, 1999); *The Rose and the Blade: New and Selected Poems 1957–1997* (Belfast: Lagan Press, 1997).
3. Paddy Doherty, *Paddy Bogside* (Dublin: Mercier Press, 2001), p. 59f.
4. 1 December 1970.
5. *The Committee: Political Assassination in Northern Ireland*, 2nd edition (Boulder, Colorado: Roberts Rinehart Publishers, 1998).
6. It seems that this was also the opinion of Richard Needham. Looking back on a long career as a British minister in Northern Ireland, he stated: '…what I did find infuriating was the way in which the British Treasury tried to frustrate our plans to curb building frauds, because to them deregulating the construction industry and breaking the power of the unions [in England] was much more important than destroying terrorist-run rackets in Belfast housing estates.' *Battle for Peace: Richard Needham, Northern Ireland's Longest Serving British Minister* (Belfast: Blackstaff Press, 1998), p. 132.
7. See Appendix 1.
8. Cardinal Daly had contacted Abbot Kevin Smith in February 1990, when the allegations first came to his attention; and again in March 1990, February 1991 and August 1992. Each time, the abbot undertook to deal effectively with the matter. The Cardinal was following Canon Law in respecting the day-to-day autonomy of a religious (i.e. non-diocesan) order (i.e. Canon 586). In the final analysis, however, he had the power to over-rule the abbot (i.e. Canon 683.2) and finally did so, ordering Smyth to present himself to the civil authorities in the North.
9. In 1962, Cardinal Ottaviani, Secretary of the Sacred Congregation of the Holy Office (whose head was Cardinal Ratzinger, the present Pope) sent a confidential letter, *Crimen Sollicitationis*, to 'all Patriarchs, Archbishops, Bishops and other Local Ordinaries, including those of the Eastern Rite' detailing procedures for priests who had used the confessional to solicit penitents. Its main aim was to safeguard the secrecy of the confessional rather than the welfare of victims, who were obliged to perpetual secrecy.
   A further confidential instruction was issued to bishops worldwide by Cardinal Ratzinger on 18 May 2001 as Head of the Congregation for the Doctrine of the Faith and personally signed by him. It asserted the Church's right to hold inquiries into the activities of paedophile priests behind closed

doors and under the highest level of Vatican secrecy, the 'pontifical secret'. The evidence was to remain confidential for up to ten years after the victims reached adulthood (i.e. the age of twenty-eight). Breaches of this secrecy carried the threat of excommunication.

Archbishop Tarcisio Bertone, co-signatory of the letter, said in 2004 that in his opinion, Church authorities were not obliged to inform the civil authorities of instances of clerical paedophilia. The decision of the American Church leadership to reject this ruling in favour of total cooperation with the civil authorities and to adopt a policy of 'zero tolerance' was greeted in Rome with consternation. One may conjecture that, in the case of the Church in Ireland, Cardinal Daly went to some lengths to explain to the Vatican authorities why it was necessary to cooperate with the civil authorities here.

10. T. Rhodes, 'Sociology of Health and Illness' (Blackwell Publishing, 1994).
11. Appendix 1.
12. See Chapter 12.
13. Appendix 2.
14. *The Sunday Times*, 14 January 2007.
15. *Report on the Murder of Raymond McCord: Operation Ballast*, published 22 January 2007.
16. At their trial, the owner of the coach, Robert McDowell, and co-driver Marc McCullough were acquitted after the jury accepted that they had been intimidated by paramilitaries and forced to undertake the trip.
17. *Belfast Telegraph*, 16 October 1997.
18. 20 December 2007.
19. *RTE News*, 21 December 2007.
20. 12 December 2001.
21. Denis Donaldson had operated the Sinn Féin office at Stormont. He and two colleagues were accused of using their position to gather information likely to be of use to the IRA in what became known as 'Stormontgate' (a Northern Ireland version of Watergate). In December 2005, the spy charges were dropped on the grounds that the trial was no longer in the public interest. Two weeks later, claiming that he was about to be 'outed' by a local newspaper, Donaldson confessed to the Sinn Féin leadership that he had worked for twenty years as a paid agent for British intelligence (MI5) and Special Branch. Shunned by colleagues, he spent his final months in exile, in a cottage at Glenties in County Donegal, where he was murdered by a person or persons unknown.
22. Their names have been omitted for legal and security reasons. Both men had a number of serious previous convictions for robberies.
23. *Report on the Murder of Raymond McCord: Operation Ballast*, published 22 January 2007, 30.8 and 30.10.

INDEX